WORLD EDUCATION PATTERNS IN THE GLOBAL NORTH

INTERNATIONAL PERSPECTIVES ON EDUCATION AND SOCIETY

Series Editor: Alexander W. Wiseman

Recent Volumes:

Series Editor from Volume 11: Alexander W. Wiseman

INTERNATIONAL PERSPECTIVES ON EDUCATION
AND SOCIETY   VOLUME 43 PART A

WORLD EDUCATION PATTERNS IN THE GLOBAL NORTH: THE EBB OF GLOBAL FORCES AND THE FLOW OF CONTEXTUAL IMPERATIVES

EDITED BY

C. C. WOLHUTER
North West University, South Africa

ALEXANDER W. WISEMAN
Texas Tech University, USA

United Kingdom – North America – Japan
India – Malaysia – China

Emerald Publishing Limited
Howard House, Wagon Lane, Bingley BD16 1WA, UK

First edition 2022

Reprints and permissions service
Contact: permissions@emeraldinsight.com

British Library Cataloguing in Publication Data
A catalogue record for this book is available from the British Library

ISBN: 978-1-80262-518-9 (Print)
ISBN: 978-1-80262-517-2 (Online)
ISBN: 978-1-80262-519-6 (Epub)

ISSN: 1479-3679 (Series)

Printed and bound by CPI Group (UK) Ltd, Croydon, CR0 4YY

ISOQAR certified
Management System,
awarded to Emerald
for adherence to
Environmental
standard
ISO 14001:2004.

ISOQAR
REGISTERED
Certificate Number 1985
ISO 14001

INVESTOR IN PEOPLE

CONTENTS

ABOUT THE AUTHORS

Tímea Ceglédi received her PhD degree in Educational Studies (2018). In her research work, she focusses on the Sociology of Resilience. She researches students with outstanding achievements despite their social disadvantages. These students are also known as resilient students. She has vast experience in the field of educational sociology thanks to participating in 35 national and international research projects related to public and tertiary education such as resilience, family, mentoring, graduate career tracking, shadow education, social cohesion, teacher training, disadvantaged backgrounds, catching up programs, talent development, and added value. Currently, she is an Assistant Lecturer at the University of Debrecen and researcher at the Centre for Higher Education Research and Development (CHERD-Hungary). She worked as a Researcher in the Hungarian Institute for Educational Research and Development, and other research centers.

Tatiana Dubayova, PhD, graduated from Psychology at the Faculty of Arts of Prešov University in Prešov in 2001; in 2010, she completed the PhD study at the Faculty of Medical Sciences, University of Groningen, Groningen (the Netherlands) in the area of health sciences focusing on the quality of life of Parkinson's patients. Since 2006, she has been with the Department of Special Education of the Faculty of Education of Prešov University in Prešov, Slovakia. She is the Author and Co-author of several research studies published in peer-reviewed journals. Since 2013, she has cooperated with the Roma Education Fund in Prešov as a Lecturer of Mentorship Courses in which she has been preparing high school teachers for the mentor's role. She worked at the civic organization Victim Support Slovakia (*Pomoc obetiam násilia*) for several years and underwent a long-lasting training in systemic therapy. At present, she also provides distant consulting to children in the civic organization *Spoločnosť priateľov detí Li(e)nka* (Children's Friends Society).

Klara Skubic Ermenc is an Associate Professor and Head of the Department of Educational Sciences, Faculty of Arts, University of Ljubljana, Slovenia. She teaches several undergraduate and graduate courses: comparative pedagogy, intercultural education, strategies of education development, and integration of theory and practice in vocational education. Her fields of research are: European trends in vocational education; the role and the development of comparative pedagogy; intercultural and inclusive education. As a Researcher or Consultant, she has participated in 17 domestic and European projects. In 2016, she worked as a Visiting Professor at the University of Belgrade. She also lectured at the University of Wroclaw, Poland; North-West University, Potchefstroom, South Africa; Comenius University Bratislava, Slovakia. She has published more than

50 scientific articles and edited chapters in scientific monographs worldwide, (co)authored three scientific and seven professional monographs. She is a Consultant for the Development of Vocational Education and Training in Slovenia, and a Member of Government Expert Team for the development of the Slovenian qualifications framework. Between 2015 and 2017, she was an Editor-in-Chief of the scientific journal *Sodobna pedagogika/Journal of Contemporary Educational Studies*, and between 2018 and 2020, she was the President of the Association of Slovenian Educationalists.

Belén Espejo-Villar has been Professor of Education Policy at the Department of Theory and History of Education, Faculty of Education, University of Salamanca. She is a Member of GIPEP, the Transdisciplinary Research Group of the University of Salamanca. She currently holds the position of Deputy Secretary of the Spanish Comparative Education Society (SEEC). She is a Member of the Editorial Board of the *Spanish Journal of Comparative Education* (REEC). She has management experience at the Department of Theory and History of Education. She is the Coordinator of the Bachelor's Degree in Pedagogy. Her research areas focus on public policies and educational reforms, with particular emphasis on the research of the transfer market and new management models in socioeducational policies. Specialized teaching in political economy of education, socioeducational policies, governance and research on educational developments, and the employment dimension of pedagogy.

Katalin Godó is affiliated with the University of Debrecen, Doctoral School of Education, Debrecen, Hungary.

Hedviga Hafičová, PhD, completed her doctoral studies in Theory of Teaching Lower Primary Level Subjects at the Faculty of Education at Prešov University in Prešov, Slovakia, in 2010 and focused on the application of information and communication technologies in primary education. She works at the Department of Natural and Technical Disciplines of the Faculty of Education of Prešov University in Prešov. Her research work focusses on the application of modern technologies in the education of pre-school and young school-age children. She was the Co-investigator in several grant projects. As a Lecturer, she concentrates on the continuous education of teachers of pre-primary, primary, and secondary education levels and develops methodologies of pedagogical practices. Within the projects organized by the Roma Education Fund, she lectured courses covering preparation of teachers for mentoring, co-authored the programme of specialization education and a university textbook for this course.

Moon Suk Hong is an Assistant Professor and the Head of the newly established International Development and Cooperation Major, Busan University of Foreign Studies (BUFS), Korea. Prior to Busan, she taught South-east Asian studies, global development, and education theories and methodology at Seoul National University. Also, she worked as an Adjunct Professor at the Graduate School of Pan-Pacific International Studies, Kyung Hee University, and a Visiting Professor at the Department of Anthropology at the University of Yangon. Holding a PhD in Global Education from the Seoul National University (SNU), and an MA in Anthropology and Development from the Australian National University (ANU), she has extensively worked in East and South-east Asia in the areas of international development and education. For Korea's international studies community, she currently serves as an External Advisor of the Presidential Committee on New Southern Policy, a Policy Advisor of the Evaluation Committee for the Prime Minister Office's Committee for International Development Cooperation (CDIC), as well as a Co-Chair of the research committee, Korean Association of International Development and Cooperation (KAIDEC).

Martin Kaleja, PhD, works as the Head of the Research Centre for Social Inclusion at Silesian University in Opava, Czech Republic. He is a Special Educational Needs Teacher and Social Pedagogue. In 2001, he started teaching at a primary school as a Roma Teaching Assistant, becoming a Teacher in 2002. Currently, he is a Polish "Profesor Uczelni" at Jan Dlugosz University in Czestochowa. He managed several projects focusing on school inclusion in four Czech cities, with his tasks including provision of support in education, building teams and connecting them, establishment of a good communication mode, making school environment socially fair for the marginalized students in their education. His academic, research, pedagogical, lecturing, and other professional activities concentrate on the following areas: inclusive approaches at school and social context, special educational needs of people with conduct disorder, manifestations of risk behavior; social justice in education, and multi- and intercultural education.

Yuto Kitamura is a Professor at the Graduate School of Education, The University of Tokyo, Japan. He graduated from Keio University and received his MA and PhD, both in education, from the University of California, Los Angeles (UCLA). He worked in the Education Sector of UNESCO in Paris as an Assistant Education Specialist and taught as an Associate Professor at the Graduate School of International Development, Nagoya University and Department of Education, Faculty of Human Sciences, Sophia University. He is specialized in comparative education and educational development studies. He has conducted his research extensively on education policy in developing countries, particularly in South and Southeast Asia, focusing on Cambodia.

Edina Kovács is a Hungarian Literature and Pedagogy Teacher and Educational Researcher. She received her PhD degree at the University of Debrecen within the Educational Sciences Doctoral Program. Her main research topics include commitment and achievement of in-service and pre-service teachers, and different aspects of teacher training. The dimension of gender is important in this field, because of the feminization of the teaching profession. She won the grant of the International Visegrad Fund in 2014 and examined Slovak and Hungarian students in teacher training. She also won grants of the National Excellence Program in 2013 and 2016. She is a Member of the Editorial Board of the *European Journal of Educational Research* since 2018. During the last six years, she has researched the development of students' attitudes and the options for reducing their prejudices toward Roma people, and especially Roma students.

Jing Liu is an Associate Professor at the Graduate School of Education, Tohoku University, Japan. Prior to the current position, he served as an assistant professor at the Graduate School of International Development, Nagoya University, Japan, from 2013 to 2017. Then, he worked as a Japan Society for Promotion of Science (JSPS) research fellow at the Graduate School of Education, The University of Tokyo between 2017 and 2019. His research areas include sociology of education, international comparative education and development, and education for sustainability. His current research projects include school collaboration for school improvement in China and Japan, small-scale schools and quality education in rural China, and transformation of higher education for sustainability in Asia.

María-Jesús Martínez-Usarralde has been a Professor of Comparative Education and International Education at Department of Comparative Education and History of Education of the Faculty of Education at the University of Valencia (UV, Spain) since 1998. Member of the Spanish Comparative Education Society (SEEC), she currently holds the position of Deputy member of its board of Directors from 2008 to 2010. She has been Vice Dean of Innovation and Educational Quality in the Faculty of Philosophy and Science of Education of the UV, from 2009 to 2011. From 2015 to 2018, she has been the Director of the Training Center Manuel Sanchis Guarner of the University of Valencia, from which she has been responsible for the policies of university teacher training and educational innovation of the UV. Her research interests focus on the topics of Comparative and International Education and questions related to its methodology, Cooperation for Educational Development, intercultural issues as mediation and educational policies of migration, as well as methodologies of learning and innovation at university like the Service Learning and its relation with Social Responsibility and inclusive policies, having been researcher of various national projects of these topics.

Irina Maslo specializes in the promotion in out-school activities for active work-life participation. Habilitation in individualization of the schooling pedagogical process on the base of international accreditation of national level innovations. Creator and implementer of master programme on Educational Treatment of Diversity. Head of the LU Doctoral school on human capacity and life wide learning in inclusive contexts of super diversity. Supervising of doctoral theses (15 defenced and five in development), for example, on youth participation in integration process in multicultural environment; the learning outcomes approach in formal second chance education; opportunities of applying continuing bilingual, intercultural and inclusive education: experiences for inclusion of third-country nationals; transversal skills and main attributes of constructivist transformational learning activities for promoting excellence in adult education and training. The directions of scientific research: LLL strategies for improving of motivation of 18–24 aged early school leavers and 25–36 aged gifted adults to participate in LLL in diverse inclusive contexts in Asia and Europe. Around 200 publications, 25 years' education and training experiences. Ten years' education and training national and international founded research experiences. The Programme committee convener and reviewer in European Education Research Association (Research network 11 on Educational Improvement and Quality Assurance); University of Latvia management representative in University Council of ASEM Education and Research Hub for Lifelong Learning (ASEM HUB LLL). Last four years – Independent National Experts Network Member in the area of adult education/adult skills, consulting experience in ECORYS and Horizon 2020 program EduMAP – Adult Education as a Means to Active Participatory Citizenship project.

Adam Nir is a Professor of Educational Administration Policy and Leadership and the Abraham Shiffman Chair in Secondary Education at The Seymour Fox School of Education, the Hebrew University of Jerusalem Israel. He is the former Chair of the Department of Education at the Hebrew University and the past President of the International Society for Educational Planning (ISEP). His scholarship focuses on school autonomy decentralization and School-Based Management, educational planning, leadership and human resource management in public education.

Alexander W. Wiseman, PhD, is a Professor of Educational Leadership & Policy in the College of Education and Director of the Center for Research in Leadership and Education (CRLE) at Texas Tech University, USA. He holds a dual-degree PhD in Comparative & International Education and Educational Theory & Policy from Pennsylvania State University, a MA in International Comparative Education from Stanford University, a MA in Education from The University of Tulsa, and a BA in Letters from the University of Oklahoma. He taught secondary English in both the United States and Japan before returning to higher education. He conducts comparative educational research on educational policy and practice using large-scale education datasets on math and science education, information and communication technology (ICT), teacher preparation, professional development and curriculum as well as school principal's instructional leadership activity, and is the Author of many research-to-practice articles and books. He serves as a Senior Editor of the online journal, *FIRE: Forum for International Research in Education,* and as Series Editor for the *International Perspectives on Education and Society volume series* (Emerald Publishing).

C. C. Wolhuter, PhD, studied at the University of Johannesburg, the University of Pretoria, the University of South Africa and the University of Stellenbosch. His doctorate was awarded in Comparative Education at the University of Stellenbosch, South Africa. He is a former Junior Lecturer of History of Education and Comparative Education at the University of Pretoria and a former Senior Lecturer of History of Education and Comparative Education at the University of

Zululand. Currently he is a Comparative and International Education Professor at the Potchefstroom Campus of North-West University, South Africa. In the winter semester of 2012, he taught Comparative and International Education as Visiting Professor at Brock University, Canada. He is the Author of several books and articles in the fields of Comparative and International Education and History of Education, and has served as President of SACHES, the Southern African Comparative and History of Education Society.

ABOUT THE EDITORS

C. C. Wolhuter, PhD, studied at the University of Johannesburg, the University of Pretoria, the University of South Africa and the University of Stellenbosch. His doctorate was awarded in Comparative Education at the University of Stellenbosch, South Africa. He is a former Junior Lecturer of History of Education and Comparative Education at the University of Pretoria and a former Senior Lecturer of History of Education and Comparative Education at the University of Zululand. Currently he is a Comparative and International Education Professor at the Potchefstroom Campus of North-West University, South Africa. In the winter semester of 2012, he taught Comparative and International Education as Visiting Professor at Brock University, Canada. He is the Author of several books and articles in the fields of Comparative and International Education and History of Education, and has served as President of SACHES, the Southern African Comparative and History of Education Society.

Alexander W. Wiseman, PhD, is a Professor of Educational Leadership & Policy in the College of Education and Director of the Center for Research in Leadership and Education (CRLE) at Texas Tech University, USA. He holds a dual-degree PhD in Comparative & International Education and Educational Theory & Policy from Pennsylvania State University, a MA in International Comparative Education from Stanford University, a MA in Education from The University of Tulsa, and a BA in Letters from the University of Oklahoma. He taught secondary English in both the United States and Japan before returning to higher education. He conducts comparative educational research on educational policy and practice using large-scale education datasets on math and science education, information and communication technology (ICT), teacher preparation, professional development and curriculum as well as school principal's instructional leadership activity, and is the Author of many research-to-practice articles and books. He serves as a Senior Editor of the online journal, *FIRE: Forum for International Research in Education,* and as Series Editor for the *International Perspectives on Education and Society volume series* (Emerald Publishing).

PREFACE

World Education Patterns
Global North Volume

The shape and form of education worldwide is the product of many varied as well as intersecting phenomena. As a result, the shapes, forms, and intersections of phenomena that affect education comprise the bulk of the scholarship, research, practice, and evaluation of education within as well as across educational systems around the world. These companion volumes look at the ebb and flow of both context and agenda to both identify and distinguish those educational patterns that may be shared or may conflict among countries and regions. Given that the world is too broad of a landscape to cover in a single volume, there are two companion volumes of *World Education Patterns: The Ebb of Global Forces and the Flow of Contextual Imperatives*. The first volume introduces the phenomenon of world education patterns and examines those patterns in countries and regions that may be broadly characterized as the Global North. The second volume establishes and examines ways that countries and regions in the broadly defined Global South experience education within their unique contexts as well. The goal is that through a thorough examination of educational patterns worldwide, the shapes and forms of education in context can be better understood for improved scholarship and practice worldwide.

Each chapter in both volumes of World Education Patterns explains and investigates the educational impact of as many of the following contextual elements as possible, including: geography, demography, economy, technology, society, politics and policy, religion, and culture. Some chapters go beyond this foundation of contextual elements and introduce others or intersect them in ways that make more sense or create unique meaning in their particular context, but all of the chapters in both volumes are grounded in Wolhuter's three aligned chapters included in the Global North volume.

In this volume, C. C. Wolhuter's chapter, "Terra Invicta: Comparative and International Education," introduces and explores the importance of context to the scholarship and practice of comparative and international education. Wolhuter also clarifies the impact of globalization on education in this first chapter. In his second chapter, "Terra Incognita: The Challenging Forces of the Unprecedented Twenty-first Century Globalized Societal Context," Wolhuter continues his examination of globalization and introduces several of the contextual elements mentioned above as a way of outlining a framework not only for further chapters across both volumes, but also to identify and interrogate the global forces that shape and form education worldwide. Wolhuter's third chapter, "Terra Nova: The Global Education Response," looks specifically at ways that educational experiences, expectations, practices, and policies have responded to not only globalization but also the unique intersections of context and agendas shaping education worldwide.

Other chapters in this volume focused on the Global North include Alexander W. Wiseman's chapter on globalization and educational trends in North America. This chapter examines the diversity of contexts and difficulties of identifying recognizable patterns across such a decentralized and multicultural landscape. María-Jesús Martínez-Usarralde and Belén Espejo-Villar investigate Western European education systems to determine the degree to which there is a coherent political agenda or European strategic framework when it comes to education. Irina Maslo explains the transformation of education in Baltic countries from post-socialist to new-liberal education. Edina Kovács, Hedviga Haficova, Tatiana Dubayova, Tímea Ceglédi, Katalin Godó, and Martin Kaleja focus on the experiences of Roma students as a way to investigate the influence of globalization on education in Central Europe. Klara Skubic Ermenc examines education in South-East European countries in relation to the Europeanization process. Yuto Kitamura, Jing Liu, and Moon Hong highlight school education, in particular, in China, Japan, and Korea, and the ways that socioeconomic inequality and new teaching and learning approaches are transforming it. Finally, Adam Nir, looks at the influence that policy borrowing in the form of school-based management policy has on both the Israeli education system and the Israeli society, more broadly, as well.

Through the thorough introduction and framing work of Wolhuter's first three chapters, the rest of this volume's focus on the Global North becomes more clearly recognizable in terms of educational patterns and intersecting contexts. Yes, there are unique elements in every national educational system and regional educational culture or practice, but the shared expectations and practices are overwhelmingly obvious as well. Those shared experiences are often overlooked because they are taken-for-granted aspects of education worldwide, but they become even more apparent when the practice of education becomes increasingly decoupled from the contexts of education. This may be less apparent in the Global North as investigated in this volume, but will be even more apparent in the companion volume focused on education in the Global South.

Alexander W. Wiseman
Series Editor

TERRA INVICTA: COMPARATIVE AND INTERNATIONAL EDUCATION: A FIELD OF SCHOLARSHIP TESTING UNPRECEDENTED FRONTIERS IN THE TWENTY-FIRST CENTURY

C. C. Wolhuter

ABSTRACT

This opening chapter sets a frame for the chapters of this volume, dealing with how the dynamic dialectic interplay between forceful global societal forces and context shape humanity's education response in various parts of the world. "Context" as a perennial threshold concept in Comparative and International Education is explicated. It will then be explained how, during its long histori-cal evolution, scholars in the field each time had to contend new contexts, or reconceived the notion of "context" in a new way. Subsequently the problems of an overly fixation on the historical and the present, to the detriment of the future, and inertia are extant in the field, will be explained. The unprecedented, seismic changes currently impacting on the societal context worldwide, will then be enumerated. These changes can be subsumed under the collective name of globalization. The concept globalization is then clarified, and the take of the scholarly community on the impact of globalization on education is then mapped and interrogated. The authors' stance on this is stated, namely that a dynamic interplay between global focus and contextual realities shape edu-cation in various parts of the world. It is in this theoretical frame that the

World Education Patterns in the Global North:
The Ebb of Global Forces and the Flow of Contextual Imperatives
International Perspectives on Education and Society, Volume 43A, 1–17
Copyright © 2022 by C. C. Wolhuter
Published under exclusive licence by Emerald Publishing Limited
ISSN: 1479-3679/doi:10.1108/S1479-36792022000043A001

remainder of the chapters of the volume is presented, combing out the main features of education development in each part of the world, as a dialectic between global forces and contextual imperatives.

Keywords: Comparative and international education; context; globalization; glocalization; world regions; paradigm

INTRODUCTION

Comparative and International Education is a dynamic and growing field found in all corners of the world. In a recent volume edited by the editors of this volume: *Comparative and International Education: Survey of an infinite field* (Wolhuter & Wiseman, 2019), the field is described as an infinite field. Indeed, and in the context of the present world, the field is testing unprecedented frontiers, where education, and therefore also the field of Comparative and International Education, is accorded new relevance and value. The aim of this volume is to zoom in on that frontier, surveying the contextual imperatives, the education response, and the new vistas these are creating for the scholarly field of Comparative and International Education.

This aim of this opening chapter is to provide a frame for the chapters following in the volume. First "context" as a perennial threshold concept in Comparative and International Education is explicated. It will then be explained how, during its long historical evolution, scholars in the field each time had to contend new contexts, or reconceived the notion of "context" in a new way. Subsequently the problems of an overly fixation on the historical and the present, to the detriment of the future, and inertia are extant in the field, will be explained. The unprecedented, seismic changes currently impacting on the societal context worldwide, will then be enumerated. These changes can be subsumed under the collective name of globalization. The concept globalization is then clarified, and the take of the scholarly community on the impact of globalization on education is then mapped and interrogated. In conclusion, a stance of the authors regarding this impact is formulated and this position will provide the frame for the chapters in the rest of the volume.

CONTEXT AS PERENNIAL THRESHOLD CONCEPT IN COMPARATIVE AND INTERNATIONAL EDUCATION

The term threshold concept is here used as it had been introduced in the publication of Meyer and Land (2003). It has since then been belabored in a constant stream of publications, for example by Land et al. (Eds.) (2016). Similarly the use of the concept has been found useful in a range of scholarly fields, under scholars reflecting upon and interrogating their fields (cf. Rodger et al., 2015, p. 546).

A threshold concept is more than just a key concept or core concept in a scholarly field. Meyer and Land (2006, p. 3) describes it as:

> [...] akin to a portal, opening up a new and previously inaccessible way of thinking about something. It represents a transformed way of understanding, or interpreting, or viewing something without which the learner cannot progress. As a consequence of comprehending a threshold concept there may thus be a transformed internal view of subject matter, subject landscape, or even world view. This transformation may be sudden or it may be protracted over a considerable period of time .... a transformed view or landscape ...

One of the properties of threshold concepts is that they are *integrative:* hitherto separate concepts are brought together into a unified whole, revealing the interrelatedness of these concepts (Townsend, 2016, p. 24).

While there are many different views as to what Comparative Education or Comparative and International Education is, here it is understood as a field of scholarship studying education from a three in one perspective (see Wolhuter, 2020):

- An education system perspective.
- A contextual perspective.
- A comparative perspective.

First, Comparative Education has as its subject of study the education *system.* However, the subject of study of Comparative Education transcends the narrow perimeters of the education system as such. The education system is studied as embedded within its societal context and is regarded as being shaped by, or as being the outcome of societal contextual forces (geographic, demographic, social, economic, cultural, political, and religious). Second, not only is the shaping influence of the societal context on education in the focus of study but also the other way around: the societal outcomes of education, that is, the effect of education on for example the economy (e.g., the effect of education on the incomes of people), or on the political system (e.g., the effect of education on entrenching democratic values) (Wolhuter, 2020). Third, Comparative Education scholarship does terminate with studying one education system in its societal context in silos. Different education systems, as shaped by their societal contexts, are compared and that is the comparative perspective.

Precipitated by trends in both the worlds of scholarship and in education, there recently developed a contention that the name of the field should change to Comparative and International Education. While the term International Education has a long history and has taken on many meanings, here International Education is used as described by Phillips and Schweisfurth (2014, p. 60), namely that International Education refers to scholarship studying education through a lens bringing an international perspective. With the scholarly field of Comparative Education then evolving into Comparative and International Education, the idea is that single/limited area studies and comparisons then eventually feed the all-encompassing, global study of the international education project.

While this occupation with context (as shaping force) of education system has been a perennial feature of Comparative Education, the conceptualization of *context* has evolved during the course of the historical development of the field, reflecting changes in both the world (the subject of study) and in the scholarly field itself, becoming ever more refined and sophisticated.

TESTING NEW FRONTIERS: EVOLUTION AND REFINEMENT OF THE *CONTEXT* CONCEPTUAL TOOL

Marc-Antoine Jullien (1175–1848) has created the term *Comparative Education*. Together with Isaac Kandel (1881–1965), he shares the title of "The father of Comparative Education" and 1817, the year of the publication of his book *Esquisses and Vues Preliminairés d'un Ouvrage sur l'Education Comparée*, is taken as year one of a science or scholarly field of Comparative Education. What inspired Jullien was the socio-political turmoil he saw in the world, in his day and age of Europe since the French Revolution to 1848, and he saw in education, international cooperation in education, and a field of scholarship of Comparative Education an instrument of ameliorative potential in sanitizing the world from such turmoil (see Wolhuter, 2017). Hence, in the conceptualization of a rationale for Comparative Education, *context* is visible, albeit not being spelled out explicitly or profoundly analyzed, neither in structure nor in terms of education–context interrelationships.

After 1900, and reaching its zenith in the decades after 1930, Comparative Education entered the "factors and forces" stage inaugurated by Sir Michael Sadler's (1865–1943) 1900 Guilford Lecture, societal context became very salient in conceptualizing the subject of study of the field, although now in the opposite direction than implied in Jullien's scheme: no longer the societal effect or outcomes of education was the focus, but societal context as antecedent or shaping force of national education systems became the focus of attention. Taking it further than Isaac Kandel's (1881–1965) rather vague-diffuse premise that "national character" shapes the kind of national education system of a nation, put forward in his landmark 1933 volume, *Studies in Comparative Education* (Kandel, 1933), various scholars in the field, such as Nicholas Hans, Friedrich Schneider, Arthur Moehlman, Vernon Mallinson, Ph Idenburg devised their elaborate schema as to the set of societal contextual forces shaping national education systems. German comparativist Friedrich Schneider (1881–1969), for example, in his volume *Triebkräfte der Pädagogik der Völker: Eine Einführung in die Vergleichende Erziehungswissenschaft* (1947), distinguished between the following sets of factors giving rise to (the particular nature) of (national) education systems: national character, geographical environment, economy, culture, religion, social differentiation, influence of other countries, and endogenous factors. University of Leiden, Netherlands, comparativist Phil Idenburg (1921–1991) distinguished between the following shaping forces of national education system: geography, demography, science and technological development, social system, economy, politics and religion, and life- and world-philosophy (Idenburg, 1975). While these schemes vary, more or less the biggest common denominator is the following set of factors: geography, demography, technological development, social system, economy, politics, and religion and life and world-philosophy (see Wolhuter et al., 2018). This classification will also be used as ordering rubric in the next and ensuing chapters in this volume.

In the 1960s, in what Harold Noah and Max Eckstein (1969) calls the "social science phase" another Copernican revolution took place in the field. Once again, what interest the leading exponents in the field was not the societal context as a shaping force of national education systems, but the societal outcomes of education. Noah and Ecsktein (1969) probably best articulate this mission comparativists set for themselves when they state that the core occupation of comparativists is to test society–education interrelationships. An example of this strand of Comparative Education at this time is the publication of Harbison and Myers (1964), in which they calculated the relation between education development and economic strength in 75 countries, so as to demonstrate the effect of education on economic growth.

In these times, from the mid-twentieth century but especially from the 1960s, a ceilingless belief in the power of education to effect any kind of desired social change, such as education to stimulate economic growth, education to eradicate poverty, education to reduce the number of road accidents, or education to combat drug abuse. This belief in the societal elevating power of education also gained a grip in the field of Comparative Education. The fashionable paradigm in Comparative Education shifted from the "factors and forces" mold to structural-functionalism and its derivate modernization, theoretical frameworks which dominated the social science phase. Structural-functionalism views society as consisting of a set of interconnected systems (economic system, social system, political system, etc.) and interconnected institutions. Change in one system will result in all other, connected systems, moreover, change can be planned in one system to bring about desired change in other systems. Hence, education can be used to effect change in other systems, for example, education can be used to effect economic growth (economic system). When looking at the emerging nations of the Third World, the paradigm of Modernization contended that education is the main instrument to be used to bring about development and modernization in these nations.

As from the 1970s, more so since the late 1980s, as Comparative Education its two ultimate phases what Rolland Paulston (1997) calls the phases of heterodoxy and heterogeneity, the field was characterized by its *avant garde* scholars introducing an ever increasing variety of paradigms. Each (or at least the majority) of these paradigms zooms in on, and explicates, a particular facet of the education–context interrelationships, at one or more level of education (for now the national state is no longer conceived as constituting the perimeter of the scope of interest of comparativists, Comparative Education is now seen to focus on a whole hierarchy of geographical levels, see Bray & Thomas, 1995; Wolhuter, 2008). For example, the paradigm of Human Capital focuses on the effect of education on economic productivity. The paradigm of critical ethnography focuses on how power relations in the (political, economic, and social) context shapes the (lived) experience of learners and teachers.

Hence, as developed hitherto, the concept of societal *context* has always been at center-stage in the activity of comparativists. This concept has, along with the field and the development in the world, evolved, from an unnamed diffused world in the time of Jullien, to being subjected to analysis as to what this context comprise of in the "factors and forces" phase, to being subjected to rigorous, exact testing, in the social science phase, to lately when a plethora of paradigms each zooms in on one or more specific facets of this context in its interrelationship with education. Yet it is now difficult to point out a number of concerns in scholars in the field and their handling of this context, in the present, unfolding world. It is to these problematic facets that this chapter will not turn to.

DEFICIENCIES IN COMPARATIVE EDUCATION SCHOLARS' CONCERN WITH CONTEXT

Criticism about comparativists current concern with context revolves around paradigm fix, the fragmentation of field, rear mirror traditions, and inertia and nominalism characterizing the field.

That the proliferation of paradigms constitute the signature feature of the field at the current day and age has been criticized repeatedly by scholars in the field, beginning with George Psacharopoulos' 1990 CIES (Comparative and International Education Society) presidential address (Psacharopoulos, 1990). First, the feeling is that a fixation on paradigms distracts attention from the actual supposed subject of study, namely education, and, second, that in a post-modern mode of "anything goes," any paradigm acceptable, the field has lost its moral compass (see Wolhuter, 2015). Related to this is the fact that the proliferation of, and celebration of a diversity of paradigms, makes for the fragmentation of the field. In his publication dealing with a parallel predicament in the field of Organizational Theory, Lex Donaldson (1995) explains how such a state of affairs can promote the disintegration of a field and of a scholarly community, with an absence of standard concepts, information overload to students of the field, and a dilution of replication which is possible. Furthermore, the scholarship body-collective in a particular field is a zero-sum game, and the multiplication of paradigms distracts attention from the actual subject of study.

Then scholars in the field show an unbalanced orientation toward the past. In the factors and forces stage, this orientation is strongly visible in the landmark volume of Harvard scholar Robert Ulich (1961) *The education of nations: A study in historical perspective*, although in most of the schema of the factors and factors protagonists, the historical as shaping factor of education systems is, in one way or another, present. In the pages of journals in the field articles, a historical slant (in explaining the present education make-up) can be found, for example, such as Dana Holland's (2010) article on higher education in Malawi. While the present also received its fair attention from scholars in the field, it would be very hard to find negotiation with the approaching future to the same extent as the past. This despite that ever since the publication of Alvin Toffler's *Future shock* (Toffler, 1970), the thesis of that book, that the key feature of the modern age is one of change, and accelerating change at that (see also Rosa, 2005).

There is also the problem of inertia in the field. Despite the spelling out by scholars in the field that the current age is one of diminishing power and importance of the nation-state (see Wolhuter, 2017), and that in the vacuum created by the fading nation-state, the locus of power is shifting in two opposite directions, upward toward international/global and supra-national structures, and downward toward sub-national, regional, and local structures right down to the empowerment of the individual; and despite theoreticians mapping out a whole hierarchy of geographical levels for comparative education studies to take place (in this regard the Bray and Thomas cube (Bray & Thomas, 1995) is the trial-blazing publication in this regard), research in the field stays tenaciously stuck at the level of the nation-state (see Wolhuter, 2008).

Finally the factors and forces' stage emphasis on the particularity of education systems has placed the field on a trajectory where extreme nominalism has characterized the field. One of the driving forces of science, to find unity in an apparently large diversity, has been subdued in Comparative Education. Taxonomy, which typically occupies a pivotal position and key organizing framework in fields of scholarship, has bypassed Comparative Education. The first elaborate taxonomy of education in Comparative Education was published only in 1997 (Wolhuter, 1997), and even after that never took center stage in the field.

To summarize, while the notion of the context has always been present in the field and is a threshold concept and very important conceptual tool, and while the term context has been explicated and refined, attention to the field has been distracted by a fascination by paradigms and a fixation on the nation state as unit of analysis, and an overbalanced attention to the past to the neglect of the future and the extreme nominalism characterizing the field also mean that the intellectual grip on this context is deficient. In the meantime, seismic changes are taking place in the world (i.e., the context). These changes can be subsumed under the collective name of globalization.

THE UNPRECEDENTED SEISMIC SHIFT IN CONTEXT IN THE EARLY TWENTY-FIRST CENTURY: GLOBALIZATION

There is no universally accepted conceptualization of globalization (Pan, 2013, p. 18). Globalization has many facets, and a large variety of trends in the contemporary world could be related to globalization (as will be explained in the next chapter). The Peterson Institute for International Economics (2020) describes globalization as "the growing interdependence of the world's economies, cultures, and populations, brought about by cross-border trade in goods and services, technology, and flows of investment, people, and information." Held (1991, p. 9) describes globalization as "the intensification of worldwide social relations which link distant localities in such a way that local happenings are shaped by events occurring many miles away and vice versa." Oxford Globalisation Professor Ian Golding and Mike Mariathasan (2014) coined the term "the butterfly defect" to describe how in the new world of hyper global connectivity, systemic risks – from cyberattacks and pandemics to financial crises and climate change – need to be managed.

While traces of globalization can be traced back at least till the time of explorations and discoveries in the fifteenth century, and Magellan's circumnavigation of the earth in 1519 (and historians of globalization has reconstructed the historical evolution of globalization identifying globalization 1.0, globalization 2.0, globalization 3.0, and globalization 4.0 as successive waves of globalization), it was after the fall of the Berlin Wall and the dissolution of the Cold War in 1990, when the disappearance of the Iron Curtain and the possibilities of the information, communication, and transport technology revolution set in motion a turbocharged globalization.

This compelling force of globalization has also attracted the attention of the Education research community, the Comparative Education scholarly circle in particular, although, as will be argued in this book, their attention was thus far somewhat lopsided. The journal *Compare* for example, ran a special issue in 2000 (volume 40 number 1) on the theme "Education in the context of Globalisation: Shifting identities, transforming cultures," while the title of Noel Mc Ginn's (1996) Comparative and International Education Society 1996 Presidential Address was "Education, democratization, and globalization: A challenge for comparative education." The journal *Globalisation, Societies and Education* commenced in 2002, and volumes such as F. Rizvi and B. Lingard (2010) *Globalizing Education Policy* and Karen Mundy et al.'s (Eds.) (2016) *Handbook of Global Education Policy* have begun to appear. It has been stated above that calls have been made for the field of Comparative Education to be superseded by Comparative and International Education; David Phillips and Michelle Schweisfurth (2014) understand International Education as studying education through a lens bringing an international perspective.

The responses of the Comparative and International Education scholarly community to the force of globalization could be arranged along two dimensions (Wolhuter, 2019). The first dimension represents a range of value-judgments of globalization, similar to those found in other social sciences and in the public discourse. University of Ghent (Belgium) comparativist Roger Standaerdt (2008) distinguishes between three stances: anti-globalization, pro-globalization, and other-globalization. The first then represents a negative judgment on globalization (and its effect on education), the second judge globalization to be a benevolent force, while protagonists of the third see in globalization *per se* potential advantages, but plead for a different kind of globalization than that currently manifesting itself in the world (Wolhuter, 2019). In Comparative Education literature, the anti-globalization stance seems to dominate (cf. Wolhuter, 2008, pp. 334–335).

The 1996 CIES Presidential Address of Noel Mc Ginn (1996) cited above is an example of a publication from the anti-globalization camp. Here globalization is seen as nothing but a tool of the neo-liberal economic revolution, now exporting the corporate rule of industry and business (multinational companies), that is, of the possessing class, to a world-scale, resulting in growing inequality on a global level, the shrinking of democratic space, undermining the autonomy of civil society, and severing the links between community and education institutions.

Examples of scholars celebrating the trend of globalization include Lidewey Van der Sluis and Sylvia van de Bunt-Kokhuis (Eds.) (2009) on the development and the circulation of global talent, Wildawsky (2010) on how globalization makes possible the development of transnational higher education, and Mark Bray's (2003) article in which he identifies new opportunities, roles, and vistas opened by globalization for the scholarly field of Comparative and International Education.

The second dimension focuses with the relative importance or agency accorded to global versus local contextual forces shaping education. On the one hand, there are those proclaiming isomorphism, seeing a homogenization of education all over the world, under the influence of the (uniform) forces of globalization. In the Comparative and International Education scholarly community, the most well-known advocates of this position are the Stanford comparativists John W. Meyer, John Boli, and FO Ramirez, a classic publication in this regard is their 1985 article published in the *Comparative Education Review* (Meyer et al., 1985). Since then they and collaborators have taken this theme further (e.g., see Zapp & Meyer, 2019). This position is also taken by scholars using the theoretical framework of neo-institutionalism, which is by no means uncommon in the field of Comparative and International Education (cf. Wiseman et al., 2014).

On the other end of the spectrum, there are those scholars who tenaciously hold on to the position of the "local" as being immune to the forces of globalization in giving shape to education systems. In the political science, there is the book of Dani Rodrik, *The globalization paradox: Why global markets, states and democracy can't co-exist* (2011), in which he argues that globalization contains within it a force which will see to its collapse and capitulation to national sovereignties. In the Education science(s), as an example of those on the pole opposite to globalization, the publication of Takayama (2010) could be cited. In her 2010 Comparative and International Education Society (CIES) Presidential Address, dealing with international policy transfer or borrowing, Gita Steiner-Khamsi (2010, p. 332) suggests that what is proclaimed to the transfer of best policy tends to be rather policies devised from the exigencies of local context, as these are understood by local actors. Urwick and Elliott (2010) show how the global trend of mainstreaming of children with special needs education strand on the rocks of the contextual realities of a low-income country such as Lesotho. The salience of context continues to be accorded importance, in one way or another, by eminent scholars in the field. Klees et al. (2020, p. 60) for example critics the World Bank's SABER (Systems Approach for Better Education Results) Study Report's recommendations for improving education in developing countries, for ignoring the context of developing countries being different from the countries from which the World Bank had extracted its list of best practices. Some scholars tenaciously cling to a attaching all value to context. Green and Mostafa (2013) concluded in their study of 25 OECD countries that there was no significant convergence in 13 of 25 policy arenas, and often trends were not as would have been predicted from global policy discourses. Archer and Cottingham (1996), in a comparative study of adult literacy campaigns, came to the conclusion that the success of adult literacy campaigns is totally a function of political commitment, that is, contextual factors, according to value to that education factors (such as pedagogy).

Other scholars have attempted to meet out in their schema place for both global and local forces. Bruno-Jofré (Ed.) (2012), for instance, use the metaphor of the "refraction": that is global forces refracted by different spaces (i.e., contexts). The use of this metaphor suggests a rather passive role for the local (contextual forces), and no dynamic interaction between local and global. The metaphor of the "dialectic between the local the local," appearing in the sub-title of R. F. Arnove, C. A. Torres, and S. Franz' (Eds.), *Comparative education: The dialectics of the global and the local*, do allocate a place for both global and local, as well as for the dynamic interplay between the two. But, from the point of view of the issue of discussion here, the main deficiency of that book, which is the most common prescribed text for Comparative Education courses at universities in the world, is that the chapters nowhere unpacks the notion of the dialectic of the local and the global in education.

At this point in time, when comparativists are shaken out of their comfort zone and set ways by the compelling force of globalization, many have seized at the notion of the "glocal," following a trend in other social sciences and in the public discourse at large (see Niemczyk, 2019; Wolhuter, 2019). The lexical meaning or definition of "glocal" is "reflecting or characterized by both local and global considerations" (Oxford Living Dictionary, 2019). "Glocal" when used by comparativists suggests according recognition to both "local" and "global" context in shaping education; although the role of each as agency is not clearly specified. Furthermore, the exact meaning of "local" is not clear. "Local" in its general use in public and scholarly discourse in the social sciences certainly has a much more, narrower circumscribed meaning than "national" which is presumably the meaning in Comparative Education discourse, given the persistent place of the nation state as dominant unit of geographical analysis (Wolhuter, 2019). However, in line with the theoretical exposé of Comparative Education comparing education in contexts at different levels (the Bray & Thomas (1995) cube, see also Manzon, 2014), Comparative Education literature contains examples of studies demonstrating the salient and active role of context as shaping force of education, at a range of levels: global, supra-national, national, sub-national (province/state), district and even local community level (cf. Wolhuter, 2008), the dominance of the nation-state as unit of analysis notwithstanding.

There is also the paradigm of historical institutionalism, which places emphasis on the role of historically developed national institutions in locking in education policies, rendering the implantation of or infection by foreign (global) policies difficult (e.g., see Fulge et al., 2016; Hall & Taylor, 1996; Simola et al., 2013; Verger, 2014). David Phillips and Kimberly Ochs (2003) constructed a four phase model for the indiginization of borrowed education policies in new contexts.

EDUCATION IN THE CONTEMPORARY WORLD

It is not only a changed context that the field of Comparative and International Education has to contend with. The subject of study of the field, education, too has taken on enhanced, unprecedented, and unbounded importance in the modern world, after having existed for long on the fringe of society.

Schools appeared for the first time in history in Ancient Mesopotamia and Egypt, by approximately 3,000 BCE, not long after the invention of writing, to train scribed (Bowen, 1982, p. 8). Two explanations exist in the scholarly literature as to the emergence of schools, namely that of the anthropologist Yehudi Cohen (1970) and that of Peter Gray (2013). Cohen offers a political rationale:

schools were created for the first time in what he calls: "civilization states." Such states, such as Mesopotamia, ancient Egypt, ancient China, ancient Athens, and the like, always entailed state formation, where smaller political units were amalgamated to form a larger political entity. The consolidation and continual existence of the state required that an elite bureaucracy, who had the assignment to administer or manage the state, had to develop a loyalty toward the state. Where Cohen ascribed a political mission to the first schools, Gray has identified an economic rationale. According to him, the economic order which came with the agricultural revolution required a new kind of person, namely a disciplined, submissive person, in contrast to the hunting and collecting economy in which an independent-minded, autonomous person had thrived. In order to cultivate the kind of person required by an agricultural economy, schools were established. It is difficult to determine the exact reason as to why schools were called into existence. At least, when mass systems of public schooling appeared for the first time in the nineteenth century, the overwhelming body of evidence and scholarly opinion today is in favor or the political motive being the dominant (without denying the existence of economic considerations too). But even if schools were created to serve the purpose Cohen ascribed to them, for very long the school stood outside the limelight of the political arena (and the economic arena and public life at large). The word "school" has after all been derived from the Classical Greek word meaning "free time use." As an illustration as to how much education was disconnected to political developments, the seismic changes of the seventeenth and eighteenth centuries can be cited. These developments such as the Glorious Revolution in England in 1789, the American independence of 1776, and the French Revolution of 1789 did after all lay the bases of the modern day political dispensation, such as the acceptance of parliamentary sovereignty and the acceptance of manifestoes of human rights. Neither those who were the intellectual *avant garde* of the American Constitution (Thomas Jefferson, Thomas Paine) nor the intellectual track layers of the French Revolution (Montesquie, Jean-Jacques Rousseau, Voltaire) were attached to a university or had themselves any university education. The role of education in economic development has an even less impressive record. As an example can be cited the (first) industrial revolution (1750–1850) – in England, adult literacy decreased from one-third to one-quarter of the adult population during this century of the first industrial revolution (Cipolla, 1969, p. 1). In Adam Smith's *An enquiry into the nature and causes of the wealth of nations* (1776, 2013) – base text and declaration of belief of capitalism and free market economics – education is not acknowledged as a production factor at all. On the contrary, the only reference to education in that book is a negative reference to education as places where young people are kept away from places of productive labor, and thus education impacts negatively on economic growth. On the other end of the economic-ideological spectrum, radical historian Neil Faulkner (2018, p. 36) casts an equally strong negative verdict on the economic role of education in earliest history. According to Faulkner (2018, p. 36), the earliest schools and education systems, which were call into existence for the purposes of government administration (tax collection and administration) in Ancient Egypt and Mesopotamia, served as a gear in a machine for the control and distribution of production in an extractive, exploitive economy, and played no role in the production of creation of wealth. While it is difficult to disprove Faulkner's point, it is equally difficult to deny Yehudi Cohen's (1970) where he also connects the formation of national education systems in the recently created nation-states in Western Europe and North America in the nineteenth century, also to the goals of forging national unity and the creation of national unity in these nascent states. Also to deny that education played no role in the putting in place the scientific-technological bases of economic progress, particularly during the industrial revolution(s).

While the publications of George Counts' (1932) and Cubberley (discussed in Chapter 15) and H.G. Wells' prophecy (discussed in Chapter 3) present interesting precursor to new ideas, it was during the second half of the twentieth century that a Copernican revolution took place as to how education was viewed as an instrument to change for the better the lives of individual and of societies. Three causal factors or at least catalysts of this change will be highlighted here.

The first is that in the year 1955, the global aggregate adult literacy rate reached the 50% level (Wolhuter & Barbieri, 2017). This means that in that year, for the first time in the history of humanity, the majority of people could read and write. That surely should have contributed to the idea that to reach people, in order to improve or to change them or society, education offers a way. The second causal factor is the creation of the United Nations' education, scientific and cultural arm or UNESCO (United Nations Educational Scientific and Cultural Organization) in 1945.

After the destructive Second World War, and the sword of a nuclear war (with the potential of wiping out the entire human species), the idea got hold that as wars start in the minds of people, the stockades against a repetition of a war should similarly be constructed in the minds of people (UNESCO, 2019). For this purpose, UNESCO was established. UNESCO was the force behind a synchronized, muscular effort of the international community for the expansion of education. Third, in the area of the relation between education and economics in particular, was the rise of the Theory of Human Capital. In his 1961 Presidential Address to the American Association of Economists, Theodor Schultz set out his theory of Human Capital. This Theory – for which Schultz was awarded the Nobel Prize of Economics in 1979 – acknowledges education- and skills levels of human resources as a production factor in economics, besides other production factors, namely labor, capital, entrepreneur, client, and land. This Theory then presented education as a production factor (or investment) rather than as a consumption factor, and resulted in a revolution in economic thought (Sobel, 1978). An empirical validation of this theory was supplied by the seminal book of Harbison and Myers (1964): *Education, manpower and economic growth: Strategies of human resource management*, in which the authors investigated the correlations between the strength or size of education systems or investment in education, on the one hand, and, on the other hand, economic power or growth, in 75 countries. At that point in history when first large parts of the Global South (particularly in Africa and South and South East Asia) gained independence, and were undeveloped or underdeveloped, and stood before the task to develop and to consolidate as newly created nation states, and second when large parts of the world (especially in the Global South) were undeveloped or underdeveloped and when the two superpowers of time competed against each other to win the favor of the nations of the Global South, Modernization Theory came to the fore. Modernization Theory postulated that large parts of the Global South stood before the challenge to modernize (in the 1960s the terms "modernization" and "development" have not yet become controversial and even discredited, the fate they suffered in later decades). Moreover, education was taken to be the main instrument to modernize nations (Fägerlind & Saha, 1984; Todaro & Smith, 2011).

Education was not only viewed as an instrument to effect economic growth and modernization. Soon it was also seen as a way to promote international peace, and the belief in education grew to the point where soon education was seen as panacea for the total round of problems or challenges facing society. German Education scholar Brezinka (1981) put it as follows: "if someone wants to reduce the number of traffic accidents, he propagates road safety education, the person wanting to eradicate drug abuse propagates anti-drug abuse education […]."

Now it is so that a voluminous body of published empirical research, based on large data sets, boasts findings similar to that of Harbison and Myers *at aggregate level* regarding the individual and societal dividends of education. Both individual and social rates of return to education have for example been calculated in a variety of contexts, and each time a positive figure is derived at (see Lozano, 2011). Lutz and Klingholz (2017) present an interesting list of studies calculating correlation coefficients between education (as independent variable) and a diverging series of individual and social indicators. One study in Malawi for example found a positive correlation between the level of people's health and the education level of their nearest neighbors. Research in Indonesia, Cuba, and Haiti found that education is a strong predictor of people's chances of surviving a hurricane or a tsunami disaster.

At the same time, the proviso has to be added that while these are aggregate figures, there is no deterministic, universal law as to the (individual and social) elevating power of education. The power or education to effect whatever change is mediated by contextual factors (economy, political factors, demography, social system, religion and life philosophy, geography). As an example can be taken the challenge of aligning the world of work with the world of education – the Gordnian knot in education systems no society has ever been successful in. While the German model of Dual Education and Vocational Training (*Duale Ausbildung*) has worked reasonably well in the German context, attempts to export it have always got stranded on the contextual impediments of the importing society (see Wolhuter, 2003). So while the unlimited belief in education gained new meaning in the framework of the seismic societal changes taking place in the current, the early twenty-first century – changes discusses in the next chapter – has spurred a stellar rise of education expansion worldwide, detailed in Chapter 3, a full understanding of this expansion requires a refinement as per context. Thus, from Chapter 4 how this expansion of education found expression in the contextual contours of the contextual landscapes of various parts of the world will be the subject of discussion.

CONCLUSION

This book is based on the premise that both the global (i.e., global forces) and the local are salient in shaping education. The local is then taken to exist as an hierarchy, at different levels as suggested in the Bray and Thomas cube (2008). The metaphor of a dialectic between the global and the local is also accepted. Mindful of the shortcomings in the field identified above – a persistent overly fixation on the nation state as unit of analysis, nominalism, too much attention to the past and relative neglect of the future – this volume investigates the dialectic interplay of forces of globalization and context in each of the world regions: North America, Western Europe, Eastern Europe, Middle East and North Africa, Central Asia, South Asia, East Asia, South East Asia, Oceania, Sub-Saharan Africa, Spanish speaking Latin America, and Portuguese speaking Latin America. As such, this book is meant to serve as an update of the first volumes which viewed education worldwide from a global optique, namely the two publications of Philip Coombs: *The world education crisis: A systems approach* (1968) and *The world crisis in education: The view from the eighties* (1985). But in also duly recognizing contextual variations, it is a refinement of the analysis presented by Coombs. And as such, it is also an update of the edited volume, *Essays on world education: The crisis of supply and demand*, edited by one of the doyens in the field, George Z. F. Bereday (1969), 50 years ago; of course then with a more refined and updated division of world regions, and with new issues and dynamics (notably globalization) receiving attention. In the next chapter, the set of global societal forces defining early twenty-first century, and sweeping all over the globe will be surveyed. In the third chapter, humanity's response by education, from a global optique, will be outlined. In subsequent chapters, the dialectic interplay between the global forces and context, and how these have shaped education responses, will be zoomed into.

It is well to remember that a main reason why there is in the world at large, or then in the public discourse of education, an interest in comparative studies of education, is to improve the domestic education project. This is evident by just casting a glimpse to the two books from the scholarly field of Comparative and International Education that did make it to the top-selling book lists amongst the reading public at large. The first was Arthur Trace's *What Ivan knows that Johny doesn't* (1961). This book appeared just after the *Sputnik* shock – when in the days of the Cold War the USSR beat the USA in becoming first to launch a satellite around the earth, in the USA, this was widely ascribed to the alleged inferiority of the education system of the USA, something that arouse a feverish interest in Soviet education (see Noah, 1986, p. 153). The second was Pasi Sahlberg's *Finnish lessons: What can the world learn from educational change in Finland?* (2010). In this case, Finland's unexpected coming out tops in the first round of PISA tests in 2001, instantaneously drew the attention of the public (as well as the scholarly) discourse on education to Finland. While the problem with government policy decision, as with the public discourse on education at large is the indiscriminate borrowing of what appears to be best international policy and practice, without factoring in contextual similarities and differences between education importing and exporting country, and while the author of this chapter subscribe to the Jullien notion of the philanthropic mission of serving humanity as a higher goal of Comparative Education, learning from others is a legitimate rationale for practicing Comparative Education. The chapters in this volume should also be read against this rationale (improvement of education in service of humanity) and the proviso of factoring-in of contextual specificities. Global trends (i.e., the global context) will be surveyed in the next chapter, followed by the education response of humanity to these challenges in a globalized world, first from a global optique (Chapter 3), the as from Chapter 4, how these global forces and education responses are co-shaped by the contextual contours in various world-regions.

REFERENCES

Archer, D., & Cottingham, S. (1996). Action research report on reflect—The experience of three REFLECT pilot projects in Uganda, Bangladesh, El Salvado. *Education Research Paper*, 17.

Bereday, G. Z. F. (Ed.). (1969). *Essays on World Education: The crisis of supply and demand*. Oxford University Press.

Bowen, J. (1982). *A history of western education* (Vol. 1). Methuen.

Bray, M. (2003). Comparative education in the era of globalisation: Evolution, missions and roles. *Policy Futures in Education*, *1*(2), 209–224.

Bray, M., & Thomas, R. M. (1995). Levels of comparison in educational studies. *Harvard Educational Review*, *65*(3), 472–490.

Brezinka, W. (1981). The limits of education. *Logos*, *1*(1), 2–5.

Bruno-Jofré, R. (Ed.). (2012). *The global reception of John Dewey's thought: Multiple refractions through time and space*. New York, NY: Routledge.

Cipolla, C. M. (1969). *Literacy and development in the west*. Pelican.

Cohen, Y. (1970). Schools and civilization states. In Fischer (red.) *The social sciences and the comparative study of educational sciences*. International Textbook Company.

Coombs, P. H. (1968). *The world education crisis: A systems approach*. Oxford University Press.

Coombs, P. H. (1985). *The world crisis in education: The view from the eighties*. Oxford University Press.

Counts, G. S. (1932). *Dare the school build a new social order?* John Day Company.

Donaldson, L. (1995). *American anti-management theories of organization: A critique of paradigm proliferation*. Cambridge University Press.

Fägerlind, I., & Saha, L. J. (1984). *Education and national development: A comparative perspective*. Pergamon.

Faulkner, N. (2018). *A radical history of the world*. Pluto.

Fulge, T., Bieber T., & Martens, K. (2016). Rational intentions and unintended consequences: On the interplay between international and national actors in education policy. In K. Mundy, A. Green, B. Lingard & A. Verger (Eds.), *Handbook of global education policy*. John Wiley.

Goldin, I., & Mariathasan, M. (2014). *The Butterfly Defect: How globalization creates systems risks, and what to do about it*. Princeton University Press.

Gray, P. (2013). *Free to learn: Why unleashing the instinct to play will make our children happier*. In *More self-reliant, and better students for life*. Basic.

Green, A., & Mostafa, T. (2013). The dynamics of education systems: Convergent and divergent trends, 1990 to 2010. In J. G. Janmaat, M. Duru-Bellat, A. Green & P. Mehaut (Eds.), *The dynamics and social consequences of education systems* (pp. 160–181). Palgrave.

Harbison, J., & Myers, C. A. (1964). *Education, manpower and economic growth: Strategies for human resource management*. McGraw Hill.

Held, D. (1991). *Political theory today*. Stanford University Press.

Holland, D. G. (2010). Waves of educational model production: The case of higher education institutionalization in Malawi, 1964–2004. *Comparative Education Review*, *54*(2), 199–222.

Hall, P. A., & Taylor, R. C. R. (1996). Political science and the three new institutions. *Political Studies*, *44*(5), 936–957.

Harbison, F., & Myers, C. A. (1964). *Education, manpower and economic growth: Strategies of human resource development*. McGraw-Hill.

Idenburgh, Ph. J. (1975). *Theorie van het onderwijsbeleid*. Tjeenk Willink.

Kandel, I. L. (1933). *Studies in comparative education*. Howard Mifflin.

Klees, S. J., Ginsburg, M., Anwar, H., Robbins, M. B., Bloom, H., Busacca, C., & Corwith, A., et al. (2020). "The World Bank's SABER: A Critical Analysis". *Comparative Education Review, 64*(1), 46–65.

Land, R., Meyer, J.G.H. & Flanagan, M. T. (2016). *Treshold Concepts in Practice*. Dordrecht: Sense.

Lozano, R. (2011). Investigating Returns to Investments in Education: An empirical study estimating returns to primary, secondary and tertiary education for countries at different levels of development. Unpublished Ph.D. Dissertation, Texas A&M University.

Lutz, W., & Klingholz, R. (2017). *Education first! From Martin Luther to sustainable development*. SUNMEDIA.

Manzon, M. (2014). Comparing places. In M. Bray, B. Adamson & M. Mason (Eds.), *Comparative education research: Approaches and methods* (2nd ed., pp. 97–138). Springer and Comparative Education Research Centre, University of Hong Kong.

Mc Ginn, N. (1996). Education, democratization, and globalization: A challenge for comparative education. *Comparative Education Review, 40*(4), 341–357.

Meyer, J., Boli, J., & Ramirez, F. (1985). Explaining the origins and expansion of mass education. *Comparative Education Review, 29*, 145–168.

Meyer, J. F. H., & Land, R. (2003). Threshold concepts and troublesome knowledge: Linkages to ways of thinking and practising within the disciplines. In C. Rust (Ed.), *Improving student learning: Theory and practice—10 years on* (pp. 412–424). Oxford Centre for Staff and Learning Development.

Mundy, K., Green, A., Lingard, B., & Verger, A. (Eds.). (2016). *Handbook of global education policy*. John Wiley.

Niemczyk, E. (2019). Glocal education in practice: Teaching, researching, and citizenship. In N. Popov, C. Wolhuter, L. De Beer, G. Hilton, J. Ogunleye, E. Achinewhu-Nworgu & E. Niemczyk (Eds.), *Glocal education in practice: Teaching, researching, and citizenship* (pp. 11–18). Bulgarian Comparative Education Society.

Noah, H. J. (1986). The use and abuse of comparative education. In P. G. Altbach & G. P. Kelly (Eds.), *New approaches to comparative education* (pp. 153–165). University of Chicago Press.

Noah, H. J., & Eckstein, M. A. (1969). *Toward a science of comparative education*. Macmillan.

Oxford Living Dictionary. (2019). Glocal. Retrieved January 25, 2019, from https://en.oxforddictionaries.com/definition/glocal

Pan, N. S. (2013). Globalization in one world: Impacts on education in different nations. In N. Popov, C. Wolhuter, P. A. Almeida, J. Ogunleye & O. Chigisheva (Eds.), *Education in one world: Perspectives from different nations* (pp. 17–27). Bulgarian Comparative Education Society.

Paulston, R. G. (1997). Comparative and international education: Paradigms and theories. In T. Husén & T. N. Postlethwaite (Eds.), *The international encyclopedia of education* (2nd ed.). Pergamon.

Peterson Institute for International Economics. (2020). What is globalization? Retrieved March 30, 2020, from https://www.piie.com/microsites/globalization/what-is-globalization Accessed on.

Phillips, D., & Ochs, K. (2003). Processes of policy borrowing in education: Some explanatory and analytical devices. *Comparative Education, 39*(4), 451–461.

Phillips, D. P., & Schweisfurth, M. (2014). *Comparative and international education: An introduction to theory, method and practice* (2nd ed.). Bloomsbury.

Psacharopoulos, G. (1990). Comparative education: From theory to practice, or are you a:\neo*, or b:*ist? *Comparative Education Review, 34*(3), 369–380.

Rizvi, F., & Lingard, B. (2010). *Globalising education policy*. Routledge.

Rodger, S., Turpin, M., & O'Brien, M. (2015). Experiences of academic staff using threshold concepts within a reformed curriculum. *Studies in Higher Education, 40*(5), 545–560.

Rodrik, D. (2011). *The globalization paradox: Why global markets, states and democracy can't co-exist*. Oxford University Press.

Rosa, H. (2005). *Beschleunigung: Die Veränderung der Zeitstrukturen in der Moderne*. Frankfurt am Main: Suhrkamp.

Schneider, F. (1947). *Triebkräfte der Pädagogik der Völker: Eine Einführung in die Vergleichende Erziehungswissenschaft*. Salzburg: Otto Müller.

Simola, H., Rinne, R., Varjo, J., & Kauko, J. (2013). The paradox of the education race: How to win the ranking game by sailing to headwind. *Journal of Education Policy, 28*(5), 612–633.

Smith, A. (1776, 2003). *An enquiry into the nature and causes of the wealth of nations*. Bantam.

Sobel, I. (1978). The human capital revolution in economic development: Its current history and status. *Comparative Education Review, 22*, 278–308.

Standaerdt, R. (2008). *Globalisering van het onderwijs in contexten.* Acco.

Steiner-Khamsi, G. (2010). The politics and the economics of comparison. *Comparative Education Review, 54*(3), 323–342.

Stephanie, Hang, M. Le, Primo, Heidi, & Reedy, Timothy E. (2020). The World Bank's SABER: A critical analysis. *Comparative Education Review, 64*(1), 46–65.

Takayama, K. (2010). Provincializing the World Culture Debate: Critical insights from the margin. *Globalisation, Societies and Education, 15*(1), 34–57.

Todaro, M. P., & Smith, S. C. (2011). *Economic development.* Pearson.

Toffler, A. (1970). *Future shock.* Penguin Random House LLC.

Townsend, L. (2016). Identifying threshold concepts for information literacy. *Communications in Information Literacy, 10*(1), 23–49.

Trace, A. S. (1961). *What Ivan knows that Johny doesn't.* Random House.

Ulich, R. (1961). *The education of nations: A study in historical perspective.* Harvard University Press.

UNESCO. (2019). Constitution. Retrieved July 23, 2019, from https://en.unesco.org/about-us/introducing-unesco

Urwick, J., & Elliott, J. (2010). International orthodoxy versus national realities: Inclusive schooling and the education of children with disabilities in Lesotho. *Comparative Education, 46*(2), 137–150.

Van der Sluis, L., & Van de Bunt-Kokhuis, S. (Eds.). (2009). *Competing for talent.* Van Gorcum.

Verger, A. (2014). Why do policy-makers adopt global education policies? Toward a research framework on the varying role of ides in education reform. *Current Issues in Comparative Education, 16*(2), 14–29.

Wildawsky, B. (2010). *The Great Brain Race: How global universities are reshaping the world.* Princeton University Press.

Wiseman, A. W., Astiz, M. F., & Baker, D. P. (2014). Comparative education research framed by neoinstitutional theory: A review of diverse approaches. *Compare: A Journal of Comparative and International Education, 44*(5), 688–709.

Wolhuter, C. C. (1997). Classification of national education systems: A multivariate approach. *Comparative Education Review, 41*(2), 161–177.

Wolhuter, C. C. (2003). Die beoogde stelsel van tweeledige beroepsonderwys en –opleiding in Suid-Afrika: Potensiaalbepaling vanuit 'n vergelykende perspektief. *Suid-Afrikaanse Tydskrif vir Opvoedkunde, 23*(2), 145–152.

Wolhuter, C. C. (2008). Review of the review: Constructing the identity of comparative education. *Research in Comparative and International Education, 3*(4), 323–344.

Wolhuter, C. C. (2015). *Quisnam Sum Ego?* Crises of identity in comparative education and the call for comparison of comparative studies. In A. W. Wiseman & N. Popov (Eds.), *Comparative Sciences: Interdisciplinary Approaches* (pp. 15–35). Emerald.

Wolhuter, C. C. (2017). The philanthropic mission of comparative and international education bequethed by Jullien: Continuing capstone of the field. *Compare: A Journal of Comparative and International Education, 47*(3), 303–316.

Wolhuter, C. C. (2019). Problematizing "Glocal" as a catchword in comparative and international education. In N. Popov, C. Wolhuter, L. De Beer, G. Hilton, J. Ogunleye, E. Achinewhu-Nworgu, & E. Niemczyk (Eds.), *Glocal education in practice: Teaching, researching, and citizenship* (pp. 19–24). Bulgarian Comparative Education Society.

Wolhuter, C. C. (2020). The significance of the BRICS countries as International Datum Line and Data Bank for South African education. In C. C. Wolhuter (Ed.), *Critical issues in South African education: Illumination from international comparative perspectives from the BRICS countries* (pp. 29–58). AOSIS (forthcoming).

Wolhuter, C., & Barbieri, N. (2017). Is the ideal of universal adult literacy in the world by the year 2030 statistically attainable? *Revista Internazionale Scienze Sociali, 2017*(1), 87–102.

Wolhuter, C., Van Jaarsveld, L., & Challens, B. (2018). Die Oorkoming van Kontekstuele Beperkinge in Leierskap aan Toppresterende Skole. *Litnet Akademies, 15*(3), 866–892.

Wolhuter, C. C., & Wiseman, A. W. (Eds.). (2019). *Comparative and international education: Survey of an infinite field.* Emerald.

Zapp, M., & Ramirez, F. O. (2019). Beyond internationalisation and isomorphism – The construction of a global higher education regime. *Comparative Education, 55*(4), 473–493.

TERRA INCOGNITA: THE CHALLENGING FORCES OF THE UNPRECEDENTED TWENTY-FIRST CENTURY GLOBALIZED SOCIETAL CONTEXT

C. C. Wolhuter

ABSTRACT

The aim of this chapter is to survey present globally present societal trends in the era of globalization, which are creating a new context for education and for the field of Comparative and International Education. The trends include the ecological crisis, the population explosion and demographic dynamics, increasing mobility, the technological revolution, especially the ICT revolution, growing affluence, the neo-liberal economic revolution, the rise of a knowledge society, the fourth industrial revolution, changing social relations, democratization, the demise of the once omnipotent nation-state, the persistent but new presence of religion, and the rise of the Creed of Human Rights. These powerful, interrelated set of societal changes, which are getting spread worldwide on the wings of globalization, is creating a new world, of (in Comparative Education nomenclature) an unprecedented new context, forcing the scholars in the field to tread unknown territory. These forces depicted in this chapter constitute a framework for subsequent chapters in the book, where the response of humanity in the education sector, to meet the challenges these forces constitute, will be the theme.

Keywords: Comparative and International Education; democratization; interculturalism; human rights; knowledge economy; multicultural education; neo-liberal economic revolution

World Education Patterns in the Global North:
The Ebb of Global Forces and the Flow of Contextual Imperatives
International Perspectives on Education and Society, Volume 43A, 19–34
Copyright © 2022 by C. C. Wolhuter
Published under exclusive licence by Emerald Publishing Limited
ISSN: 1479-3679/doi:10.1108/S1479-36792022000043A002

INTRODUCTION

In the first chapter, it was explained that Comparative and International Education perennial subject of interest is the societal context in its interrelationships with education; and that at the present point in time, this context is undergoing unprecedented, seismic changes. While these changes can be subsumed under the collective name of globalization, these are actually a wide array of forces, meriting a full exposition and discussion before the education response of humanity can be understood and interrogated. The aim of this chapter is to survey present societal trends visibly globally. As an analytical framework, these trends will be grouped using the customary rubrics used in the field when analyzing context shaping education systems, namely geography, demography, scientific and technological development, economy, social system, political system, and religion and life and world philosophy.

THE SEISMIC CONTEXTUAL CHANGES OF THE EARLY TWENTY-FIRST CENTURY

Geography: The Ecological Crisis

Ever since the publication of Rachel Carson's *The Silent Spring* (1962) (the topic of this book is the devastating effects of the unbounded use of insecticides) social scholars have cautioned, with increasing seriousness, that the most urgent crisis of challenge faced by humanity is that of the ecological crisis. For example, in his book, *Hot, flat and crowded: Why the world needs a green revolution—And how we can renew our global future*, Thomas Friedman (2009) argues that this is one of the three pivotal issues which will shape the trajectory of humanity through the present century, while Ian Mortimer (2014) ends his brilliant survey of the history of humanity the past millennium, explaining that the present unsustainable, overuse of the natural habitat puts the survival not only of humanity, but even of the planet earth at stake.

The burgeoning global population and increasing industrial activity and consumption of an ever more numerous and affluent global population, made possible by growing technological prowess (all these trends are unpacked in subsequent sections in this chapters) result in increasing use and pressure and use of environmental resources, and in increasing amounts of waste products. In his publication, *Our final century?: Will the human race survive the twenty-first century?* Cambridge astronomer Martin Rees (2003) gives humanity a fifty–fifty chance of surviving the twenty-first century.

The major dimensions of the ecological crisis are air pollution (and the resulting global warming), deforestation, pollution of marine resources, depletion and pollution of fresh water resources, soil depletion, and the destruction of biodiversity. The number of automobiles in the world has now passed the one billion mark (this mark was reached in 2010), releasing (as long as they run on fossil fuels) an inordinate amount of carbon dioxide in the atmosphere, fanning global warming. It is estimated that 750,000 people die in China every year due to air pollution (Conserve

Energy Future, 2020). J. V. Jacks and R. O. White's *The rape of the earth* (1939) and Richard Leakey and Roger Lewin's *The sixth extinction: Biodiversity and its survival* (1996) portray the frightening proportions that respectively the soil erosion and the destruction of biodiversity take on in the world at present. Estimates of the number of species that are wiped out of existence each year (the clearing of the tropical forests being the main cause) vary from 17,000 to 100,000 (Leakey & Lewin, 1996, p. 236) (estimates of the total number of species on earth vary from 10 million to 100 million (Leakey & Lewin, 1996, p. 123). An striking example of how humanity is overtaxing the stock of natural resources is that every day, humanity uses enough water to fill a convoy of trucks lining up from the earth to the moon (482 million kilometers) above the amount of fresh water replenished by rain (mainly borehole water or groundwater) (Gribbin, 2006). The world lost more than 26 million hectares of trees – an area the size of Britain – each year from 2014 to 2018 (Rowling, 2018).

Global Footprint Network calculates an indicator called "Earth Overshoot Day," that is the day in the year in which humanity has extracted from the earth what can be replenished by natural regeneration in one year. In 2019 that date was 29 July – the earliest ever (Global Footprint Network, 2019). According to Global Footprint Network (2019), humanity is currently using nature 1.75 times faster than our planet's ecosystems can regenerate, equivalent to 1.75 Earths.

The unexpected outbreak of the COVID-19 virus in 2020 shows that despite boasts of the levels of technological progress and the unlimited potential of a nascent Fourth Industrial Revolution, respected societal analyst Yuval Noah Harari (2015) claims that humanity has passed the age when the outbreak of disease poses a danger and that humanity has taken control – and rational control at that – of the forces of nature, is, sadly, probably premature.

Demographic Trends

Salient demographic trends are the population explosion, changing age profiles, migration patterns, and increased population mobility.

Demographic Trend: (i) Population Explosion

While the first acclaimed publication predicting catastrophe if population growth go on unchecked was that of English cleric Thomas Malthus in 1798, *An essay in the principles of population* (Malthus, 1798) (Malthus' thesis was that population in the world rises faster than food production, and the world is therefore inevitably heading for mass starvation and misery), the equivalent of Carson's ecology book on population growth was Stanford scholars' Paul and Anne Ehrlich's 1968 *The Population Bomb: Population control or the race to oblivion* (Ehrlich & Ehrlich, 1968). Since about mid-way through the twentieth-century a global population explosion took off, although now slowing down. The global population now (beginning of 2020) totals 7.8 billion and is projected to reach 8 billion in 2023, 9 million in 2037, and 10 billion in 2056 (Chamie, 2020). The annual population growth rate has peaked at 2.1% per year in 1968 and currently stands at 1.0% per year. Each year 81 million people are added to the global population, dropping from the 93 million peak reached in 1988. According to the projections of the United Nations Population Division (2020), the global population will stabilize at 11 billion by the year 2100.

The epicenter of the global population growth is in the countries of the Global South. The present annual population growth rates for the various parts of the world are: 2.49% for Africa (2.63% for Sub-Saharan Africa), Oceania: 1.31%, Asia: 0.86%, South America: 0.83%, North America: 0.62%, and Europe: 0.06% (World Population Review, 2020). In 2006, the numbers of births on the various continents were as follows: Asia: 76 million, Africa: 44 million, North America: 8.5 million, South America: 7.6 million, Europe: 7.2 million, and Oceania: 628 thousand (Reddit, 2020). These differential growth patterns have strong effects for migration patterns and for the supply of education, to which will be returned to later in this chapter and in this volume.

Demographic Trends: (ii) Changing Age Profile

The average human lifespan in the developed countries has been increasing at a rate of three months per year ever since the year 1840 and keeps on increasing at the same rate (Dyer, 2015). With decreasing births and increasing longevity, the global trend is toward a population increasing in age. However, this general global pattern also masks notable regional differences. The age pyramid is changing: in the countries of the Global North there is an aging or "greying" of the population, as the biggest growth is in the 65 year plus age group. In the Global South, the biggest growth is in the adult population sector, i.e., those 15–65 year of age making up an increasing part of the population and becoming the sector with the majority of people. The median age per continent currently stands at 18 years in Africa, 31 years in Asia, 31 years in South America, 33 years in Oceania, 35 years in North America, and 42 years in Europe (Desjardins, 2019). The different age profiles are one of the reasons a continent such as Europe places more emphasis on lifelong learning than any other world region, while in the Global South, the population pressure focuses attention to striving to supply primary education or basic education to all.

Demographic Trends: (iii) Migration

The globalized world is one of the increasing demographic migration, facilitated by the information, communications and transport technology (ICT) revolution (to be discussed in more detail later in this chapter). The number of international migrants in the world (i.e., those residing in a country other than the country of their birth) stands at 258 million, or 3.4% of the global population (Institute National d'Etudes Demographiques, 2020). This number of international migrants in the world rise at a rate of 2.4% per year (Institute National d'Etudes Demographiques, 2020). The countries in the world have immigrants making up various percentages of their population, rising to 88.4% in the case of the United Arab Emirates. The country with the largest number of immigrants is the United States of America with 49.8 million. The two countries with the largest number of emigrants are India and Mexico with, respectively, 17 million and 11 million per year. Two strong global vectors in migration patterns are from South (Global

South) to North (Global North) and from East (Asia) to West (Western Europe and North America). Here push (unemployment, poverty, war, political instability in the countries of the South and East) and pull (political stability, economic affluence, employment opportunities in the West or Global North) factors are at work.

Demographic Trends: (iv) Increasing Population Mobility

The ICT revolution also meant that one of the features of the globalized world is that people are becoming increasingly mobile. The world's population has become increasingly mobile. While in 1,800 people in the United States of America traveled on an average 50 meters per day, by the beginning of the twenty-first century they have traveled 50 kilometers per day (Urry, 2007, pp. 3–4). British Sociologist John Urry spells out the radical implications of this increasing mobility for the scholarly field of Sociology (loosely defined as the study of societies) in his publication *Sociology beyond societies: Mobilities for the twenty-first century* (Urry, 2000).

Economic Trends

Compelling economic trends in the world are: economic growth and affluence, internationalization, the neo-liberal economic revolution, the growth of the informal economic sector (in especially the Global South), the rise of a knowledge economy, and the fourth Industrial Revolution.

(i) Economic Growth and Affluence

Ian Mortimer's (2014) survey of a history of a millennium portrays history as one rising line of economic progress. In the long run, disruptions since the South Sea Bubble in the Seventeenth Century and the Tulip Crash in the Eighteenth Century, right through to the crises of the twentieth-century (Great Depression, Two World Wars, Oil Crisis) and twenty-first century 2008 economic crisis, could make no dent in this line. In fact, since the beginning of the twentieth century the rising curve has been steeper. In the 10-year period 2005–2015, the global annual economic output has more than doubled, from US$29.6 trillion to US$78.3 trillion (World Bank, 2016). This rise has continued to reach US$84.4 trillion in 2018 (World Bank, 2020). While mindful that this growth has occurred concomitantly with rising inequality (graphically explained by Thomas Piketty, 2014), the numbers and percentages of the global population living under the poverty line are diminishing (World Bank, 2016, 2020), and the overall picture is one of growing and wider-spreading affluence. Eight hundred and thirty-six million people in the world survive on less than US$1.25 per day (down from 1.923 billion in 1990) (World Bank, 2016). The growing affluence in the world has placed education, higher education in particular, within reach (affordability) of increasing numbers of people. The scope of inequality in the world is simply but starkly portrayed in the web-page: "If the world were a village of 100 people," then, for example, only one would have a university degree, only 20 will have access to clean, drinkable water, and 59% of the wealth would be concentrated in six people (all living in the United States of America) (Meadows, 2020).

(ii) The Neo-liberal Economic Revolution
Growing and unsustainable budget deficits by the 1980s made it clear that the
Western welfare state that had been growing for about a century was unsustainable. For example, by 1990 the public budget of the United States of America
was US$200 million, and while the Gross Domestic Product was expanding at
a rate of 8% per year, government debt was growing at a rate of 11% per year
(Davidson & Rees-Mogg, 1992, p. 394). Conservative governments in especially
the United Kingdom (Margaret Thatcher) and the United States of America
(Ronald Reagan) took the lead and scaled down expenditure and the range of
activities of the state, giving the forces of the market and the private sector freedom of reign. This neo-liberal economic revolution spilled over to the East Bloc
after its implosion since November 9, 1989, and with the dissolution of the Cold
War, and nations in the Global South no longer having the trump card to play-
off the superpowers of the West and the East Bloc for aid and grants, and in any
case having growing and unsurmountable foreign debt levels, forcing them to go
to the World Bank and International Monetary Fund for bail-outs, the countries
of the Global South followed suit. Africa's total debt, for example, increased from
US$14 billion in 1973 to US$125 billion in 1987 (Kennedy, 1993, p. 214). By the
mid-1980s, payments on loans consumed about half of Africa's export earnings.

(iii) Economic Internationalization (see Redwood, 1993)
The world economy has become more and more integrated, due to, among other
things, the communication technology revolution, the diminishing power of the
powerful nation-state (to be discussed below), and the role of institutions such
as the World Bank and the International Monetary Fund. Multinational companies are becoming increasingly prominent, and a massive international financial
market, which operates 24/7, is evolving. The surge in global capital flows is connected to the revolution in global communications: computers, mobile phones,
computer software, satellites, the web, skype, and high-speed electronic transfers.
Across the world, millions of investors, companies and banks speculate, many of
them automatically follow computer-generated indicators.

(iv) The Rise of the Informal Economic Sector (See Alcock, 2015)
A noteworthy development in the current economic development of the nations
in the of the Global South is the rise of the informal economic sector, made
possible by the space created by economic liberalization and withdrawal of
state dominance (discussed above) and the contraction of the state and its range
of activities. Mills et al. (2020, p. 193) write that the ease of doing business in
Vietnam resulted in the majority of the urban poor setting up informal shops on
sidewalks. Around 1.2 million people migrate to the cities in Vietnam each year,
where about a quarter of the workforce now make up informal street vendors sell-
ing Vietnamese *bahn mi*, a twist of the French baguette. A clean-up campaign in
2017 failed, resulting in the resignation of Ho Chi Minh City's District 1 Deputy
Mayor (Mills et al., 2020, p. 193).

(v) Rise of Knowledge Economies
In the histories of (national) economies, the following stages can be discerned. In most primitive ages or economies, a phase of hunting and gathering existed, where hunting and gathering were the only economic activities. After the Agricultural Revolution, which commenced 10,000–12,000 years ago, agricultural economies arose, where agriculture and/or other extractive industries, such as mining, fishing, or forestry for trade and profit, became the main economic activity. Next, after the Industrial Revolution, which began in England from about 1,760, industrial economies came into being, where manufacturing became the economic base. Next, a phase of services, where services constitute the majority of economic activities, appeared in North America and Western Europe in the twentieth century. Now, in the most advanced economies, a phase of a knowledge economy is dawning, that is, an economy where the production and consumption of new knowledge has become the driving axis of economic development. At the beginning of the new millennium, the World Bank issued two reports, dealing with the implications of knowledge economies for respectively the tertiary education sector and for education in the developing world (World Bank, 2002, 2003).

(vi) The Fourth Industrial Revolution
The term Fourth Industrial Revolution has been coined by Klaus Schwab (2016), describing its quintessential feature the blurring or fusion of the physical, biological, and digital/technological worlds; to distinguish it from previous waves of industrialization, namely the first industrial revolution (based on steam, from 1750), the second (based on electricity, from 1850), and the third (based on computers and digitalization, from 1960). This revolution offers at once frightening and exciting possibilities for humanity, including the development of artificial intelligence, biotechnology, robotics, automated vehicles, and many others.

Trends in Scientific and Technological Development: (i) Continued Scientific and Technological Progress
For long social scholars, attempting to mark out the present era has identified technology or technological development of the technological revolution as the or one of the key features of contemporary times. In 1980, Alvin Toffler (1980) writes in his book *The third wave* that human history has been marked by three key developments (or three waves as he termed them): the development of agriculture 10,000 years ago, the industrial revolution 250 years ago, and the technological revolution of the second half of the twentieth century. When referring to the advancing twenty-first century became vogue, Paul Kennedy (1993) in *Preparing for the twenty-first century* argued in his future scope that the two fundamentals which will drive the world in the twenty-first century will be demography and technology.

The ever-expanding frontiers of science, and the exponential increase in technological innovations, will have a significant influence on the future, if the trajectory of the twentieth century is anything to construct a projection from. While the Covid-19 virus cautioned that Harari's (2015) description of the present age as

Homo Dues (human being attaining omnipotence) may be exaggerated, it would be difficult to argue with Murray Thomas (1990), when surmising about the future of the field, this Comparative Education scholar wrote in 1990 that even our best educated guess will most likely fall short of envisioning the technological marvels lying ahead. Particular areas of the unabated scientific and technological progress are agricultural development and transformation, biotechnology, the robot revolution, and above all, the ICT (Information, Communications and Transport Technology Revolution).

Trends in Science and Technological Development (ii): The Information, Communication and Transport Technology (ICT) Revolution

J. D. Davidson and W. Rees-Mogg (1992) view the three main events in human history as the agricultural revolution (ca. 8000 BCE), the Gunpowder Revolution (in the fifteenth century) and the present information revolution. Currently an instant 24-hour planetary information network is rapidly taking shape, due to free access to and widespread use of the personal computer, the Internet, the fax machine, and the mobile telephone. Currently more than 200 billion emails are sent across the world each day (Dijkstra, 2017, p. 62). Mobile ICT technology is the latest wave and on its own represents a quantum leap in ICT technological development. M. Castells (1997), named this the "network society" in his book with the same title.

The information and communication technology revolution has radical implications for knowledge. For the purposes of this chapter, information refers to data that have been grouped into categories, or classes, or other patterns. Knowledge refers to information that has been further refined into general patterns and interpreted within a framework, or structure, of other existing knowledge. The stock of knowledge is multiplying at an ever-increasing rate. In his 1982 book, *Critical Path*, R. Buckminster Fuller (1982) estimated that up until 1900, human knowledge doubled approximately every century. By 1945, it was doubling every 25 years, and, by 1982, it was doubling every 12–13 months. IBM estimates that in 2020, human knowledge will be doubling every 12 hours (Hart, 2020). Furthermore knowledge is become democratized, as everyone has access to knowledge, by means of electronic media and sources.

One Effect of the ICT Revolution: Rise of English as International Lingua Franca

One result of the ICT revolution, within the context of current power relations (with the United States of America as undisputed super power; buttressed by the United Kingdom as the second-order world power, and Canada and Australia also no insignificant factors in the global power equation) and historically developed patterns (a large percentage of countries till recently British Colonies, and, in many of these for various sound reasons, English is still *de facto* and in some cases also de jure the official language) is the rise of English as global lingua franca (see Crystal, 2003). The central nerve center of the web and of the ICT world is the United States of America. But with 52% of the web material being English, and only 25% of the global population literate enough in English to benefit from that, this obviously creates a new inequality in the world.

Social Trends

Salient social trends are the diminishing importance of primary and secondary groupings in society, and the rise of importance of tertiary groupings, and the emergence of multicultural, diverse societies.

(i) Fading Importance of the Primary Social Grouping

The pervasiveness of the primary social grouping in society – the nuclear family, is declining. For example, whereas two or three generations ago, the family was a production unit (e.g., on a farm in a rural area) as well as a consumption unit (i.e., taking meals together), it has now for long no longer been a production unit, while the family as a consumption unit is also fading. The nuclear family has become only one of many options of lifestyles; others being the solo household (where a single person lives), single parents, and cohabitations. In 1960, 76% of children lived with two parents, in 1980, this percentage decreased to 61%, and, by 2014, this figure was 46% (Pew Research Center, 2015). Only 34% of South African children are living with both parents, 23% were living with neither, and 148,000 households are headed by a child of 17 years or younger (Kenny, 2009, p. 13).

(ii) Diminishing Importance of the Secondary Social Grouping

The second leg of the current social relations revolution is the declining importance of the secondary social grouping, or the workplace. The neo-liberal economic revolution, with its attendant decrease in number of fixed (tenured) appointments, the number of people with a "job for life" and the rise of temporary appointments and fixed term appointments; the rise of self-employment, outsourcing and contract work, and the rise of the informal sector, as well as the effect of technological advances and in particular, robotics, and the fourth industrial revolution, rendering many jobs obsolete, mean that the job as beacon of stability, security, and of identity, just does not exist to the extent that it existed in the past. The World Bank Development Report of 2019 carries the title and covers the theme of *The changing nature of work* (World Bank, 2019), unpacking these trends in the world of work, and while maintaining its belief in the primacy of human capital development in the world, highlights the imperative for society to respond to these trends with appropriate social policy and reorganization (including education).

(iii) Surge of Tertiary Social Groupings

In contrast to the family and work place, tertiary social groupings, that is, functional interest groups (sport clubs, hobby clubs, common interest groups, etc.), are rising in prominence and in importance as a result of the emancipation and empowerment that such groups enjoy under the ICT revolution, the emerging trends of diversity and multicultural societies (to be discussed in the next section), and the trends of democratization and individualism and the Creed of Human Rights (all discussed in subsequent sections in this chapter).

(iv) The Emergence of Multiculturalism and Minority Interest Groups
The persistent stream of immigrants from the Global South to the countries of
the Global North, the present day Creed of Human Rights and the denudation of
the power of the centralized nation-state (both discussed in subsequent sections
of this chapter) all have contributed to a change in ideas about the incorpora-
tion of immigrants and of viewing diversity in societies. Historically there have
been three phases regarding policies toward immigrants, these were especially
conspicuous in immigrant countries such as the United States of America (and
Canada and Australia and New Zealand). First there was a policy of assimilation, whereby immigrants were expected to take over the culture of their countries
of immigration. That was so because alien cultures were seen to be a threat to
national unity and to the integrity of the state. Cultural life of minority groups
and immigrant communities was suppressed. That philosophy and such ideas
were echoed in the treatment of all kinds of diversity: the state enforced a narrowly defined official version of culture.

The phase of assimilation was followed by phase when the ruling philosophy
and policy was that of integration ("melting pot" philosophy), whereby the idea
was that the existing culture in the immigration country and the culture(s) of
immigrants should integrate and melt together to form a new culture. Lately, in
the last phase, the "melting pot" idea has been replaced by a philosophy and by
policies of multiculturalism, that is by state and society giving positive recognition to cultural (be it linguistic, religious, or otherwise) diversity and respecting
the rights of minorities. The loss of power of central governments and the global
information network (bypassing the authority of the state) have contributed to
the empowerment of minority interest groups, such as women's rights groups,
eco-conscious groups, animal rights groups, or other single-issue groups. In contemporary society, diversity is valued and no longer frowned upon. Davidson and
Rees-Mogg (1992, p. 304) write about the "fracturing of culture": the ICT revolution with the resulting increase in volumes and types of information will tend to
fragment culture. Persons living in close proximity to each other may no longer
share the common experiences in culture, and central governments will no longer
be in a position to enforce a uniform culture. The ICT revolution has facilitated a
market choice of channels of instruction, entertainment, information, etc., with
the result that people who live within blocks of one another may have radically
different habits and values. The ICT revolution, the Creed of Human Rights,
democratization, and individualization have produced a division of cultures. It is
no longer possible to identify a person's culture, lifestyle or tastes simply from the
country in which he/she lives.

Political Trends

Conspicuous political trends are the demise of the once omnipotent nation-state,
the rise of supranational and international structures, and subnational structures
filling the vacuum left by the nation-state, decentralization, democratization, and
individualization.

(i) The Demise of the Once Omnipotent Nation-State
The ICT revolution, discussed above, the globalization of economies, and downscaling of the activities of the state out of necessity and subsumed under the name of the neo-liberal economic revolution, all contribute toward the denudation of the power of the state.

At the same time, it should be stated that many nations in the Global South, in particular, face the challenge of building the efficiency of the state to be able to fulfill those core functions that do pertain to the state (give the state its *raison d'être*, functions no other institution can fulfil) such as fighting terrorism, corruption, drug trafficking, and securing the security of the lives and property of its citizens. In many Global South societies, weak, incompetent or non-existent governments (the term "failed state" has gained currency) are the source of severe problems (see Fukuyama, 2004).

(ii) Rise of Supranational and International Structures, and Sub-national Structures
With the vacuum created by the erosion of the power of the nation-state, the locus of power is shifting from the nation-state in two opposite directions: upward toward supranational (of which the European Union is perhaps the best example) and international structures (examples of this include the role of the World Bank and the International Monetary Fund in effecting the neo-liberal economic revolution, and the United Nations, for example, in mobilizing the international community behind the Millennium Development Goals), and downward in a process of decentralization and the affirmation of the autonomy by civil society, toward subnational and local structures, and eventually right to the level of the individual.

(iii) Democratization
The empowerment of the individual, the loss of control by the state, and the current wave of economic liberalization have also ignited a process of democratization, which first (in the 1990s) swept conspicuously through the countries of the erstwhile Eastern Bloc, followed by the countries of the Global South. The information and communication revolution, too, has played its role in democratizing the world, and in democratizing the influence of the individual. In the early 1990s, with the then recently passed Cold War Era, Francis Fukuyama, in his book *The end of history and the last man* (1992) predicted the end of history as the democratic system of government together with free-market economics (discussed above under the neo-liberal economic revolution) are winning the ideological war and become the universal political-economic order. While the world and history has proved to be more complex (as will be expatiated on in the next paragraph and in subsequent sections and chapters), he does capture the essence of a first-order trend in the modern world.

While Daron Acemoglu and James Robinson convincingly argue in their book *Why nations fail: The origin of power, prosperity and poverty* (2012) that the key difference between prosperous, winning nations and poverty-stricken losing nations, is the existence of a system and culture of transparent, accountable, functioning democracy, and notwithstanding the macro-trend (over the past 35 years) of democratization; political analysts have detected a decline in the advance of democracy in many countries in recent years (see Lührmann & Lindberg, 2019) and Steven Levitsky and Daniel Ziblatt, in their book *How democracies die* (2018) identify a number of alarming threats to democracy in the contemporary world. This underscores the role of education to deepen and secure democracy – a theme which will be returned to in subsequent chapters in this book – once again.

(iv) Individualization
Customized manufacturing, individual access to a variety of information, the breakdown of state-controls, and the rise of the Creed of Human Rights, all contribute to individualization (empowering the individual and raising the importance of the individual). Through the advertising industry, business has added to this feeling of self-importance of the individual. This was well depicted in the 2002 BBC Documentary "The Century of the Self," which was followed by millions around the globe. During recent decades, the explosion of CD's, Walkman, videos, the Internet, Facebook, and the like all added to the growing sense of self-centeredness, because each individual can make his/her own choices without consulting others. Some social science scholars caution about the emergence of a culture of narcissism becoming visible in modern society (and how easy that can go over into sociopathologies such as greed, corruption, a sense of entitlement, and the evasion of personal responsibility, and the like), and point that the difference between positive self-esteem and narcissism should be recognized (e.g., see MacDonald, 2014; Twenge & Campbell, 2010) – something also of relevance when education is coming under the spotlight. For example, in the higher education sector, the academic profession finds itself increasingly sandwiched between the demands of management and government from above, and from beneath from students (now names "clients") with a growing sense of entitlement, not only distorting the historic master–student relationship, bit distracting the academic profession and academe from its unhindered pursuit of truth (see Lukianoff & Haidt, 2018).

Religious and Life-philosophical Trends
Salient religious and life-philosophical trends in the early twenty-first century society include the persistent but changed presence of religion, the rise of the Creed of Human Rights, interculturalism, and individualism, materialism, and consumerism.

(i) The Persistent But Changed Presence of Religion
Despite the frequently made claim that the present age is a post-religious age, religion persists in being an important factor of the life of people and in societies. The survey of the Pew Research Center in 2012 found that 84% of the global population regard themselves as belonging to some kind of religious affiliation. The Pew

Research Center's data and projections indicate that this will continue till at least 2050. However, the presence of religion in society is changing and is becoming more varied and complicated than in the past. First, multireligious societies, which is part of the multicultural make up of modern societies, as explained above, is taking on form. Second, many people consider themselves to be religious but do not belong to an organized religious community. Third, people no longer fit into neat categories such as "Christian" or "Sikh Muslim" but put together their own individualized belief systems. Fourth, there is spirituality and its appearance. Some people regard themselves as religious but not spiritual, some as neither religious or spiritual, some as spiritual but not religious, and some as both religious and spiritual, somewhere on a continuum regarding where they place the relative importance of these two in their lives.

Religion has exerted an important force on the lives of individuals, societies, and history. In the scholarly literature, this has for the first time graphically been depicted by Max Weber in his 1905 *The Protestant ethic and the spirit of capitalism* (Weber, 1905), and recently again by Samuel Huntington (1996) in his 10 "civilization blocks" (i.e., religious regions in the world) which he contended will constitute the fault lines in a post-Cold War world. In Comparative Education too, as has been explained in the previous chapter, religion (and life and world view) has always been acknowledged as one of the contextual forces shaping education systems. With the persistent, and more complicated manifestation of religion in society, it is little wonder that edited volumes on the topics of the relation between religion and education keep on appearing in the field of Comparative and International Education (e.g., see Sivasubramanian & Hayhoe, 2018; Wolhuter & De Wet, 2014).

Two other life-philosophical trends are the spread of the Western, individualistic, materialistic outlook to all corners of the world, and likewise, the Creed of Human Rights finding subscription virtually all over the world.

(ii) The Rise of the Creed of Human Rights

Ever since the seventeenth century leading philosophers and political theorists have tabled the idea of Human Rights, that is, that all human beings have a set of basic rights, beyond the will of any king or sovereign or democratically elected majority. In the twentieth century, and especially after the Second World War, the Creed of Human Rights was internationalized. In 1948, the United Nations General Assembly accepted its *Universal Declaration of Human Rights* (United Nations, 1948). Based on this concerted statement by the international community, Manifestoes of Human Rights became part of the Constitutions and Legal Frameworks of many countries. In this manner, the Creed of Human Rights became the reference point of a new moral order in the world (Prozesky, 2018). In one form or another, education, especially Basic Education, is commonly in these Manifestoes of Human Rights pronounced as a Human Right.

(iii) Interculturalism

While the increasing individualism, multiculturalism and empowerment of minority groups have spawned a value revolution in society, that is, a diversity of value systems, replacing the historically more homogenous societies, already in 1996,

Dalin and Rust (1996, p. 65), in one of the first publications in field of Comparative Education to carry the term "twenty-first century" in its titles, cautioned that there will have to be some limits to and reconciliation between the plurality of value systems, to ensure peaceful co-existence. Francis Fukuyama (1999, p. 16) writes about the need for "social capital," which he defines (i.e., other than the Bourdieuan definition of the term) as a set of informal values or norms adhered to by a group that permits cooperation between them (Fukuyama, 1999, p. 16).

In recent years, particularly after the terrorist attacks of 9/11, it seems as if the philosophy of multiculturalism and the pedagogy of multicultural education have been superseded by a philosophy of interculturalism (and the pedagogy of intercultural education). Markou (1997) explains the four principles of intercultural education as follows:

- Education with empathy, which means showing deep understanding for others, and trying to understand their position.
- Education with solidarity, which means that an appeal is directed to the cultivation of a collective conscience, and to the promotion of social justice.
- Education with intercultural respect.
- Education with ethicist thinking, which assumes the presence of dialogue.

(iv) Individualism, Materialism, Consumerism
A final trend that can be discerned as part of the globalization process is the spread of individualism, materialism, and consumerism. Individualism and its antecedents have been discussed above. Some scholars also relate these trends to the neo-liberal economic revolution, and some portray these as Western values permeating the rest of the world (notwithstanding equally discerning trends of diversification of value systems, as discussed above), carried by the processes of globalization.

CONCLUSION

A powerful, interrelated set of societal changes, which are getting spread worldwide on the wings of globalization, is creating a new world, of (in Comparative Education nomenclature) an unprecedented new context, forcing the scholars in the field to tread unknown territory. As was explained in the first chapter, since the mid-twentieth century, humanity looks onto education to equip itself for the world. In the next chapter, changes in education in response to the new context will be surveyed, from a global optique.

REFERENCES

Acemoglu, D., & Robinson, J. A. (2012). *Why nations fail: The origin of power, prosperity and poverty.* Profile Books.
Alcock, G. G. (2015). *Kasinomics: African informal economics and the people who inhabit them.* Tracey McDonald Publishers.

Carson, R. (1962). *The silent spring*. Houghton Mifflin.

Castells, M. (1997). *The network society*. Blackwell.

Chamie, J. (2020). World Population: 2020 Overview. Retrieved April 4, 2020, from https://yaleglobal.yale.edu/content/world-population-2020-overview

Crystal, D. (2003). *English as a global language*. Cambridge University Press.

Conserve Energy Future. (2020). Air Pollution Facts. Retrieved March 28, 2020, from https://www.conserve-energy-future.com/various-air-pollution-facts.php

Dalin, P., & Rust, V. D. (1996). *Towards schooling for the twenty-first century*. Redwood Books.

Davidson, J. D., & Rees-Mogg, W. (1992). *The great reckoning: How the world will change in the depression of the 1990s*. Sidgwick & Jackson.

Desjardins, J. (2019). Median age of population per continent. *Virtual Capitalist*, February 15. Retrieved April 6, 2020, from https://www.visualcapitalist.com/mapped-the-median-age-of-every-continent/

Dijkstra, A. (2017). *Wie (niet) reist is gek*. Prometheus.

Dyer, G. (2015). Three months a year. *New Vision*, January 29. Retrieved April 6, 2020, from https://www.newvision.co.ug/new_vision/news/1319823/months

Ehrlich, P., & Ehrlich, A. (1968). *The population bomb: Population control or the race to oblivion*. Ballantine.

Friedman, T. L. (2009). *Hot, flat and crowded: Why the world needs a green revolution—And how we can renew our global future*. Penguin.

Fukuyama, F. (1999). *The great disruption: Human nature and the reconstitution of social order*. The Free Press.

Fukuyama, F. (2004). *State building—Governance and world order in the twenty-first century*. Profile Books.

Fuller, R. B. (1982). *Critical paths*. St. Martins Press.

Global Footprint Network. (2019). Earth Overshoot Day 2019 is July 29th, the earliest ever. Retrieved April 7, 2020, from https://www.footprintnetwork.org/2019/06/26/press-release-june-2019-earth-overshoot-day/

Gribbin, J. (2006). The meaning of the 21st century by James Martin. *The Independent*, November 3. Retrieved January 1, 2019, from https://www.independent.co.uk/arts-entertainment/books/reviews/the-meaning-of-the-21st-century-by-james-martin-422636.html

Harari, Y. N. (2015). *Homo Deus: A brief history of tomorrow*. Penguin.

Hart, J. (2020). *Modern workplace learning*. Modern Workplace Learning Centre.

Huntington, S. P. (1996). *The clash of civilization and the remaking of world order*. Simon and Schuster.

Institute National d'Etudes Demographiques. (2020). World Migration Patterns. Retrieved April 6, 2020, from https://www.ined.fr/en/everything_about_population/demographic-facts-sheets/focus-on/migration-worldwide/

Jacks, J. V., & White, R. O. (1939). *The rape of the earth*. Faber.

Kennedy, P. (1993). *Preparing for the twenty-first century*. Fontana Press.

Kenny, A. (2009). Fathers and roots of failure. *The Citizen*, August 11, p. 1.

Leakey, R., & Lewin, R. (1996). *The Sixth Extinction: Biodiversity and its survival*. Weidenfeld and Nicolson.

Levitsky, S., & Ziblatt, D. (2018). *How democracies die*. Broadway Books.

Lührmann, A., & Lindberg, S. I. (2019). A third wave of autocratization is here: What is new about it? *Journal of Democratization, 26*(7), 1095–1113.

Lukianoff, G., & Haidt, J. (2018). *The coddling of the American mind: How good intentions and bad ideas are setting up a generations for failure*. Penguin.

MacDonald, P. (2014). Narcissism in the modern world. *Journal of Psychodynamic Practice, 20*(2), 144–153.

Markou, G. (1997). *Introduction to intercultural education*. Pappas Bros.

Malthus, T. R. (1798). *Essay on the principles of population*. J. Johnson.

Meadows, D. (2020). If the world were a village of 100 people. Retrieved May 3, 2020, from http://www4.uwm.edu/ptb/africology100/worldvillage.pdf

Mills, G., Obasanjo, O., Desalegn, H., & Van der Merwe, E. (2020). *The Asian aspiration: Why and how Africa should emulate Asia*. Picador Africa.

Mortimer, I. (2014). *Human race: 10 Centuries of change on earth.* Vintage.

Pew Research Center. (2012). The global religious landscape. Retrieved December 12, 2017, from www. pewforum.org/2012/12/18/global-religious-landscape-exec/

Pew Research Center. (2015). Social and demographic trends. Retrieved April 10, 2020, from https:// www.pewsocialtrends.org/2015/12/17/1-the-american-family-today/

Piketty, T. (2014). *Capital in the twenty-first century.* Harvard University Press.

Prozesky, M. (2018). Tomorrow's ethics in a globalizing world. *Journal for the Study if Religion, 31*(1), 307–317. Retrieved April 12, 2019, from http://dx/doi.org/10.17159/2413-3027/2018/v31n1a17

Reddit. (2020). Number of babies born per continent in 2016. Retrieved April 6, 2020, from https:// www.reddit.com/r/MapPorn/comments/6z77b4/number_of_babies_born_in_each_continent_ in_2016/

Redwood, J. (1993). *The global marketplace: Capitalism and its future.* Harper Collins.

Rees, M. (2003). *Our final century?: Will the human race survive the twenty-first century?* William Heinemann.

Rowling, B. (2018). World losing battle on 2020 goal to cut deforestation. Thomson Reuters Foundation. Retrieved April 9, 2020, from https://news.trust.org/item/20190912123534-rteig/

Schwab, K. (2016). *The fourth industrial revolution.* Penguin.

Sivasubramanian, M., & Hayhoe, R. (Eds.). (2018). *Education and religion: Comparative and international perspectives.* Symposium Books.

Thomas, R. M. (1990). Postscript C into the future: What developments may lie in the decades ahead? In R. M. Thomas (Ed.), *International comparative education: Practices, issues and prospects.* Pergamon.

Toffler, A. (1980). *The third wave.* Pan.

Twenge, J. W., & Campbell, W. K. (Eds.). (2010). *The narcissism epidemic.* Free Press.

United Nations. (1948). *The Universal Declaration of Human Rights.* [Online]. Retrieved April 12, 2019, from http://www.un.org/en/universal-declaration-human-rights/

United Nations Population Division. (2020). World population prospects. Retrieved April 6, 2020, from https://population.un.org/wpp2019/Graphs/DemographicProfiles/Line/900

Urry, J. (2000). *Sociology beyond societies: Mobilities for the twenty-first century.* Routeldge.

Urry, J. (2007). *Mobilities.* Polity Press.

Weber, M. (1905, 2002). *The protestant ethic and the spirit of capitalism.* Penguin.

Wolhuter, C. C., & De Wet, C. (Eds.). (2014). *International comparative perspectives on religion and education.* Sunmedia.

World Bank. (2002). *Constructing knowledge societies: New challenges for tertiary education.* The World Bank.

World Bank. (2003). *Lifelong learning in the global knowledge economy: Challenges for developing countries.* World Bank.

World Bank. (2016). *World development indicators.* The World Bank.

World Bank. (2019). *The changing nature of work (2019 World Development Report).* The World Bank.

World Bank. (2020). *World development indicators.* The World Bank.

World Population Review. (2020). World population. Retrieved April 6, 2020, from https://worldpopulationreview.com/continents/

TERRA NOVA: THE GLOBAL EDUCATION RESPONSE

C. C. Wolhuter

ABSTRACT

This chapter will now focus on humanity's response to the seismic contextual changes brought about by globalization at the cusp of the twenty-first century. The signature feature of this response is an enrollment explosion. Other features are four driving policyscapes (that aligned to capabilities theory, neo-liberal economics, the Creed of Human Rights, and social justice), education for sustainable development, managerialism, decentralization, Global, Citizenship Education, Multicultural and Intercultural education, Multilingualism and the rising importance of English as international lingua franca, Human Rights Education, from STEM to STEAM education and a reappreciation of the social sciences and the humanities, the divergent calls for relevance, new ways of production and packaging of knowledge, a shift from teaching to learning, new learning theories, and the rise of international testing regimes. In many ways, these responses are incomplete and still searching for the perfect fit in each context. It is in this regard where the value of Comparative and International Education comes to the fore.

Keywords: Enrollments; capabilities theory; education for sustainable development; global citizenship education; human rights; neo-liberal economics; social justice

INTRODUCTION

As was explained in the first chapter, since the mid-twentieth century, education has looked onto by humanity as the panacea for every societal ill or challenge. This chapter will now focus on humanity's response to the seismic contextual

World Education Patterns in the Global North:
The Ebb of Global Forces and the Flow of Contextual Imperatives
International Perspectives on Education and Society, Volume 43A, 35–52
Copyright © 2022 by C. C. Wolhuter
Published under exclusive licence by Emerald Publishing Limited
ISSN: 1479-3679/doi:10.1108/S1479-36792022000043A004

changes brought about by globalization at the cusp of the twenty-first century. These responses are summarized in table form in Table 1, next to a summary of the contextual forces discussed in the preceding chapter. Subsequently these responses will now be unpacked.

Table 1.   Global Societal Trends and Humanity's Response in
terms of Education.

Global Forces	Education Patterns
Signature feature: Globalization	*Signature feature:* Enrollment swell
Ecological crisis	Global expansion drives
Population explosion	Lifelong education
Changing age pyramid	Distance education and e-learning
Migration	
Mobility	
Economic growth and affluence	*Driving policyscapes*
Internationalization	Capabilities theory, neo-liberal economics, Creed
Neo-liberal economic revolution	of Human Rights, Social justice
Informal economic sector	*Objectives*
Knowledge economy	Education for sustainable development
Fourth Industrial Revolution	
Technological progress	*Governance and organization*
ICT Revolution	Managerialism
English as international lingua franca	Decentralization
Declining importance of primary and	Privatization
secondary social groupings en rise of	
importance of tertiary social groupings	
Rise of multicultural societies	
Demise of once omnipotent nation state	School ladder
Supra-national and international structures	
Decentralization	
Individualization	
Democratization	
Persistent but changing nature of religion	*Curriculum*
Creed of Human Rights	- Global Citizenship Education
Individualism	- Multicultural and Intercultural education
	- Multilingualism and the rising importance of
	English as international lingua franca
	- Human Rights Education
	- STEM to STEAM and a reappreciation of the
	social sciences and the humanities
	- The divergent calls for relevance
	New ways of production and packaging of
	knowledge
	Modes I, II, and III Knowledge
	Teaching and learning
	-shift in emphasis from teaching to learning
	-new pedagogies
	-new theories and views on learning
	(from information absorption to evaluation and
	creation of knowledge)
	Assessment
	-Rise of international test series

SIGNATURE FEATURE: ENROLLMENT SWELL

The population growth, the increasing affluence, democratic rights, and emphasis on the individual, as well as the new value which a knowledge economy attach to education, all contributed to an enrollment swell becoming the signature feature of humanity's response, in the education sector, to the exigencies of globalized century. The proportions of this enrollment swell are portrayed in Table 2 (enrollment figures) and Table 3 (enrollment ratios).

The figures in Tables 2 and 3 speak of a massive education expansion. While in every part of the world this expansion is visible, the exact expansion (as per numbers and percentages per level) differ from region to region, according to population dynamics, level of affluence and historical factors. While the countries in the Global North, for example, are well in the stage of mass higher education (in 2012 Canada became the first country in the world where more than 50% of the adult population have a higher education qualification, followed soon after by Russia, and currently Israel is approaching that status too), many countries in the Global South at the other end of the spectrum do not even have universal adult literacy at present or even on the horizon (as is pointed out elsewhere in this chapter).

A massive education expansion project got off the ground since the mid-twentieth century. This expansion has by no means abated or run out of steam, in fact, in the twenty-first century, it made a quantum leap and went into an even higher orbit. This stellar rise of the international education expansion project is unprecedented in history. Since 75 years ago, education has expanded worldwide more the than the entire preceding human history. Indeed, and mindful of the societal trends depicted in the previous chapter, HG Wells' (1866–1946) prophecy that the future is "… a race between education and catastrophe" has turned out to be true.

Table 2. Global Enrollments at Education Institutions.

Year Level	1950	2000	2018
Primary education	177,145,000	657,302,902	750,739,389
Secondary education	38,040,000	452,347,430	594,663,192
Higher education	6,317,000	100,159,487	223,671,873

Sources: UNESCO (1971, 2020).

Table 3. Global Gross Enrollments Ratios in Education (Percentages).

Year Level	1950	2000	2018
Primary education	59	98.77	103.95
Secondary education	13	57.93	75.56
Higher education	5	19.08	38.04

Sources: UNESCO (1971, 2020).

Global Expansion Drives

In an age of globalization, it was not only national governments which initiated education expansion drives, these drives were also launched by the global community in a concerted mode. While this idea of international cooperation in education for the betterment of humanity, and precursors can be found in the earliest work of UNESCO, such as the UNESCO Experimental Literacy Project in the 1960s, and the UNESCO Literacy for All in 2000 Project in the last part of the twentieth century, it got off in full motion with the *Education for All* movement or the Jomtien Declaration of 1990 and its follow-up, the Dakar Framework for Action in 2000, the education part of the United Nations Millennium Development Goals (in 1990 set for 2015), and after the lapse of 2015, the education part of the United Nations Sustainable Development Goals.

At a meeting organized by UNESCO, the Ministers of Education of the world met at Jomtien, Thailand, from March 3 to 5, 1990, and issued the World Declaration on Education for All (Jomtien Declaration) which stated that: "Every person – child, youth and adult – shall be able to benefit from educational opportunities designed to meet their basic learning needs" (UNESCO, 1990).

One of the eight millennium development goals dealt with education. This goal was "to promote universal primary education." Goal 4 of the Seventeen Sustainable Development Goals, "access to inclusive, equitable quality education for everyone," was packed out at an international conference held on May 19–22, 2015 in Incheon, South Korea, attended by 1,600 delegates from 160 countries, including 120 Ministers of Education (cf. UNESCO, 2015b). This conference resulted in the INCHEON Declaration, where the goal, "inclusive and equitable quality education and lifelong learning opportunities for all" is unpacked as the Vision for Education for 2030 by the international community (UNESCO, 2015b). This vision includes:

> [...] the provision of 12 years of free, publicly funded, equitable quality primary and secondary education, of which at least nine years are compulsory, leading to relevant learning outcomes. We also encourage the provision of at least one year of free and compulsory quality pre-primary education and that all children have access to quality early childhood development, care and education. (UNESCO, 2015b)

Lifelong Learning

In an age of the rapid multiplication of knowledge, and an aging population, education is more and more no longer conceived as an once-off event (taking place in the childhood and adolescent phases) in a lifetime, but something spanning the entire life cycle.

The development of policies of lifelong learning has been most advanced in the Global North (where universal primary and even universal secondary education have been attained, as has mass higher education) and where the population is aging. In a country such as Germany, *Umschulung* (second chance) education has long been part of the education dispensation, and with the formation of the European Union, and the idea of a knowledge economy becoming its trademark in the work, already in 2000 (i.e., on the even before the official inception of the European Union) a policy document entitled *A Memorandum of Lifelong Learning* (European Commission, 2000) was released. Outside the formal education system, chapters of the "University of the Third Age" are flourishing.

Distance Learning

Distance learning, and in its latest version, e-learning, has given the expansion of education, higher education in particular, further momentum. It is especially in the Global South where distance education has given many people access to higher education, who would not have enjoyed such access otherwise (see Perraton, 2005; Young et al., 1980). Tellingly, the University of the South Africa (currently with 420,000 students the largest university in Africa), world pioneer in distance tuition, commenced in 1947, two decades before the Open University in the United Kingdom commenced, and the biggest university in the world today, with over four million students, is Indira Gandhi National Open University in India. In recent decades, national open universities have opened in one country after the other, from Hagen University in Germany to the Open University of Tanzania, and recently, the growth of MOOCS (Mass Online Open-Access Courses) (cf., e.g., the Khan Academy) in especially the global north has opened up a new dimension of making higher education more accessible by using technology for distance education (see Ogden et al., 2020). At the time of writing (April 2020), the worldwide COVID-19 threat has forced universities (and even education institutions below the tertiary echelon) worldwide to go more on-line (this will probably permanently alter the face of higher education, although exactly how and how much is at the time of writing not yet clear).

POLICYSCAPES DRIVING THE SCHOLARLY AND THE PUBLIC DISCOURSE AND WORLDWIDE EXPANSION OF EDUCATION

Four salient policyscapes driving the scholarly and the public discourse on education; that is finding a rationale and motivation for this drive, and for assessing education initiatives, can be discerned, namely the capabilities approach, the neoliberal economic revolution policyscape, the Creed of Human Rights policyscape and the social justice policyscaoe (see Wolhuter et al., 2022, forthcoming).

The Philosophy of Human Capabilities, as formulated by Amartya Sen (1999), Martha Nussbaum (2000), and others, views human beings as having huge potential, capabilities, and that conditions should be created so that capabilities can flourish. The core idea is that of individual self-actualization or individual excellence, while the idea of creating space for creativity (see Grigorenko, 2019) fits in comfortably with this approach of human capabilities too. The human capabilities narrative will table the argument that education institutions and systems should be crafted so as to offer maximum opportunities to each individual learner, or to individualize maximally; to make possible the development of individual talent and to make space for creativity to flourish.

The neo-liberal economics narrative views the human being as a production and consumption unit. Economic performance or output is the *summum bonum*. Key concepts in the neo-liberal economics discourse on education include the contribution of education to human capital, rates of return analyses, quality assurance, managerialism and performativity. Other favorite themes of scholarship include the privatization of education, ranking of universities, rates of return analyses, educational outcomes and the determinants or correlates thereof, and, as a source for such studies, the use of international test series data. Publications of the World Bank (and it should be noted that, according to Philip Altbach (1991, pp. 502–503), by the early 1990s, the World Bank has emerged as the largest producer of Comparative Education literature in the world) is typically in the mold of this neo-liberal economics narrative.

This policyscape is built on the fundamental principle that human beings are being endowed with basic, natural, unalienable rights. A good idea of the scope of Human Rights Education, as the message of the human rights narrative can be gleaned in the United Nation's Declaration on Human Rights Education and Training, dated December 20, 2011. Article 2 of this Declaration describes Human Rights Education as entailing education *about* human rights, education *for* human rights, and education *through* human rights:

(a) Education about human rights, which includes providing knowledge and understanding of human rights norms and principles, the values that underpin them and the mechanisms for their protection..
(b) Education through human rights, which includes learning and teaching in a way that respects the rights of both educators and learners..
(c) Education for human rights, which includes empowering persons to enjoy and exercise their rights and to respect and uphold the rights of others (United Nations, 2011).

In this narrative fits also a large part of the discourse on Peace Education and Intercultural Education. A long standing justification for the field among its practitioners, ever since the time of Marc-Antoine Jullien (1775–1848), was that one of the purposes of Comparative and International Education is to contribute to international understanding and international cooperation. In this narrative fits also the whole issue of Peace Education, and of intercultural education. The policyscape of Human Rights contends that education should socialize students into the new global order organized according to the Creed of Human Rights, education should serve to strengthen this nascent society and its moral code.

If the publications on education of the World Bank are part of the Neo-liberal economics policyscape, then that of the United Nations Education Scientific and Cultural Organization (UNESCO) is an example of an international body actively producing literature on education in the Human Rights policyscape. A very salient example is the 2006 UNESCO document on a Plan of Action for Human Rights Education (UNESCO, 2006).

Social Justice refers to the distribution of wealth, opportunities, and privileges within a society. The main theme of propounders of social justice is that human beings should be treated equally; opportunities and resources to be equally accessible to all. Social equality is of major concern, and power relations are a key concept. When it comes to education, views expressed in this narrative can be placed upon a spectrum. At the one end, education is seen as instrument to equalize opportunities (albeit normally in a different form of education prevalent in societies today). On the other end of the spectrum, the contention is that education can be an instrument empowering people and opening opportunities, but not in the present society (where education benefitting the already privileged only and/ or serves as an instrument to suppress the powerless). An example of the latter is the classic publication of Swedish scholar Torsten Husen *The school in question: A comparative study of the school and its future in Western society* (1979) ends with the conclusion that the school, promoted as "the great equalizer of society" (i.e., an instrument of social mobility), has proved itself to be rather a "great sorting machine" of society. Another example is Michael Apple's (2013) *Can education change society?*, in which the author contends that education cannot change society, before society itself changes. On the other and, Geoffrey Walford's edited volume (2016) on private schooling contains chapters expressing a range of views: some chapter authors view privatization of schools as a potential way to effect social justice in education (though often with the proviso that it should be another form of privatization than what they see in the countries they are writing about), while other chapter authors are against the principle of privatization, contending that it unavoidably works against social justice. Thus, a feature of this narrative is a strong criticism of the kind of schools/education in a society and/or the kind of society, and the contention that one or both of these should change for education to be an agent of more social justice in society.

Objectives of Education. Education for Sustainable Development

From each of the narratives of education highlighted above, one or more objective or rationale for education supply or education expansion can be found. For the capabilities narrative, the neo-liberal economic, the human rights narrative, and the social justice narrative, their respective objectives of education could be summarized as offering maximum opportunities to each individual learner to make possible the development of individual talent and to make space for creativity to flourish, pursuing maximum efficiency and profit, creating a world where the human rights of everyone are respected, and the promotion of social justice.

Without denying the embodiment of these objectives in education systems in the world, as pursued by various lobby groups in society, or the force of objectives which governments pursue with education systems (and which will be returned to later in this chapter and in subsequent chapters of this volume), however, in its concerted effort, the objective of education proclaimed by the global community is formulated in goal 4 of the Sustainable Development Goals (the international community's vision for the world of 2030), and unpacked in the INCHEON Declaration of 2015, namely, to "ensure inclusive and equitable quality education and promote lifelong learning opportunities for all" (UNESCO, 2015b). If this is, then the intrinsic aim of education, the extrinsic objective is to ensure sustainable development. Thus, the ecological challenge has given rise to a response, "sustainable development" which has become a collective noun under which the total response of humanity to the challenges of a globalized era is subsumed.

While Education for Sustainable Development has become a catchphrase for the global community's concerted education response to the challenges of the twenty-first century globalized world, the ecological crisis, more narrowly conceived, too has given rise to interesting education innovations, such as the Natur- und Waldkindergärten (nature and wood Kindergartens) in continental Europe: a most greenest version of Montessori kind of schools (see Häfner, 2003).

GOVERNANCE AND ORGANIZATION
Managerialism

One result of the neo-liberal economic revolution, and specifically its wholesale transportations of the principles of the neo-liberal economic revolution into the education sector, is rising managerialism. Managerialism is evident in especially the higher education sector, so much so that it is beginning to threaten the very essence of the mission of the university, namely the unhindered quest for truth and societal critique (see Locke et al., 2011). Growing managerialism is, however, by no means absent in the secondary and primary education levels, as is evident in the deprofessionalization of the teaching profession.

To counter this ominous trend of managerialism, what has become vogue in especially the scholarly discourse and in teacher education and school principal education programs, is the concept of Education Leadership. This ties in with other imperatives emanating from the twenty-first century globalized context, such as the need for creativity, for innovation, and individualization. How much teachers and principals are given space to exercise leadership is, however, a moot point.

Decentralization

Chiming in with the global trend of democratization and the denudation of the power of the nation-state, a worldwide movement of decentralization can be detected in education. From the National Agreement to Modernize Basic Education between the President, the Governors of all 31 States and the Teachers Union in Mexico in 1992, to post-1990 education reform in Russia (see Balzer, 1991) to the 1995 Education and Training Policy in Tanzania (signaling a major shift in post-independence education policy), policies of decentralization of education to sub-national levels of government can be detected. In 2011, Pakistan changed her Constitution in order to abolish the central Ministry of Education and shift all education responsibility to the four provinces. Taken to its logical end, this decentralization has resulted in the trend toward school autonomy, equally conspicuous worldwide, from the United States of America (see Keddie, 2016) to Israel (see Nir et al., 2016) to the 1996 Schools Act in South Africa and the 2001 Education Act of Namibia. Furthermore, there is a strong growth of private schools worldwide, as well as trends such as the Charter Schools Movement in the United States of America, community run schools such as the *Minban* schools in the People's Republic of China and voucher systems such as in Sweden and which was used in Chile for a few decades (until abandoned recently).

It should be noted, however, that the managerialism (and other manifestations of neo-liberalism in education) do pose a counter-force to decentralization. Hawkins (2000) analyzing decentralization in the People's Republic of China concludes that it is not so much decentralization of authority as it is a transfer of tasks. With the hold of managerialism and perfomativity, of centralized testing and international test series, it is not difficult to extrapolate this conclusion to beyond China. The effect of the 1988 Education Act in England (setting in place for the first time in the history of English education a national curriculum) and the standardized testing that came with the 2001 "No Child Left Behind" Act in the United States of America come to mind here.

EDUCATION LADDER

The effect of the American example as a superpower, and of recent global initiatives are evident in developments regarding the education ladder in the world. Not only is the American term "grades" being adopted by more and more countries (e.g., replacing the historically English terms "standard" or "form" in Anglophone African countries such as in the primary school cycle in Zimbabwe or both primary and secondary school cycles in South Africa and Namibia after, respectively, 1994 and 1990), but the American 6-6 school ladder is becoming more and more ubiquitous (replacing, e.g., the seven years primary school cycle in Anglophone African or the shorter primary school cycles in Francophone and Lusophone Africa which these countries inherited from, respectively, France and Portugal).

The global collective began to peddle with the idea of "basic" education by the last part of the twentieth century. This term is very prominent in, for example, the Jomtien Declaration. It superseded the fixation on "universal primary education" very prominent in, for example, the Addis Ababa, Santiago and Karachi Conferences, and Plans which UNESCO held to map out an education blueprint for respectively Africa, Latin America and Asia in 1960. "Basic" education came to be understood as primary and lower secondary education (i.e., 9 or 8 years schooling) and the term began to appear in education restructuring plans, and the compulsory education block was extended to include both primary and lower secondary education in voluntary after country, for example, the 1986 Education Act instituted the nine-year compulsory school in China; while in Turkey in 1997 compulsory schooling was extended from primary to lower secondary education, and, in India, the *Right of Children to Free and Compulsory Education Act* of 2010, which introduced free and compulsory education for children between the age of 6 and 14 years.

CURRICULUM

Global Citizenship Education

Notwithstanding the four narratives and their lofty rationales for education, there is little doubt that national education systems were created at the beginning of the era of the modern nation-state, as instruments to serve the interests of those governments. Sociologists, and political scientists, commencing with Max Weber, Emile Durkheim and John Stuart Mill, recognized that national education systems came into being as a part of the apparatus of modern government on the Western world (Mundy et al., 2026). Now the demise of the nation-state and the globalization of society and of life ask for something different than loyalty and identification with the nation-state. There is a need for the cultivation of a global mindset, or of global citizenship education.

Global Citizenship Education is indeed a contested term (see Veugelers, 2020 for the range of meanings attached to this term), but the following definition of UNESCO (2015a, p. 9), can be taken as a working definition of Global Citizenship Education:

> [...] a framing paradigm which encapsulates how education can develop the knowledge, skills, values and attitudes learners need for securing a world which is more just, peaceful, tolerant, inclusive and sustainable.

At present, a book series on Global Citizenship Education is published by Routledge, with Carlos Torres, UNESCO Chair of Global Citizenship Education, UCLA, as Series Editor.

Multicultural and Intercultural Education

As was stated in the previous section, national education systems came into being to legitimize the existence of the nation state. In fact, anthropologist Yehudi Cohen (1970), in one of the few theories offering an explanation as to why schools as institutions came into being, argues that the first schools in antiquity were created in what he calls "civilization states," the reason was to safeguard the integrity of these states, by cultivating a loyalty amongst the elite (bureaucracy and priestly class) toward the state and to suppress local loyalties to the clan or family or province. Cohen uses the same thesis to explain the modern day rise of public school systems as from the nineteenth century, beginning in Western Europe and North America. For long schools socialized and coerced the youth into the straightjacket of a narrow, officially sanctioned national culture. Extreme examples of this are the residential schools in Canada (see Indian Residential School Survivors Society, 2009) and the Stolen Generation Children in Australia (see Van Krieken, 1999) – now defunct, both involved forcibly removing First Nation children from their parents to a place where they could get an education into the Western culture. However, by the end of the twentieth century, a combination of factors, such as changing demographics, the Creed of Human Rights and others explained in the previous chapter, forced national governments to abandon these policies and to begin to value diversity, cultural diversity in particular. After Anthropology professor Franz Boas and his student-followers (Margaret Mead, Ruth Benedict, Melville Herskovits, Ashley Montagu, Gregory Bateson and others) have prepared the intellectual or scholarly field – where ideas of a racial and gendered hierarchy in the world held free reign – with ideas of cultural equality and cultural relativism (see King, 2019), contextual realities further moved the scholarly and the public discourse of education toward embracing the philosophy of multicultural education.

While Canada adopting its Multicultural Policy in 1971 and its Multicultural Act in 1988 was the first nation in the world with an official, government mandated multicultural policy, and while not all nations may have such a report of gravitas as that of the Swann Commission of 1984, heralding multicultural education in England, in especially the countries of the Global North, policies embracing multiculturalism became he norm.

Multicultural education (then in the countries of the Global North in particular) went through a particular trajectory. Token inclusion of the cultural objects and heritage was the first step, followed by the acknowledgement of other cultures as fully fledged constituent of society (as recommended by the Swann Commission in England). In later phases, such multicultural education was followed first by anti-racist education and then anti-oppressive education, before finally being superseded by intercultural education (as defined in the previous chapter).

Multilingualism and the Rising Importance of English as International Lingua Franca

In the present contextual configuration, two – in many cases, opposing forces exist pertaining to the position of language in education (both teaching of language as subject and even to language of learning and teaching too). On the one hand, forces such as the rise of multicultural societies ask for the inclusion and empowerment of a variety of languages. The principals of the European Union recommends to member states that three languages be taught in schools as from the third school year (as a minimum, and in as far as that is implemented, this boils down to the official language of the country, English and one other language), while in the United States of America, the American Council on the Teaching of Foreign Languages (ACTFL) has been busy for four decades promoting the teaching of foreign languages as a way of connecting the United States of America with the rest of the world (see Heining-Boynton & Redmond, 2014). On the other hand, there is the strong call for the privileged thorough teaching of English as the de facto and still rising global lingua franca. Perhaps the best synthesis or accommodation of all these imperatives can be found in the way China has developed, with respect to the 55 minority languages acknowledged in the Constitution of China models of trilingual education, that is, Mandarin as official language, English as international lingua franca, and the minority language. The model of each depends on the particular contextual features regarding the particular minority language and its speakers, and is described in Anwei Feng and Bob Adamson's (2015) *Trilingualism in education in China: Models and challenges.*

Human Rights Education

In the previous chapter, the stellar rise of the Creed of Human Rights was explained, and in this chapter above, when the Human Rights narrative was discussed, that Human Rights education comprise education *about* human rights, education *for* human rights, and education *through* human rights, that is, it spans curriculum, pedagogy education outcomes and then the creed of human rights also includes education supply/access. The last will mean that the emphasis will vary in the world from region to region, depending on context. International convention is vague. The proto-document, the 1948 United Nations' Universal Declaration on Human Rights, states on the right to education, in section 26:

1. Everyone has the right to education. Education shall be free, at least in the elementary and fundamental stages. Elementary education shall be compulsory. Technical and professional education shall be made generally available and higher education shall be equally accessible to all on the basis of merit.
2. Education shall be directed to the full development of the human personality and to the strengthening of respect for human rights and fundamental freedoms. It shall promote understanding, tolerance and friendship among all nations, racial or religious groups, and shall further the activities of the United Nations for the maintenance of peace.
3. Parents have a prior right to choose the kind of education that shall be given to their children (United Nations, 1948).

While publications steeped deep in the Global North contain discussions as to whether higher education is a human right, at the other end, there are 16 countries in the world where the adult literacy rate is still under 50% and 40 eight countries where it is below 75% (World Atlas, 2019). BRAC, the largest non-governmental organization in the world, based in Bangladesh (one of the countries with a low adult literacy rate), does commendable work in providing by means of non-formal education programs an opportunity for basic education for those who never had such an opportunity through the regular, form school program (see Bickmore et al., 2017).

STEM to STEAM and a Re-appreciation of the Social Sciences and the Humanities

For at least, since the mid-twentieth century a privileging and esteem of the natural sciences and mathematics and engineering (and its step-sibling vocational and technical education) have gathered momentum. That can probably be related to inter alia the 1957 launch of Sputnik and the effect that has had on education thinking in the United States at a time when the space race, the nuclear arms race, the atomic race and the economic race were all manifestations of fierce rivalry between the superpowers in the era of the Cold War (see Noah, 1986, p. 153) (it is perhaps not by accident that both the first scholarly society Comparative and International Education Society, and the first journal in the field, the *Comparative Education Review*, got off the ground at this point in time). This veneration of mathematics, natural science, and engineering culminated in the lobby for STEM education. However, some features of the globalized twenty-first century society (such as the frightening prospects of seemingly unlimited technological progress, democracy, an appreciation of creativity, and the Creed of Human Rights) (vividly argued for in, e.g., Marha Nussbaum's, 2010 book *Not for profit: Why democracy needs the humanities*) have resulted in a re-appreciation of the social sciences and humanities, and a call for STEM (science, technology, engineering, and mathematics education) to be superseded by STEAM education (where A stands for arts) (see Sousa & Pilecki, 2018). There is an inspiring predecessor in the Waldorf schools worldwide (based on the philosophy of Rudolf Steiner), where learners find copious educative space for artistic self-expression (also for individualism and spirituality – two other features of the globalized twenty-first century society).

The Divergent Calls for Relevance

The severing of the world of education and the world of the life of the learner is an old theme, as are calls for relevance. However, the neo-liberal narrative in education brought the demand for relevance in higher volume and with more urgency. What constitutes relevance is a moot point. In the Global North, this question has been taken to refer mainly to aligning the world of education and the world of work. This has proven to be difficult in history (and in simpler times) and is even less clear in times of the dawning Fourth Industrial Revolution.

Besides aligning education and work (already difficult) calls for relevance in the Global South has also come to refer to decolonizing education, that is getting it out of the grips of Northern Hegemony, reforming education so as to reflect the natural and cultural heritage of the nations of the Global South, and transforming education to be an instrument of empowerment rather than of alienation and of enslavement. On its own a challenging task, more so if to be harmonized with keeping education globally relevant and turning learners into people globally competitive too.

NEW WAYS OF PRODUCTION AND PACKAGING OF KNOWLEDGE: MODES I, II, AND III KNOWLEDGE

In the contemporary, two additional modes of the production and packaging of knowledge have emerged.

Mode I knowledge is a term coined by Gibbons et al. (2003) to indicate the manner in which knowledge has been historically generated, ordered, and taught (at least in academe and in education institutions), namely in a discipline-defined format. They use this term to distinguish such knowledge from the modern day trend of what they call Mode II knowledge. Gibbons et al. (2003) then define Mode II knowledge that is no longer generated, ordered and taught in a discipline-bound format (Mode I knowledge), but in a trans- and interdisciplinary open system where knowledge is ordered and evaluated not so much in terms of scientific criteria as in terms of practical and utilitarian considerations. This trend can be related to a number of societal trends, such as the neo-liberal economic revolution, with its call for relevance, for the demonstrable immediate practical utility of knowledge.

Then even more recently, the ICT revolution, and especially the rise of social media, created a situation where anyone can produce and disseminate knowledge (or what he/she can proclaim as being knowledge). To describe this phenomenon, Strohmaier (2014) introduced the term Mode III knowledge in order to distinguish it from Gibbons et al.'s Mode I and II knowledge, and to refer to a new mode of knowledge of knowledge production and packaging with has emerged in the contemporary world, besides Mode I and II knowledge:

> With the proliferation of data, the increasing availability of rather simple tools to analyze data and an increasing number of people who can use these tools in combination with the availability of low cost publication platforms (e.g., blogs), the potential to democratize certain aspects of scientific processes – such as empirical data analysis – seems tremendous. This might give rise to the idea that everyone who can use these tools (such as Python), and publish the results from their analysis (e.g., via blog posts) can now participate in knowledge production. (Strohmaier, 2014)

As much as the rise of Mode II knowledge, if not more, the emergence of Mode III knowledge – the appearance of unverified, unchecked knowledge which can be generated and spread by anyone (the specter of fake news and its potential dangerous consequences come to mind here) – have radical implications for education. Some of these implications will be pointed out in the next three sections of this chapter.

TEACHING AND LEARNING

The Shift in Emphasis From Teaching to Learning and From Teacher to Child

The twenty-first century societal trends outlined in Chapter 1 add up to a shift from teacher to child and, related to that from teaching to learning. Even before the onset of the millennium and of globalization, there were ideas such as those of AS Neill, whose freedom without license ideas chimes in well with trends such as individualization and democratization, but, even to the extent that these were realized in Neill's model school of Summerhill, never became part of mainstream schools. Concerning teaching and learning the emphasis has shifted from teaching to teaching and learning. In the historical conceptualization of education, teaching was privileged over learning, in as far as learning figured at all. The historical view of education and teaching as the transmittance of knowledge from (omniscient) teacher to (ignorant or *tabula rasa*) learner has become obsolete in the face of the ICT revolution, which placed knowledge in reach of everyone. Democratization and individualization, and the Creed of Human Rights too dictated a shift in emphasis from the activity of the teacher (teaching) to that of the learner (learning) when deliberating and when planning and implementing education. At the same time, learning theories in vogue too went through a long and radical developmental trajectory, which will be reconstructed in a next section below.

New Pedagogies

In line with the ICT revolution and with the shift in emphasis from teaching to learning, new pedagogies have evolved, and even better pedagogies are searched for. The radio, television, and the web have all been harnessed, e-learning, and online teaching has emerged, and recently, with the rise of mobile communication technologies, m-learning. Not that technology is a magic wand for all the challenges in the world regarding education. Côte d'Ivoire's Programme d'Éducation Télévisuelle (PETV) was the world's most ambitious attempt to harness television for public education, commencing in 1971, but went dead by 1983 after having foundered on the contextual impediments in Côte d'Ivoire (see Prosperetti, 2019). Furthermore, Carnoy (2012) contends that technology could not bring the much coveted equality or access to quality education for all in the world (which many anticipated or wished for). While Friedman (2009, pp. 26–27) writes admiringly and inspiringly about teachers in India tutoring students in North America, Western Europe, and other parts of the world electronically, it seems that ICT technology is a good aid for teachers (used correctly, also consonant with the context), it cannot replace the teacher.

The individualization trend in society has found its precipitation in the advocacy for pedagogies such as Self-Directed Learning, Free Learning, and Free Choice Learning (see Falk & Dierking, 2002).

New Theories and Views on Learning: From Information Absorption to Evaluation and Creation of Knowledge

Not only has, in tune with the calls of the time, the emphasis in education shifted from teaching to learning, but views of learning have developed and have changed as well. From the primitive, rudimentary views of the child as *tabula rasa* of John Locke in the seventeenth century, to the somewhat more refined similar model of Herbart in the nineteenth century, to behaviorism in the early twentieth century, to cognitive theories later in the century to the more sophisticated and responding to the requirements of contemporary context constructivistic, social constructivistic, and intersubjectivistic learning theories have been developed, as – in terms of the taxonomy of Benjamin Bloom – the objectives of learning proceeded from memorization and reproduction to higher order objectives such as evaluation of knowledge, synthesis, and creating own knowledge.

ASSESSMENT

Rise of International Test Series

A combination of the competitiveness of a globalized economy, the ICT revolution, and the managerialism which was a by-product of the neo-liberal economy revolution, has resulted in the rise of international test series, in the tests of the IEA (International Association for the Evaluation of Educational Achievement), such as the TIMSS (Trends in International Mathematics and Science Study) tests, and especially the PISA (International Program of Student Assessment) tests since 2001. Not only have these tests become the benchmark for the evaluation of national education systems and the surrogate measurement of the success of nations, but in many countries, it gave rise to a next tier of standardized national assessments at regular intervals (as was touched upon above in the section on decentralization). These tests have attracted the attention of the scholarly community of Comparative and International Education, and have also attracted its share of criticism (see, e.g., Meyer & Benavot, 2013). In the higher education sector, a parallel development is the development of the international university rankings industry (see Shin et al., 2011).

CONCLUSION

To the new context emerging in globalized society, humanity has responded in terms of education. Some facets of this response are impressive and commendable, such as the enrollment swell. But in many respects there is evidence of huge challenges. For example, despite the call to move away from teaching to learner centered education, from teaching to learning, from learning as rote memorization to independent and critical thinking, creativity and the self-construction and evaluation of knowledge, and despite lofty policy statements to this effect, and the exemplary pioneer work done by Maria Montessori (1870–1959) and widely followed at pre-primary school level in the Montessori schools worldwide and extensions of this model such as the Reggio Emilio Approach of Loris Malaguzzi, learner-centered institutions and systems at higher levels, apart from experiments such as the Dalton Plan schools initiated by Helen Parkhurst in 1919, remain elusive, and the traditional method and practices remain in schools from deep in the Global South, such as Eswatini (formerly Swaziland) (see World Bank, 2011, p. 90) to what is hailed as the most exemplary education systems in the world, such as Finland (see Andrews, 2013). On the other hand, in Colombia and other countries in Latin America, in not the most affluent of societies and drawing on local resources, the *Escuela Nueva* schools movement has effected a remarkable transformation in this regard. Therefore, it is in thinking through and in negotiating these challenges of contemporary education that the value of Comparative Education comes to the fore. It is in this frame that the subsequent chapters in this volume are offered.

REFERENCES

Altbach, P. G. (1991). Trends in comparative education. *Comparative Education Review, 35,* 491–507.
Andrews, P. (2013). Finnish mathematics teaching from a reform perspective: A video-based case-study analysis. *Comparative Education Review, 57*(2), 189–211.
Apple, M. (2013). *Can education change society?* Routledge.
Balzer, H. (1991). From hyper centralisation to diversity: Continuing efforts to restructure Soviet education. *Technology in Society, 13*(1–2), 123–150.
Bickmore, K., Hayhoe, R., Manion, C., Mundy, K., & Read, R. (Eds.). (2017). *Comparative and international education: Issues for teachers.* Canadian Scholars Publishers.
Carnoy, M. (2012). What does more ICT in the world economy and in post-industrial societies mean for education? Paper presented at the Foro Valparaiso, Universidad Catolica de Valpariso, Chile.
Cohen, Y. (1970). Schools and civilization states. In J. Fischer (Ed.), *The social sciences and the comparative study of educational sciences.* International Textbook Company.
European Commission. (2000). *A memorandum of lifelong learning.* European Union.
Falk, J. H., & Dierking, L. D. (2002). *Lessons without limits: How free choice learning is transforming education.* Alta Mira.
Feng, A., & Adamson, B. (Eds.), (2015). *Trilingualism in education in China: Models and challenges.* Springer.
Friedman, T. L. (2009). *Hot, flat and crowded: Why the world needs a green revolution—And how we can renew our global future.* Penguin.
Gibbons, M., Limoges, C., Nowotny, H., Schwartzman, S., Scott, P., & Trow, M. (2003). *The new production of knowledge: The dynamics of science and research in contemporary societies.* Sage.
Grigorenko, E. L. (2019). Creativity: A challenge for contemporary education. *Comparative Education, 55*(1), 116–132.

Häfner, P. (2003). Natur- und Waldkindergärten in Deutschland – eine Alternative zum Regelkindergarten in der vorschulischen Erziehung. DNB 967124190 Unpublished Doctoral Dissertation, University of Heidelberg. Retrieved April 22, 2020, from https://core.ac.uk/download/pdf/32578703.pdf

Hawkins, J. (2000). Centralisation, decentralisation and recentralisation—Educational reform in China. *Journal of Educational Administration, 38*(5), 442–454.

Heining-Boynton, A. L., & Redmond, M. L. (2014). World language education: Connecting with the rest of the world. In D. E. Mulcahy, D. G. Mulcahy & R. Saul (Eds.), *Education in North America* (pp. 299–318). Bloomsbury.

Husen, T. (1979). *The school in question: A comparative study of the school and its future in Western society*. Oxford University Press.

Indian Residential School Survivors Society. (2009). Indian Residential School History. Retrieved April 1, 2012, from http://www.ewww.glob.pe/portal/enlaces

Keddie, A. 2016. Maintaining integrity of public education: A comparative analysis of school autonomy in the United States of America. *Comparative Education Review, 60*(2), 249–270. http://www.journals.chicago.edu/t-and-c

King, C. (2019). *Gods of the upper air: How a circle of renegade Anthropologists reinvented race, sex and gender in the twentieth century*. Penguin.

Locke, W., Cummings, W. K., & Fisher, D. (Eds.). (2011). *Changing governance and management in higher education: The perspectives of the academy* (pp. 107–125). Springer.

Meyer, H.-D., & Benavot, A. (Eds.). (2013). *PISA, power, and policy: The emergence of global educational governance*. Symposium Books.

Mundy, K., Green, A., Lingard, B., & Verger, A. (2016). Introduction: The globalization of education policy—Key approaches and debates. In K. Mundy, A. Green, B. Lingard & A. Verger (Eds.), *The handbook of global education policy* (pp. 34–55). Wiley Blackwell.

Nir, A., Ben-David, A., Bogler, R., Inbar, D., & Zohar, A. (2016). School autonomy and 21st century skills in the Israeli educational system: Discrepancies between the declarative and operational levels. *International Journal of Educational Management, 30*(7), 1231–1246. https://doi.org/10.1108/IJEM-11-2015-0149

Noah, H. J. (1986). The use and abuse of comparative education. In P. G. Altbach & G. P. Kelly (Eds.), *New approaches to comparative education* (pp. 153–165). University of Chicago Press.

Nussbaum, M. (2000). *Women and human development: The capabilities approach*. Cambridge University Press.

Nussbaum, M. (2010). *Not for profit: Why democracy needs the humanities*. Princeton University Press.

Ogden, A. C., Streitwieser, B., & Van Mol, C. (2020). How COVID-19 could accelerate opportunities for IHE. *University World News*, April 4. https://www.universityworldnews.com/post.php?story=20200403133447141

Prosperetti, E. (2019). Between education and catastrophe: Côte D'Ivoire's Programme Déducation Télévisuelle and the urgency of development. *Journal of African History, 60*(1), 3–23.

Perraton, H. (2005). *Open and distance learning in the developing world*. Routledge.

Sen, A. (1999). *Development as freedom*. Knopf.

Shin, J. C., Toutkoushian, R. K., & Teichler, U. (Eds.). (2011). *University rankings: Theoretical basis, methodology and impacts on global higher education*. Springer.

Sousa, D. A., & Pilecki, T. (2018). *From STEM to STEAM: Brain-compatible strategies and lessons that integrate the Arts*. Sage.

Strohmaier, L. (2014). Mode 3 knowledge production, or the difference between a blog post and a scientific article. https://mstrohm.wordpress.com/2014/02/17/mode-3-knowledge-production-or-the-differences-between-a-blog-post-and-a-scientific-article/

UNESCO. (1971). *UNESCO Statistical Yearbook*. UNESCO.

UNESCO. (1990). World declaration on education for all, Jomtien, 1990. https://bice.org/app/uploads/2014/10/unesco_world_declaration_on_education_for_all_jomtien_thailand.pdf

UNESCO. (2006). 2006 UNESCO document on a Plan of Action for Human Rights Education. Paris: UNESCO.

UNESCO. (2015a). *Global citizenship education: Topics and learning objectives*. UNESCO.

UNESCO. (2015b). *INCHEON Declaration and Framework for Action for the Implementation of Sustainable Development Goal 4*. Retrieved December 2, 2018, from http://uis.unesco.org/

sites/default/files/documents/education-2030-incheon-framework-for-action-implementation-of-sdg4-2016-en_2.pdf

UNESCO. (2020). Statistics. Retrieved March 31, 2020, from http://data.uis.unesco.org/

United Nations. (1948). *The universal declaration of human rights*. [Online]. Retrieved April 12, 2019, from http://www.un.org/en/universal-declaration-human-rights/

United Nations. (2011). United Nations Declaration on Human Rights Education and Training. New York, NY: United Nations. Retrieved from https://digitallibrary.un.org/record/715039?ln=en. Accessed on November 27, 2019.

Van Krieken, R. (1999). The 'stolen generations' and cultural genocide: The forced removal of Australian indigenous children from their families and its implications for the sociology of childhood. *Childhood, 6*(3), 297–311.

Veugelers, W. (2020). Different views on global citizenship education making global citizenship education more critical, political and justice-oriented. In D. Schugurensky & C. Wolhuter (Eds.), *Global citizenship education and teacher education*. Routledge.

Walford, G. (Ed.). (2016). *Privatization. Education and social justice*. Routledge.

Wolhuter, C. C., Spinoza, O., & McGinn, N. (2022, forthcoming). Narratives in the public and scholarly education discourse and the value thereof as a heuristic device for Comparative and International Education (forthcoming).

World Bank. (2011). *The education system of Swaziland: Training and skills development for shared growth and competitiveness*. The World Bank.

World Atlas. (2019). List of countries by literacy levels. Retrieved April 17, 2020, from https://www.worldatlas.com/articles/the-highest-literacy-rates-in-the-world.html

Young, M. F. D., Perraton, H., Kenkins, J., & Dodd, T. (1980). *Distance teaching for the third world: The lion and the clockwork mouse. Incorporating a directory of distance teaching projects*. Routledge.

THE GLOBALIZATION OF EDUCATION IN NORTH AMERICA: A DISCUSSION OF IMMIGRATION, IDENTITY, AND IMAGINATION

Alexander W. Wiseman

ABSTRACT

North America is both geographically large and demographically diverse, which makes a discussion about globalization in North America difficult to distinguish from globalization writ large. This chapter attempts to do so nonetheless by examining tangible, virtual, and envisioned versions of the globalization of education in North America specific to trends in immigration (and migration), identity, and imagination. A brief explanation of theories of globalization that intersect in the North American context includes world systems, neo-institutionalism, cosmopolitanism, neoliberalism, and post-colonialism, but could include many more. This chapter also suggests that the globalization of education in North America is not limited to the continent of North America due to the many external or global educational entanglements that North Americans have with other countries and regions worldwide.

Keywords: Globalization; North America; immigration; identity; imagination; neo-institutionalism; cosmopolitanism; neoliberalism; post-colonialism

INTRODUCTION

North America is large and diverse, and it is impossible to summarize all the ways that education has, is, and will be globalized across the continent. But there

World Education Patterns in the Global North:
The Ebb of Global Forces and the Flow of Contextual Imperatives
International Perspectives on Education and Society, Volume 43A, 53–66
Copyright © 2022 by Alexander W. Wiseman
Published under exclusive licence by Emerald Publishing Limited
ISSN: 1479-3679/doi:10.1108/S1479-36792022000043A005

are ways to address the globalization of education in North America by focusing on key themes of globalization and by discussing broadly the educational contexts that comprise the continent as well as North America's influence beyond its geographic boundaries. An obvious grouping for globalization discussions is geographic because of proximity, political and economic relationships, historical migration, and intersecting or shared social and cultural contexts. As such, the geographic proximity of Canada, the United States of America (US), and Mexico is important. While the US shares a border with Canada to the North and Mexico to the South, Canada, and Mexico do not border each other geographically, and are instead separated by a vast distance by the US, which they both border. Likewise, there have been political and economic relationships across the continent involving all three countries (e.g., NAFTA), but outside of these broad geo-political alliances, there are fewer direct links between Canada and Mexico politically, economically, socially, or culturally that do not also include the US.

Historically, there is a well-established theory about the population of North America resulting from humans crossing an ice and land bridge from Asia into northwestern North America eons ago (McGhee, 1989). But historical migration across North America is more of a hodgepodge (1) of travel by indigenous communities following herds or the seasons in search of food or conquest and (2) of colonialism by European countries that spread across wide swaths of North and South America (Amick, 2017; Greer, 2012). Even in these historical migrations, though, the area that now comprises the US is where many of the intersections eventually took place with peoples and groups either coming from or going into what is now known as either Canada or Mexico. Evidence suggests that relatively few people groups migrated across or through all three regions (Diamond, 1977). As a result, there are intersecting and shared histories and contexts in the lands that comprise each country, but those come more from recent globalizations of technology and travel rather than a prehistoric or historical community of shared experiences or locations.

This leaves the comparativist with a dilemma. Does one emphasize the globalization experience of all three national education systems that comprise North America distinctly and individually? Or does one focus the attention on the system that experienced and continues to experience the most interaction with the other North American countries overall as well as with other national educational systems outside of North America? If the latter, then the focus falls on the US experience. Then the comparativist is left with another dilemma. US interests and experiences are already amply reflected in the literature on globalization in education and across all sectors, due to twentieth and twenty-first century North American hegemony in political, economic, and socio-cultural arenas. This hegemony means that the uniquely American experience is more frequently associated with the US rather than with Canada or Mexico in discussions about the globalization of education.

This dilemma, therefore, leads an examination of the globalization of education in North America to focus predominantly on the US, but to include references to Canada and Mexico to demonstrate that many of these globalizing experiences are shared across the continent despite the uniqueness of each educational system itself. This focus on the USA with supplementary examples from Canada and Mexico also follows the population center of North America, which lies within the US (Spring et al., 2016). And the globalization of education in North America is not limited to the geographic borders of the continent but extends worldwide as well.

AGENCY AND AGENDA IN THE GLOBALIZATION OF AND BY NORTH AMERICA

How does the globalization of education in and by North America occur? There are three ways that it can and has been accomplished in North American educational systems, especially since the mid-twentieth century. First, globalization can be self-inflicted or "done to" one's own system or country. This often occurs in the form of domestic reform that relies on borrowed policies and practices from other systems recognized as more successful in achieving desired educational outcomes (which often translates to student achievement scores or as legitimized model systems within a regional or global community). Second, globalization of education can be done to others often in the form of international development agendas, policies, and practices. If the World Bank, for example, loans a country significant funds for domestic infrastructure improvement, this arrangement has been historically associated with educational development initiatives that accompanied the infrastructure funding (Heyneman, 2005). And these development aid programs or policies for education focused more on sustaining the national economic development system than on the individual returns or education for other less fiscally impactful outcomes.

Finally, globalization can be done by those North American actors on other educational systems either within North America or outside of North America. In other words, North American actors can implement change in alignment with globalizing or globalized goals and agendas outside of North America itself. For example, this could be done through the work of a development-oriented non-governmental organization (NGO) or aid organization (e.g., USAID) that has its cultural, economic, and educational foundation in one country (e.g., the United States), but through the placement of American NGO or aid workers in an external or target country, those North American agents make changes to education and influence both policy and practice in alignment with the agenda of North American political, economic, and educational organizations rather than in response to or alignment with local concerns, agendas, or needs (Makuwira, 2018).

In short, the globalization of education in North America also includes the hegemonic and often imperial externalization of educational norms, values, cultures, and expectations on national and local educational systems outside of North America itself. This is a process that directly contrasts with Schriewer's (1989) conceptualization of "externalization," which involves nation-states identifying with external cultures and systems. Instead, North American externalization is a process of assuming and imposing North American expectations, systems, and agendas on countries and communities external to North America itself. This happens through the dissemination of North American culture and values through NGOs, but also through large-scale development that takes place through multilateral organizations like the World Bank, UNESCO, and many aid organizations like CARE and Feed the Children, which have an outsized American workforce distributed all over the world.

Therefore, the globalization of education in North America is both global and local. It looks beyond the boundaries of Canada, the US, and Mexico into the educational practices, structures, policies, and beliefs implemented in formal mass schooling systems globally, but also is focused on the globalization of education within North America itself. To understand these dual processes of internal and external globalization centered on North America, it is perhaps helpful to originally recognize the foundational work of Wallerstein's (2000) world systems theory and Meyer's neo-institutional theory (1977). Both frameworks address the issues of the internationalization and externalization of globalization, but in different ways.

Wallerstein's (2000) world systems theory focuses on the conflict inherent in a colonial or post-colonial landscape, where a core of nation-states concentrates power and industrial processes while a periphery of colonized or developing nation-states provides the raw materials (Chase-Dunn & Rubinson, 1974). This process has also been used as a literal metaphor for the globalization of education (Bose, 2007), where the "raw materials" of intellectual capacity and human resources available in systems on the periphery (i.e., the Global South) are drawn to and cycled through the educational systems of core colonizing or imperial systems (i.e., the Global North). The "educated" graduates of North American higher education institutions (specifically, Canadian or US), for example, would then be recirculated either within their new North American home or back to their original communities in the periphery where they are now not-so-subtle representatives of the North American agenda, culture, way of thinking, and so on (Moosavi, 2020).

Meyer and his colleagues' approach to globalization is less about globalization and more about the dissemination of culture through institutions like education (1977). In this approach to understanding both internal and external globalization, there are more subtle forms of colonization that occur including the isomorphic shift toward legitimized models of education. One historical example of this form of isomorphic globalization is the global spread of a legitimized formal mass education model (Ramirez & Boli, 1987). Another characteristic of institutionalization of education as a form of globalization is the recognition that globalization equates with neither standardization nor homogenization (Wiseman et al., 2014). Instead, the global shift toward a shared expectation and experience in education, which often mirrors or mimics the Western and frequently North American experience in many ways, is characterized by an expected loose coupling and slow change over time into new forms of shared experiences and expectations (Schofer et al., 2012).

World systems theory and neo-institutionalism provide several key characteristics of the agency and agendas of globalization that are particularly relevant to the North American experience within North America itself as well as to the influence and impact that North America has had on the globalization of education worldwide. Wallerstein's world systems approach explains how education systems within North American countries as well as at the local levels within each country can reorient and often create a reimagining of what it means to be a person (Illich, 1971) as well as what the role and importance of a certain kind of education are (e.g., individualism) (Ramirez & Meyer, 1980). Meyer and colleagues' neo-institutional approach suggests ways that education is a cultural phenomenon more than a functional outcome or socio-economic resource alone (Frank & Meyer, 2020; Ramirez et al., 2018; Zapp & Lerch, 2020), but other theoretical frameworks related to globalization are also indicative of the North American experience and impact.

While the world systems and neo-institutional approaches can explain how North America facilitates globalization beyond its own borders, other approaches are needed to explain the intense globalization within North America. Three frameworks are at work in North America throughout the era of rapid globalization beginning in the mid-to-late nineteenth century and continuing into the twenty-first century. These frameworks include cosmopolitanism, neoliberalism, and post-colonialism, and are both complementary as well as contradictory within the North American context.

The globalization of education in North America is an intersection of both global and local values and expectations (i.e., cosmopolitanism) but is split in North America around global and national authority and power coupled with local responsibility and burden for implementation and accountability in education (i.e., neoliberalism). Globalization in North America is better characterized as cosmopolitanism because it is a crossroads event more than a universalizing event, where openness and acceptance of global ideas, cultures, and people reside alongside a loyalty to and valuing of local customs, values, norms, and communities (Cicchelli & Octobre, 2019; Spector, 2020). Likewise, neoliberalism is difficult to uniformly define but is largely based on the values of (1) the individual, (2) freedom of choice, (3) market security, (4) *laissez-faire*, and (5) minimal government (Larner, 2000; Wiseman & Davidson, 2021). In practice, neoliberalism limits the functions of government by increasing the power of centralized authority to make decisions and assess accountability while shifting responsibility for the implementation and outcomes of education to regional and local communities (Astiz et al., 2002; Lerch et al., 2021).

Within this context, there are growing voices from the post-colonial community, which highlight the internal North American imperialism resulting from European colonization, slavery, and indigenous genocide (Hickling-Hudson et al., 2004; Lee & Johnstone, 2021; Takayama et al., 2017). Post-colonial approaches to understanding the globalization of education focus on cultural imperialism as the legacy of both formal education and the school curriculum. As such, it identifies, critiques, and often transforms Western imperialist assumptions about epistemology and knowledge both in the former colonial centers (i.e., the core) as well as the communities where colonialism was applied (i.e., the periphery) (Wallerstein, 2000).

Im/Migration, Identity, and Imagination in Three Contexts

Three perspectives on the intersection of education in North America are required to understand the experience of globalization. This shared globalization experience will be specifically examined through the lens of three key globalization themes in North America: im/migration, identity, and imagination.

Immigration and migration (i.e., im/migration) in North America has been and continues to be a large-scale change process for education and society more broadly as well. Addressing the unique situations and needs of large groups of im/migrants has come in waves and altered the ways that education is offered, and the effects education has had on both teaching and learning as well as the outcomes of education, such as labor market participation and transitions to higher education (Nichols et al., 2020; Streitwieser et al., 2019). The identity of youth is a large part of the socialization process of education in North America, and as social norms and values have shifted so have the identities that are either possible or are outcomes of the educational process in North American educational systems.

How education stakeholders perceive their community, and their futures are part of the imagination of globalization that has affected North America. For example, the expansion of girls and women as examples and participants in politics, science, and other historically male-dominated fields through textbook changes, increased opportunities for girls and women in the professions (Clark Blickenstaff, 2005; Wiseman et al., 2009), and by the individualism that pervades much of North American culture, individuals and communities can imagine unique futures for themselves in ways that are different from other more collectivist communities (Darwish & Huber, 2003; Davies & Aurini, 2003).

The globalization of education in North America through im/migration, identity, and imagination occurs through three modalities, which include the tangible, digital, and envisioned. These three modalities intersect with one another and are intertwined in ways that make them difficult to separate sometimes but represent broadly the traditional and historical forms of globalization (i.e., physical or tangible), virtual modes of globalization (i.e., digital), and the merging of those two which leads to a conceptual or envisioned (and often believed) globalization.

Physical Immigration & Digital Migration
Tangible or physical modes of educational globalization occur through the physical exchange of people, goods, ideas, and services related to education. This occurs through the borrowing and lending of educational policies and practices from one community to the next as described above in relation to international perspectives on globalization (Phillips & Ochs, 2003; Wiseman, 2010). This could be through the exchange of teachers and students through study abroad programs or the physical exchange of letters by classrooms and schools in different countries (Portnoi, 2016).

Rising Immigrant/Refugee Populations. North America has a history of accepting immigrant and refugee populations (Hatton, 2020), and those populations, especially youth, have had a significant impact on the globalization of education.

Although the number of officially recognized refugees and asylees has dropped because of increasingly restrictive policies in receiving countries (Bohmer & Shuman, 2007), the large waves of immigrants coming to North America both formally and informally has risen dramatically over time (Wiseman & Bell, 2021). Both Canada and the US are major receiving countries of immigrants from former British colonies as well as from conflict zones (Donato & Ferris, 2020), and the US and Mexico have received many informal or undocumented immigrants from Central and South America who are fleeing economic, political, or civil crises (FitzGerald & Arar, 2018; Park et al., 2018).

Shift to Remote Work/Learning/Living. North American education has shifted slowly in the latter part of the twentieth and more quickly in the early parts of the twenty-first centuries to more remote education, technology-focused or -driven teaching and learning, and less exclusive reliance on attending synchronous or face-to-face schooling (Yan, 2020). This is how digital migration has contributed to the globalization of education in North America. The COVID-19 pandemic drove this trend even further by requiring remote online learning during the quarantine phase of the pandemic (Bansak & Starr, 2021), and many teachers and students still operate remotely due to shifts in workplace norms, the development of newer technologies that provide opportunities for home-based education through online mechanisms, and due to ongoing health concerns related to the pandemic (Kohli et al., 2021).

There is also a shift toward more remote or online interaction due to the proliferation of digital devices, especially mobile phones and tablets, which provide educational access and resources immediately through a technology that students and teachers already possess outside of their work or school requirements (Palvia et al., 2018). This means that teaching and learning knowledge and skills are not exclusively place-based anymore. For decades, the idea of providing laptops to students through one-to-one laptop programs and initiatives both in school districts and through development or aid organizations was a major push (Gonzales & Jackson, 2020; Kay & Schellenberg, 2019). In particular, the early 2000s saw this trend rise dramatically, but it has become increasingly obsolete in Canada and the US through the increasing ubiquity of individually owned mobile devices (Aguilera-Hermida et al., 2021). However, Mexican educators and students do not have the same experience. The COVID-19 pandemic revealed that there is a significant gap across North America in terms of access to technology for learning, which disadvantaged low income and minority communities (Dubois et al., 2021), but research is finding that in many instances accessibility of new technology was not as much of an obstacle as having the opportunity to use existing technology for teaching and learning (Francis & Weller, 2021). In other words, as many systems of North American education shifted to remote or online education and both educators and students digitally migrated to online teaching and learning, the disparity in living conditions and educational supports in communities was exposed (Donnelly & Patrinos, 2021). This showed that deep social and economic disparities were responsible for educational inequality rather than it being solely a technology issue.

Digital/Virtual – Identity
Digital or virtual modes of educational globalization occur through communication, educative, and other activities and exchanges that occur using technology
such as computers, mobile phones, and other devices or software. As discussed
above, North American educators and students have become digital migrants,
which means that their identities in school, family, community, and the nation
have become increasingly virtual or imagined as well.

North Americans largely identify with the broader community of schooled or
educated individuals. This is due to the fact that most North American youth and
even their parents and often their grandparents all have either attended or had an
opportunity to attend a government-sponsored, publicly-funded school (Schofer
et al., 2021). The expansion of mass education of this sort throughout North
America in the twentieth century has created an identity of schooling or education that may vary by demographic community, but that exists broadly across
Canada, the USA, and Mexico as well as across racial, ethnic, socioeconomic,
and gender lines in each national education system (Leander, 2002; Levinson,
1996). This ontological understanding of who we are as schooled individuals follows the broader conceptualization of globalization as an imagined and trans-
cendent understanding of interconnectivity (Bartelson, 2000).

Perhaps more significantly, the identity of individuals has outpaced the actual
educational attainment of many in North America. In other words, although not
everyone has a post-secondary degree, the broadly defined identities of North
American individuals are that they are educated and can decide what is and is not
knowledge and truth (McLeod & Yates, 2006). The evidence may not necessarily
support that all the time, but the fact is that identities related to race, class, and
gender in North America all intersect with the identity of a schooled person.

Envisioned or Believed Globalization

Anderson (2006) explained in significant detail the role of imagined communities in developing a global political, social, and economic culture through new
forms of technology, transportation, and conceptualizations of communities
beyond the immediate experiences of individuals and groups. The same outcomes
of imagined or conceptualized global education communities develop because
of the tangible and digital modalities described above. The educational experience of sitting in a classroom, smelling the chalk on the chalkboard, eating
lunch with classmates, and other signature experiences of schooling are shared
both physically and virtually by individuals all over the world. These shared
experiences – even when they occur independently from one another – create a
sense of imagined community around education, especially formal schooling.
This, in part, leads to the conceptualization and identity of a schooled individual.

But an envisioned or believed globalization of education in and by North
America is a cultural phenomenon, which relates back to the theoretical
approaches to globalization briefly described above. Through a combination of
neoliberalism, inequal world systems, and the slow institutionalization of shared
norms, values, and activities related to education across Canada, the US, and

Mexico, North American education is both globalized and a globalizing agent itself. These globalization processes are intra-national, inter-national, and trans-national. Each provides an example of how globalization occurs through the spread of shared expectations and taken-for-granted experiences in education.

Intra-national processes include the diffusion and adoption of shared expectations and experiences in education within national education systems in North American countries. This is a first and important step because it examines the vast diversity that exists in each system itself in terms of race and ethnicity, gender, culture, language, socioeconomic status, and other core characteristics. In the three North American national education systems, there are shared or borrowed educational policies and practices across Canada, the US, and Mexico as well as within each educational system itself. These borrowed policies and practices within national education systems are specifically intra-national because they provide a platform for the sharing of knowledge and skills and other educational activities from one local community to another or from one individual to another within the same national educational system.

Some of the impetus for increasing intra-national globalization processes comes from the comparison of states and school districts in each of the North American systems by student academic outcomes. These outcomes comparisons are often conflated with national economic or political status, and therefore states and districts will borrow or copy "best practice" models from other states or districts where student outcomes are higher or more consistent than their own. There is also a tendency to borrow or copy educational policies and practices when a state or district's educational activities are legitimized by national recognition or alignment with broader international norms and values (i.e., International Baccalaureate models) (Ingersoll, 2018).

In contrast with intra-national globalization processes, inter-national processes are perhaps the most aligned with traditional notions of globalization because they present the intersections among national education systems themselves with all the borrowing and lending of policies and practices that have been examined and critiqued throughout the scholarly community. International perspectives often are reactionary or focused on "best practices" even though the distinctions among educational systems, teaching, and learning in the nations in question may be too diverse or unique to productively compare let alone intersect or globalize.

Critics of educational reform in North American educational systems have suggested that international comparisons are often inappropriate comparisons and that intra-national comparisons are the better approach for making actual change in educational practice and outcomes (Weingarten, 2014). In fact, critiques of international comparisons of education have a long history within North American systems, yet those international comparisons have brought increasingly globalized educational ideas and legitimated forms of educational policy, practice, and curriculum to schools in Canada, the US, and Mexico, especially in the latter twentieth century (Baker & Wiseman, 2005). In fact, there have been decades of educational change and reform in North America that have been driven by comparisons with other national education systems. In the 1990s and into the early 2000s, comparisons with Asian countries like Japan, Hong Kong,

Singapore, and South Korea have been staples of educational reform initiatives in North America, especially around issues of instructional time, centralization of curriculum, and the training of teachers (LeTendre et al., 2001; Schmidt et al., 2011; Shimahara & Sakai, 2018).

A third and increasingly important globalization process is trans-nationalism. This perspective suggests that boundaries are porous, increasingly irrelevant, or dissolving when it comes to educational systems, policy, and practice. A trans-national perspective on the globalization of education in North America, for example, asks if education is that much more different across national boundaries compared to intra-national variation. And the evidence suggests that it is not necessarily as different or unique as individual perception might suggest. For example, transnational education can occur any time a border (either real or perceived) is crossed as a process of education. This occurs regularly through online, distance, or remote educational experiences. Any online collaborative learning experience is potentially a transnational globalizing experience (Bannier, 2016). MOOCs (i.e., massive open online courses) and other open online learning experiences, especially through higher education institutions, are some of the most common forms of transnational education in North America. Without considering political, social, or cultural borders, knowledge and skills related to both traditional educational subjects like language, science, or technology are taught, learned, and certificates of completion provided by open learning online.

CONCLUSION

After reviewing the globalization of education in North America, a few findings are especially relevant. First, it is important to note that summarizing the globalization of education across such a large and diverse continent and its national educational systems is unwieldy and perhaps not entirely possible. Instead, this chapter has attempted to identify globalization processes and outcomes using a broader and often conceptual understanding of globalization in and by North America. The recognition that globalization is not something that can happen solely within a national educational system or grouping of systems is coupled with the recognition that the global role of North America has played an outsized role in the globalization of education in other systems and communities outside of North America itself throughout much of the modern history of formal mass education worldwide.

Globalization of education in and by North America is also an intersection of tangible and virtual processes that are pushed forward by immigration, identity, and imagined communities. In this sense, globalization in North America is more genuinely a global enterprise than a geographically contained phenomenon. Immigration and migration both in the physical movement of people as well as in the digital migration of ideas and education has been influential in the interaction of ideas, teaching, and learning across boundaries as well as within systems in North America. The imagined communities that develop within and across North America are globally connected as well. Schooled individuals in

North American communities share just as many ideas, experiences, and outcomes within their local schools as they do with other schooled individuals from communities across the globe.

But, perhaps one of the most difficult globalization processes to both understand and reconcile in the North American context is the role of North America's influence on the globalization of education outside of Canada, the US, and Mexico. Much comparative research literature has addressed issues of educational imperialism, colonization, and both explicit and implicit agenda setting worldwide, but the globally institutionalized ideas, norms, values, and structures of education that have become staples of formal education in most national education systems worldwide are still often the result of North American agendas and actors either influencing or involved in the establishment and ongoing practice of formal education worldwide. This phenomenon poses yet another quandary related to the globalization of education in North America because the question is one of origin of ideas rather than the exchange of people, services, goods, and ideas related to education. Yet, this quandary may not be answerable other than to continue to ask whether North American education is a producer or consumer of globalization.

REFERENCES

Aguilera-Hermida, A. P., Quiroga-Garza, A., Gómez-Mendoza, S., Del Río Villanueva, C. A., Avolio Alecchi, B., & Avci, D. (2021). Comparison of students' use and acceptance of emergency online learning due to COVID-19 in the USA, Mexico, Peru, and Turkey. *Education and Information Technologies, 26*(6), 6823–6845.

Amick, D. S. (2017). Evolving views on the pleistocene colonization of North America. *Quaternary International, 431*, 125–151.

Anderson, B. (2006). *Imagined communities: Reflections on the origin and spread of nationalism.* Verso.

Astiz, M. F., Wiseman, A. W., & Baker, D. P. (2002). Slouching towards decentralization: Consequences of globalization for curricular control in national education systems. *Comparative Education Review, 46*(1), 66–88.

Baker, D. P., & Wiseman, A. W. (Eds.). (2005). Global Trends in Educational Policy, Volume 6 in the International Perspectives on Education and Society Series. Elsevier Science, Ltd.

Bannier, B. J. (2016). Global trends in transnational education. *International Journal of Information and Education Technology, 6*(1), 80.

Bansak, C., & Starr, M. (2021). COVID-19 shocks to education supply: How 200,000 US households dealt with the sudden shift to distance learning. *Review of Economics of the Household, 19*(1), 63–90.

Bartelson, J. (2000). Three concepts of globalization. *International Sociology, 15*(2), 180–196.

Bohmer, C., & Shuman, A. (2007). *Rejecting refugees: Political asylum in the 21st century.* Routledge.

Bose, P. (2007). 'New' imperialism? On globalisation and nation-states. *Historical Materialism, 15*(3), 95–120.

Chase-Dunn, C., & Rubinson, R. (1977). Toward a structural perspective on the world-system. *Politics & Society, 7*(4), 453–476.

Cicchelli, V., & Octobre, S. (2019). Introducing youth and globalization and the special issue: The rise and fall of cosmopolitanism. *Youth and Globalization, 1*(1), 1–18.

Clark Blickenstaff, J. (2005). Women and science careers: Leaky pipeline or gender filter? *Gender and Education, 17*(4), 369–386.

Darwish, A. F. E., & Huber, G. L. (2003). Individualism vs collectivism in different cultures: A cross-cultural study. *Intercultural Education, 14*(1), 47–56.

Davies, S., & Aurini, J. (2003). Homeschooling and Canadian educational politics: Rights, pluralism, and pedagogical individualism. *Evaluation & Research in Education, 17*(2–3), 63–73.

Diamond, J. M. (1977). Colonization cycles in man and beast. *World Archaeology, 8*(3), 249–261.

Donato, K. M., & Ferris, E. (2020). Refugee integration in Canada, Europe, and the United States: Perspectives from research. *The Annals of the American Academy of Political and Social Science, 690*(1), 7–35.

Donnelly, R., & Patrinos, H. A. (2021). Learning loss during COVID-19: An early systematic review. *Prospects*, 1–9.

Dubois, E., Bright, D., & Laforce, S. (2021). Educating minoritized students in the United States during COVID-19: How technology can be both the problem and the solution. *IT Professional, 23*(2), 12–18.

FitzGerald, D. S., & Arar, R. (2018). The sociology of refugee migration. *Annual Review of Sociology, 44*, 387–406.

Francis, D. V., & Weller, C. E. (2021). Economic inequality, the digital divide, and remote learning during COVID-19. *The Review of Black Political Economy, 49*, 00346446211017797.

Frank, D. J., & Meyer, J. W. (2020). *The university and the global knowledge society*. Princeton University Press.

Gonzales, M. M., & Jackson, I. (2020). Going the distance: What school administrators can learn from one-to-one laptop schools. *Journal of School Administration Research and Development, 5*, 55–60.

Greer, A. (2012). Commons and enclosure in the colonization of North America. *The American Historical Review, 117*(2), 365–386.

Hatton, T. J. (2020). Asylum migration to the developed world: Persecution, incentives, and policy. *Journal of Economic Perspectives, 34*(1), 75–93.

Heyneman, S. P. (2005). The history and problems in the making of education policy at the World Bank, 1960–2000. In D. P. Baker & A. W. Wiseman (Eds.), *Global trends in educational policy* (International Perspectives on Education and Society (Vol. 6, pp. 23–58). Emerald Group Publishing Limited.

Hickling-Hudson, A., Matthews, J., & Woods, A. (2004). Education, postcolonialism and disruptions. *Disrupting Preconceptions: Postcolonialism and Education, 3*(2), 1–16.

Ingersoll, M. (2018). Uncommon knowledge: International schools as elite educational enclosures. In *The Wiley handbook of global educational reform* (pp. 259–281). Wiley.

Illich, I. (1971). *Deschooling society*. Harper and Row.

Kay, R., & Schellenberg, D. (2019, March). Comparing BYOD and one-to-one laptop programs in secondary school classrooms: A review of the literature. In *Society for information technology & teacher education international conference* (pp. 1862–1866). Association for the Advancement of Computing in Education (AACE).

Kohli, H., Wampole, D., & Kohli, A. (2021). Impact of online education on student learning during the pandemic. *Studies in Learning and Teaching, 2*(2), 1–11.

Larner, W. (2000). Neoliberalism: Policy, ideology, governmentality. *Studies in Political Economy, 63*, 5–25.

Leander, K. M. (2002). Polycontextual construction zones: Mapping the expansion of schooled space and identity. *Mind, Culture, and Activity, 9*(3), 211–237.

Lee, E., & Johnstone, M. (2021). Resisting a postcolonial construction of historical trauma and healing: Critical discourse analysis of public apologies in Canada. *Critical Sociology, 48*(2), 375–375. 08969205211052326.

Lerch, J. C., Bromley, P., & Meyer, J. W. (2021). Global neoliberalism as a cultural order and its expansive educational effects. *International Journal of Sociology, 52*(2), 1–31.

LeTendre, G. K., Baker, D. P., Akiba, M., Goesling, B., & Wiseman, A. (2001). Teachers' work: Institutional isomorphism and cultural variation in the US, Germany, and Japan. *Educational Researcher, 30*(6), 3–15.

Levinson, B. A. (1996). Social difference and schooled identity at a Mexican secundaria. In B. A. Levinson, D. E. Foley & D. C. Holland (Eds.), *Cultural production of the educated person: The Critical ethnographies of schooling and local practice* (pp. 211–238). SUNY Press.

Makuwira, J. (2018). Power and development in practice: NGOs and the development agenda setting. *Development in Practice, 28*(3), 422–431.

McLeod, J., & Yates, L. (2006). *Making modern lives: Subjectivity, schooling, and social change*. SUNY Press.

McGhee, R. (1989). Who owns prehistory? The Bering land bridge dilemma. *Canadian Journal of Archaeology/Journal Canadien d'Archéologie, 13*, 13–20.

Meyer, J. W. (1977). The effects of education as an institution. *American Journal of Sociology, 83*(1), 55–77.

Moosavi, L. (2020). The decolonial bandwagon and the dangers of intellectual decolonisation. *International Review of Sociology, 30*(2), 332–354.

Nichols, L., Ha, B., & Tyyskä, V. (2020). Canadian immigrant youth and the education-employment nexus. *Canadian Journal of Family and Youth/Le Journal Canadien de Famille et de la Jeunesse, 12*(1), 178–199.

Palvia, S., Aeron, P., Gupta, P., Mahapatra, D., Parida, R., Rosner, R., & Sindhi, S. (2018). Online education: Worldwide status, challenges, trends, and implications. *Journal of Global Information Technology Management, 21*(4), 233–241.

Park, M., Katsiaficas, C., & McHugh, M. (2018). *Responding to the ECEC needs of children of refugees and asylum seekers in Europe and North America.* Washington, DC: Migration Policy Institute (MPI).

Phillips, D., & Ochs, K. (2003). Processes of policy borrowing in education: Some explanatory and analytical devices. *Comparative Education, 39*(4), 451–461.

Portnoi, L. M. (2016). *Policy borrowing and reform in education.* Palgrave Macmillan.

Ramirez, F. O., & Boli, J. (1987). The political construction of mass schooling: European origins and worldwide institutionalization. *Sociology of Education, 60*(1), 2–17.

Ramirez, F. O., & Meyer, J. W. (1980). Comparative education: The social construction of the modern world system. *Annual Review of Sociology, 6*(1), 369–397.

Ramirez, F. O., Schofer, E., & Meyer, J. W. (2018). International tests, national assessments, and educational development (1970–2012). *Comparative Education Review, 62*(3), 344–364.

Schmidt, W. H., Cogan, L., & Houang, R. (2011). The role of opportunity to learn in teacher preparation: An international context. *Journal of Teacher Education, 62*(2), 138–153.

Schofer, E., Hironaka, A., Frank, D. J., & Longhofer, W. (2012). Sociological institutionalism and world society (Vol. 33, pp. 57). *The Wiley-Blackwell companion to political sociology.* Wiley

Schofer, E., Ramirez, F. O., & Meyer, J. W. (2021). The societal consequences of higher education. *Sociology of Education, 94*(1), 1–19.

Schriewer, J. K. (1989). The twofold character of comparative education: Cross-cultural comparison and externalization to world situations. *Prospects, 19*(3), 389–406.

Shimahara, N. K., & Sakai, A. (2018). *Learning to teach in two cultures: Japan and the United States.* Routledge.

Spector, H. (2020). Trends and typologies of cosmopolitanism in education. In *Oxford research encyclopedia of education.*

Spring, A., Tolnay, S. E., & Crowder, K. (2016). Moving for opportunities? Changing patterns of migration in North America. In *International handbook of migration and population distribution* (pp. 421–448). Springer.

Streitwieser, B., Loo, B., Ohorodnik, M., & Jeong, J. (2019). Access for refugees into higher education: A review of interventions in North America and Europe. *Journal of Studies in International Education, 23*(4), 473–496.

Takayama, K., Sriprakash, A., & Connell, R. (2017). Toward a postcolonial comparative and international education. *Comparative Education Review, 61*(S1), S1–S24.

Wallerstein, I. (2000). *The essential Wallerstein.* The New York Press.

Weingarten, R. (2014). International education comparisons: How American education reform is the new status quo. *New England Journal of Public Policy, 26*(1), 8.

Wiseman, A. W. (2010). The uses of evidence for educational policymaking: Global contexts and international trends. *Review of Research in Education, 34*(1), 1–24.

Wiseman, A. W., Astiz, M. F., & Baker, D. P. (2014). Comparative education research framed by neo-institutional theory: A review of diverse approaches and conflicting assumptions. *Compare: A Journal of Comparative and International Education, 44*(5), 688–709.

Wiseman, A. W., Baker, D. P., Riegle-Crumb, C., & Ramirez, F. O. (2009). Shifting gender effects: Opportunity structures. Institutionalized Mass Schooling, and Cross-National Achievement in Mathematics. In D. P. Baker & A. W. Wiseman (Eds.), *Gender, equality, and education from international and comparative perspectives* (pp. 395–422). Emerald Publishing Limited.

Wiseman, A. W., & Bell, J. C. (2021). Education without evidence: Gaps in data availability for refugee, asylee, and humanitarian migrant students in US schools. *Research in Education*, *0*(0), 1–14. https://doi.org/10.1177/00345237211034885

Wiseman, A. W., & Davidson, P. M. (2021). Institutionalized inequities and the cloak of equality in the South African educational context. *Policy Futures in Education*, *19*(8), 992–1009.

Yan, Z. (2020). Unprecedented pandemic, unprecedented shift, and unprecedented opportunity. *Human Behavior and Emerging Technologies*, *2*(2), https://doi.org/10.1002/hbe2.192

Zapp, M., & Lerch, J. C. (2020). Imagining the world: Conceptions and determinants of internationalization in higher education curricula worldwide. *Sociology of Education*, *93*(4), 372–392.

EUROPA REGINA: A PAST, PRESENT, AND FUTURE PROJECT (A QUAM *EXPETI PROPOSITUM*)

María-Jesús Martínez-Usarralde and
Belén Espejo-Villar

ABSTRACT

This chapter shows, from a comprehensive and dynamic approach, a unitary idea of Europe that shatters the fragmentation and reification of the old continent that is being politically projected. The research, based on a brief overview of the geopolitical and territorial diversity of the Western European countries, recovers the cartographic representation of Europe made by Sebastian Münster in 1544. It aims to represent a renewed area that has strengthened its international presence, based on the legitimization of divergent trajectories explained through interactive logics.

The political agenda for socio-educational issues portrays the contextual diversity that rules the governance of the Western European education systems. At the same time, it shows unification regarding inclusive institutional paradigms where the most significant achievements are accomplished within the European strategic framework. The research allows us to move on from the nationalist–post-nationalist option. Part of the European scene from which present and future lines of joint action are extracted in relation to sustainability, economic digitization and/or reformulation of the social system model.

Keywords: West Europe; European Union; comparative education; education governance; transnationalism perspectives; educational equity; political agenda

World Education Patterns in the Global North:
The Ebb of Global Forces and the Flow of Contextual Imperatives
International Perspectives on Education and Society, Volume 43A, 67–83
Copyright © 2022 by Emerald Publishing Limited
ISSN: 1479-3679/doi:10.1108/S1479-36792022000043A006

INTRODUCTION

Sebastian Münster's *Cosmographia* (1544) is home to the reference with which we wanted to entitle our chapter: "Europa Regina." This concept of a united Europe, that had already been dreamed of by emperor Charles I of Spain and V of Germany, is also recalled in Heinrich Bunting's *Itinerarium sacrae scripturae* (or "The Travels of the Holy Patriarchs, Prophets, Judges, Kings, Our Savior Christ and His Apostles, as They Are Related in the Old and New Testaments") of 1592, which contains a print of a symbolic map of Europe, this time as a virgin.

Of these two evocations, we wish to refer to the more political image that is transmitted by *Europa Regina* – from the Latin "Reina Europa" [Queen Europe, in English] – representing the European continent as a queen in the form of a map. Introduced and popularized during the Mannerism Period (Late Renaissance), Europe is drawn as a woman standing upright. In this representation, the Iberian Peninsula represents her head wearing a crown and Bohemia represents her heart. Her imperial attributes, meanwhile, are located above Sicily and Northern Germany.

We also wish to link and flesh out this suggestive initial metaphor with our support for Adoumié's belief (2013) that, before anything else, to question Europe is,

indeed, inevitably, to question its idea: the fact that it cannot be defined by geography or history, nor by language or by any other specific feature. The mere fact of its plurality forces us to admit that, if nothing else, "Europe is an idea." (pp. 142–143)

Based on this dual concept of Europe as a queen and Europe as an idea, we shall now review all of the aspects that characterize the so-called Western Europe, written in a unique space and time frame that we shall now analyze in greater detail.

REGIONAL CONTEXT

Geography

The consideration of Europe as a geographical concept leads us, from the regional focus, to the concept of "Continental Europe" that is widely accepted in modern-day society, with its variable geography being an additional idiosyncratic feature (Le Monde Diplómatique, 2012). The fundamental features of European geography are characterized by the variety and moderation of its physical features; its largely maritime nature; its cultural heterogeneity, in all meanings of the term; the high level of socio-economic development, with regional contrasts; the division into areas of stability and instability; its prominent role in the history of mankind in recent centuries; the great dynamism of its components and the continued transformation of its structures; the permanence of links and imprecision of borders with neighboring regions (López-Palomeque & Plaza, 2020). The spatial and social precision of this current reality allows us to conceive various "Europes" on an intra-continental scale: contrasts and heterogeneity that are also based on the social inequalities and territorial imbalances that are manifested in the European space, whose explanatory factors go beyond qualitative geographical attributes, whether geo-cultural or geo-natural.

Demography

One of the most significant trends with regard to Europe is its ageing population which, according to European Union and GlobalStats (2019), will have a clear impact on the future of Western European countries. The population is rapidly ageing, driven by increased life expectancy and lower fertility rates than in previous years. Population growth is slowing down, and increasing numbers of elderly people are dependent on others to look after them. These factors have serious consequences in areas such as the job market, health, and pensions (Prskawetz et al., 2007).

On the other hand, freedom of movement within the EU, in particular the East-West movement of citizens from this area, has increased, with this migration increasing the population of some EU member states and decreasing that of others. We must also consider the increased population as a result of migration over the last few decades (OECD, 2019a).

Politics

Europe is the only continent on the planet with a project that seeks to construct a multinational and multistate geopolitical system that is original, autonomous and globally influential. The European Union (EU) – without being imperial or subject to a dominant state, as it is governed by a system of contractual relations which all member states – has become the political, economic and institutional heart of the continent (López-Palomeque & Plaza, 2020).

Since the nineteenth and twentieth centuries, the pan-European idea of Europe as a political project has been developing and showing a certain continuity, spreading from the West to the central and eastern parts. The EU, following the signing of the Maastricht Treaty in 1992, the Amsterdam Treaty in 1997 and its various additions, now consists of 27 member states. In a referendum held on June 23, 2016 on whether or not the UK wished to remain in the EU (the so-called "Brexit" referendum), the campaign advocating Britain's exit from the EU was victorious. This has shaped a new political landscape upon which Europe has managed to articulate the necessary instruments to continue building a common project formed by post-national governments, despite dissent from certain countries.

Economy

After the World War II, European economies were totally devastated and Europe was strategically divided into two parts. The West – including countries such as Germany, France, England and Mediterranean Europe – developed institutional democracy, albeit at different speeds, and began to open markets. The East, meanwhile, continued to cling onto communism. In the 1950s, the Marshall Plan and the ensuing transfer of American funds to the continent helped to rebuild Europe, albeit with restrictions on the movement of capital. It was this plan which led Western European countries to participate in the Organization for European Economic Cooperation (OEEC), which was the precursor to the

Organization for Economic Cooperation and Development (OECD). Later on, the Treaty of Rome (1957) led to the formation of a common market with established economic objectives (strengthening cooperation in trade relations between the member states while adopting a synergetic trade policy *vis-à-vis* the rest of the world) and political objectives (ensuring peace and security). This would later forge the European Economic Community (EEC), under which the EU as we know it would be created.

The creation and evolution of the EU is the most successful example of international economic and political cooperation (Valle, 2006), exemplifying how trade liberalization, the free movement of people and capital and the promotion of market competition can have a positive impact on economic scenarios. In 2018, according to the World Bank's most recent World Development Indicators, the EU's GDP (in PPP USD) amounted to $15.9 trillion.

Social System

The European Social Model (ESM) consists of

> a political project articulated around the values of social equity (equality), collective solidarity (redistribution) and productive efficiency (optimisation), and is the result of contemporary processes of conflict and cooperation in the "Old Continent." As a general strategic objective, the MSE supports sustained and sustainable economic growth based on the promotion of social and economic equality, although this success has not led to the homogeneous and unique institutional embodiment of a certain type of welfare state in all European countries. (Moreno, 2019, p. 292)

Currently, authors such as Sánchez and Díaz (2017), following the classification made by Esping-Andersen, differentiate between four welfare regimes: the liberal model, including the Anglo-Saxon European countries, characterized by a residual role of the State in the provision of welfare; the social democratic model, implemented in the Nordic countries, whose basic features are the de-commercialization and universalization of social rights; the conservative model, whose core principle is to insure risks, which ultimately depend on the working conditions of individuals, as is the case in France, Germany, Belgium, Austria, and the Netherlands; finally, the model of the southern European countries (Greece, Italy, Spain, and Portugal), which hold similar values to continental countries but with greater inter-generational solidarity (fundamentally in terms of the family).

Religion and World and Life-view

Religious beliefs, alongside language, have become decisive elements in the shaping of a European culture (Azcárate & Sánchez, 2013). Currently, in the EU, according to a 2006 Eurobarometer survey and studies published at a later date (Fundación Alternativas & Ebert-Stifung, 2019), 46% of European citizens consider religion to occupy a very important position in society. This is despite the fact that European governments have imposed the most religious restrictions in recent years (between 2007 and 2017), as noted in the study published by Pew Research (2019).

Europe has a varied history in this regard, ranging from the ancient religions of the pagan people to the Greek and Roman religions, through to the various branches of Christianity, which is its official religion (one of which, Catholicism, is the predominant religion in Italy, Spain, France, and Ireland) nevertheless, a secular state is culturally and politically dominant in both France and Ireland. However, this religiousness coexists with a growing trend of secularization (Delanty, 2011). Alongside this, as a result of certain migration patterns, Islamism also holds an increasing presence in Europe. In a multicultural Europe, religion, which is perceived in times of tension as an element of social and cultural disagreement, assumes capital value for political management in societies which have become diverse and plural.

THE INCOMING TIDE OF GLOBAL TRENDS
Ecology and Sustainability

European trends in terms of sustainability are reflected in various different treaties and documents that seek to strengthen the common principles and values of democracy, human rights, and the rule of law in order to consolidate the European tradition, democratic culture and the quality of life of its citizens in a world that is constantly changing. European citizens are faced with challenges such as environmental degradation and climate change, demographic transition, migration, inequality, and pressure on public finances, which will affect future generations and result in an ecological debt with universal repercussions (European Commission, 2019). These challenges transcend borders, both inside and outside the EU, and put jobs, prosperity, living standards, freedom, and health at risk.

It is clear that economic aspects such as science, financing, taxation and governance are crucial in meeting the Sustainable Development Goals (SDGs). The high-level political forum on the SDGs, created by the European Commission in 2016, has played a very positive role in achieving cross-cutting ideas. Today, more than ever before, in light of the COVID-19 pandemic, the values of the EU, in line with the United Nations, must be consolidated to ensure the quality of life of European citizens with tolerance, equality, inclusion, and solidarity.

Economy

In a world of growing complexity, uncertainty and rapid change, combined with the vulnerability presented by global issues such as the COVID-19 pandemic, the EU, and therefore Western Europe – the region being studied here – is characterized by five trends with economic repercussions (ESPAS, 2016) that remain valid. First, as seen in the previous section, the EU has an ageing population. Meanwhile, as the European middle class continues to grow, social inequalities are increasingly pronounced. It seems that migration and social policies could be a way of addressing these inequalities. When strengthened and balanced, these policies can serve to restore the two detected imbalances. Second, the sustained development of the global economy is increasingly vulnerable to the difficulties and weaknesses of globalization; as such, the European economy will need to continue overcoming this inertia *vis-á-vis* its Asian counterpart. Third, the EU must draw up economic digitization plans that can address all of the challenges that it is currently struggling with. Fourthly, the management of scarce natural resources will force us to take action towards a sustainable Europe that seeks, through the 2030 Agenda, to meet the Sustainable Development Goals. Finally, the interdependence of countries – now a reality of global life – will force the EU to strengthen global governance, as we analyzed in the political section.

Languages

The distribution, diversity, and number of languages and dialects in the European area constitute a genuine cultural mosaic (López & Plaza, 2020): the EU has 24 official languages, in addition to around fifty non-official languages and hundreds of dialects. These are split across the Romance languages, which are spoken in the southern countries, and the Germanic and Slavic languages spoken in Central and Eastern Europe (Adoumié, 2013). Every time a new member country has joined the EU, the list of official languages has increased. Even after the UK's withdrawal from the EU, English remains an official language in both Ireland and Malta. According to the European Parliament (s.d.), the Parliament employs about 270 staff interpreters and can also regularly draw on a pool of more than 1,500 external accredited interpreters, about 600 translators, and about 30% of the translation work is outsourced to freelance translators.

With regard to the current use and extension of the English language, analyst Paul Butcher of the European Policy Centre stated that English "is here to stay" when asked whether or not the language could lose influence in the EU following Brexit. He notes that "English is already perceived as an international language and is by far the most common means of intercultural communication in Europe, especially amongst young people," adding that the social reality in EU institutions is that "many more people speak English than French or any other competing language, which means that it is simply inevitable that English will maintain its dominant position" (EFE, 2020).

Politics

Politically, on a formal and moral level, Europe has capitalized on a project defined by Delanty (2006) as "cosmopolitan," owing to the novelty of embodying European identity in a national context. This project, risky and ambitious in equal measure, has not been free from difficulties, which are often explained in terms of crisis (Guirao, 2019). Whether in a crisis or not, today's EU is the result of its past, and expresses, to a large extent, some of the tensions most recently experienced by this post-national project that has been shaped by solidarity.

However, the solidity of its institutions has resurfaced with greater legitimacy since the signing of the Treaty of Lisbon in 2007. This is insufficient for some in terms of legal matters, but absolutely necessary at a troublesome time in which the commitment to a model that guarantees fundamental rights has become a key issue. The digitization of the economy, together with the construction of a fairer and more social Europe, is part of the European strategic agenda set for the period up until 2024, in which divergences, which are increasingly present, can help to strengthen the EU project.

Social Trends

Within the framework of social policy, Europe represents the institutionalization of fundamental rights on a global level, both formal (civil and political, or "first generation") and social ("second generation"). Historically, the role given to the State by German and English governments (proposed by Otto Von Bismarck and William Beveridge, respectively) in terms of working rights and universal social security mean that Europe is still identified as the social paradigm *par excellence*.

However, the uncertainties caused by the economic behavior of a globalized capitalist system, together with the inequalities arising from increasingly precarious production markets, have once again put the spotlight on the effectiveness of different forms of state intervention in the management of social welfare.

On the other hand, the advance of nationalist discourses (Campani & Pajnik, 2017) and the weakening of common values around a cultural, political, and social model are raising a series of challenges in the evolution of a multicultural and global citizenship project.

Actions such as the European Pillar of Social Rights (signed in 2017 by the European Parliament, the Council and the Commission) and the establishment of institutional pro-equality frameworks (Strategy for Gender Equality 2020–2025) continue to be references in the construction of a more social and solidarity-based Europe, despite existing divergences and difficulties.

EDUCATION

The Beginnings of Formal Education

The historical evolution of education in Europe during the twentieth century presents some significant milestones, which can be grouped into three axes of development.

First, with regard to scientific knowledge, we must highlight the development of "paedocentrism," the importance placed on the student's personal autonomy, the emphasis on individualism as an objective, the link between knowledge and training programs with the current context, the criticism of the excesses of intellectualism, the interest in sentimental and volitional areas and the stimulus of active methods. The development of experimentalist teaching (Binet, Lay, and Meumann); the ideas and proposals of the New Education movement; the work of the Jean Jacques Rousseau Institute (Claparède, Ferrière, Decroly, Montessori, and Piaget); the impulse of new schools in England, France, Germany, and Austria; and the impact of German educational homes in the countryside (Koerrenz et al., 2018), also contributed to this.

From the perspective of international agreements on new educational trends and strategies and repeated guidance in UNESCO general conferences, the following have been widely adopted in European countries over the last third of a century: attention to children's education, interest in lifelong learning, the new identity of teachers, sensitivity to civic training, etc. Ideological and political orientations led to the definition of various educational ideals, such as those designed by social democracy, or which severely reinforced the debates around education: secularism/confessionalism, democracy/totalitarianism, predominance of public school/private school conditions (Jones et al., 2009).

Finally, it is worth mentioning another significant fact, even with the significant developments in the extension of free and compulsory universal basic public schooling. Namely, the incessant demand for an education that is not conditioned by economic, social, gender, or religious distinctions, from which two criticisms arise. First, that denounces the failures and injustices of a "capitalist school," considered as an ideological instrument or apparatus of the State (Bourdieu, Baudelot, Establet) which rejects the legitimizing and reproductive role of the System. The second criticism, from a social democratic perspective, promotes "understanding" policies and equal education opportunities in the wake of the World War II.

Education Objectives

At a time of great political, economic, and socio-sanitary uncertainties, England, Germany, France, Italy, and Spain are facing important challenges in the construction of a Europe that must have education as a priority. In the 1990s, looking ahead to 2020, Diez-Hotchleitner (1994) recalled Europe's role throughout history as both a crossroads and a melting pot. Twenty years later, this continues to be the mission with which educational systems are encouraged to address a more complex situation within the framework of educational governance based on processes of privatization and structural frameworks of networks and power. Some authors (García-Ruiz, 2012; Nóvoa, 2010) have written about new definitions of education that are being developed by certain actors (large corporations such as the OECD, World Bank, EU), which are increasingly acting as epistemic communities (Francesco & Guaschino, 2020). Cone and Brøgger (2020) use the term "soft privatization" to refer to a recent phenomenon in the field of education in the EU, which has succeeded in completely merging education and the economy.

Without losing sight of this reality, and precisely based on this scenario, the education system is being asked, at a time when the European project is being reconstructed, to make a commitment that will enable it to ensure an inclusive, fairer and more democratic system.

Organization and Administration

The management models under which the education systems of Western European countries are currently organized are subject to global processes of modernization in the management of public policies (Blanchenay & Burns, 2016). These reforms are related to the rise in educational success theories as legitimizers of new actors in the governance of schools.

These dynamics of change, which educational governance has capitalized on, have permeated the forms of educational regulation in each of the countries studied, reformulating the power relations between political actors and retaining the identity that each of these states has maintained, despite the development-based approaches of recent years. It comprises a historical and contextual journey that has also helped us to understand the institutional forms of power distribution in the field of education (Hall & Gunter, 2016).

We can therefore appreciate, in Western European countries, most of the governance approaches established by the OECD (2015), ranging from centralized regulatory models to multiscale decentralization trends that lend different political and/or administrative capacity to power structures. This concept of shared management is incipient in some systems and more consolidated in others, where power is shared between the regional and national levels. The most advanced decentralization occurs in countries such as Germany, which have instruments of intra-administration coordination. England fluctuates between centralizing and decentralizing trends with a tendency toward privatization, in which new concepts such as scalecraft and statecraft serve to explain the organizational levels of public policies (Naumann & Crouch, 2020).

Institutional Fabric and School Ladder

Institutional approaches are highly defined in Western European educational Systems. Largely because the three educational models with which knowledge and school structures have traditionally been associated (dual, vocational and scholar) originated in the countries that make up Western Europe (Popov & Genova, 2019).

Perceiving professional knowledge in terms of duality (education-business) as a capital value of the German education system (and of continental European countries) therefore offers, despite the controversies generated by the compulsory "early choice," new itineraries for the mandatory education may experience (Martínez-Usarralde, 2001). On the other hand, the plurality of actors and institutions present in the shaping of school careers is a central component of the English occupational model, which derives from the liberal economic system and determines, from an industrial and productive perspective, diversified actions in the struggle against early school drop-out (Hodgson & Spours, 2020).

Regardless of the model that governs the structures and organization of education systems in Western Europe, all recent reforms (Lundahl & Brunila, 2020) are incorporating extended compulsory education as a central element in the configuration of a country's social fabric, and above all, as a major factor in educational equality.

CURRICULUM

Throughout the process of building the EU, various milestones were significant in shaping Western European curricular policy. First, the convergence brought about by the signing of the Maastricht Treaty (1992), which sought to combine the European dimension with the labor modernization project through a high-quality education, which must contain professional training on its curriculum. Second, the Lisbon Strategy (2000) and its implementation in the areas of competitiveness and employment, which later appear in European Commission reports (Education and Training 2010, 2020). These are included in a project of standardized curricular skills, following the line established by the OECD and the first PISA reports.

Beyond these policies, the curricular foundation of Western European education systems is currently torn between the inclusion of hybrid learning (academic-professional) and the presence of a civic culture, with its different theoretical and applied rationalities (Pashby et al., 2020), as is the case in England.

TEACHERS

In a political context marked by managerialist structures, learning standards and accountability, many European governments have understood that teachers are a central element in achieving educational improvements in international indicators (Espejo & Lázaro, 2014). Research lines on academic success and its link to the profession of teaching (Özer, 2020) have contributed to this, serving to highlight the main trends in education systems and the working conditions of teachers.

Two ideas are particularly relevant to this debate, as reflected in some of the studies carried out in this field (Egido, 2020). On the one hand, the contextual weakness that accompanies the transfer of teaching practices between countries and, therefore, the detachment that occurs between training and the social and cultural consciousness of member states.

With regard to teaching, TALIS (OECD, 2019b) and PISA, in their latest editions, presented an image of the profession that is probably not so widely shared, that allows us to appreciate the complexity of their work. The idea of a teacher performing his/her teaching duties with a diverse range of students, where institutionally received teaching support is crucial in complex conditions, is of enormous importance in the perception of educational leadership and in the development of more collaborative work (Bowers, 2020).

LEARNERS

In terms of the student body, including adult students, the key objectives that feature in the guidelines set forth by the EU for lifelong learning are presented in documents such as the Education and Training Monitor report (2019), which is depicted in Fig. 1. This figure outlines the clear trend toward attaining a greater number of students at all levels of education. However, there is a worrying percentage of early leavers from education and training and concerning rates of skills not being acquired by primary and secondary school students (less than 15 years old) in the areas of reading, mathematics and sciences. These will need to be further addressed with policies focused on improving these percentages, as they remain low and outline the importance of equitable policies.

EU targets for 2020 in education

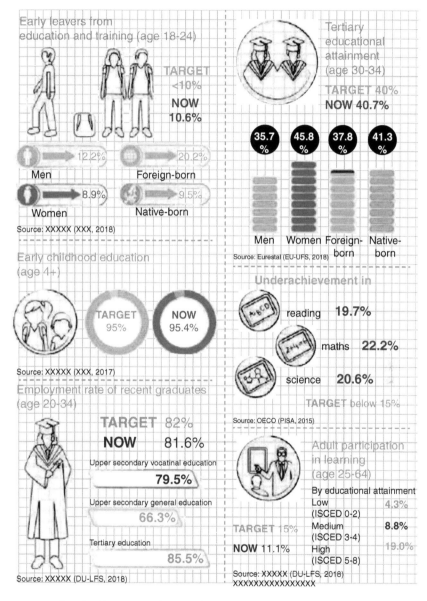

Early leavers from education and training (age 18-24)

TARGET
<10%
NOW
10.6%

12.2%
Men

20.2%
Foreign-born

8.9%
Women

9.5%
Native-born

Source: XXXXX (XXX, 2018)

Early childhood education (age 4+)

TARGET
95%

NOW
95.4%

Source: XXXXX (XXX, 2017)

Employment rate of recent graduates (age 20-34)

TARGET 82%

NOW 81.6%

Upper secondary vocatinal education
79.5%

Upper secondary general education
66.3%

Tertiary education
85.5%

Source: XXXXX (DU-LFS, 2018)

Tertiary educational attainment (age 30-34)

TARGET 40%
NOW 40.7%

35.7%   45.8%   37.8%   41.3%

Men   Women   Foreign-born   Native-born

Source: Eurestal (EU-UFS, 2018)

Underachievement in

reading   19.7%

maths   22.2%

science   20.6%

TARGET below 15%

Source: OECO (PISA, 2015)

Adult participation in learning (age 25-64)

By educational attainment

Low (ISCED 0-2)		4.3%
Medium (ISCED 3-4)		8.8%
High (ISCED 5-8)		19.0%

TARGET 15%

NOW 11.1%

Source: XXXXX (DU-LFS, 2018)
XXXXXXXXXXXXXXXX

Fig. 1. EU Targets for 2020 in Education. *Source*: EU (2019).

Matching Education and Work

It was in the late 1980s, coinciding with the impetus given to OECD education policies, that the theory of institutional reciprocity between the labor market and the formal sphere began to emerge. One specific example is the development of educational evaluation plans that were implemented in the early 1990s, on an experimental basis, in certain European educational systems. These would go on to be decisive in the interrelationship between contextual and process variables, and the results that these variables generate at different levels. This introduced an economic exchange value (EFQM model) in the organizational culture of education, and led to educational systems focusing more on job production (Lingard et al., 2016; Medne et al., 2020).

On an institutional level, this trend toward two-way education and work in European training systems was reinforced in 2008 by the European Parliament and the Council with the recommendation of developing a European Qualifications Framework for lifelong learning (EQF). This represented a political commitment to standardize qualification levels across different European countries, with the clear purpose of encouraging mobility and improving the employability of young people and the wider population (Mikulec, 2017).

Method of Teaching and Learning

School governance and the rise in theories pertaining to school autonomy in England, Germany and, to a lesser extent, Spain, is helping to re-contextualize policies of educational innovation as an expression of the identity of a type of privately-run but publicly-funded school (*freie schulen* in Germany, free schools in England, *escuelas libres/alternativas* in Spain and *écoles démocratiques* in France, which also have headquarters in other countries). However, the teaching experiences that have been reported on this subject suggest that progress is being made in all educational centers in general, regardless of the mode of management and ownership. In countries like Italy, which represent the cradle of an important tradition in teaching methodology, the alternative method is consolidated as a form of educational work.

Certain research projects (Zainuddin & Perera, 2019) outline the benefits that the principles of more innovative and collaborative methodologies, such as the "flipped classroom," can have on student motivation, enabling greater control of autonomous learning and facilitating better interaction between peers.

Language of Learning and Teaching

The narrative of a linguistically evolved and pluralistic Europe is the image that we get from the official reports on linguistic education policies. Eurydice, Eurostat, and the international documents of PISA and TALIS, for which the European Commission is jointly responsible, provide an overview that suggests that there has been a greater awareness of linguistic competence amongst member states in recent years, with this being conceived as a value of cognitive development and a capital element for social and cultural integration.

The policy actions enacted within the Common European Framework of Reference for Languages show significant progress in terms of language learning. The study of a first foreign language in primary education (normally English) is very common in France, Italy, Spain, and Germany; however, the novelty lies in the presence of other languages such as French (the second most-studied foreign language in Germany, Italy and Spain), and Spanish (studied in England and France). This allows us to speak, with certain caution, of the fact that a *transitology* (Cowen, 2001) is taking place in education language policies. The strategic development of the inter-relational role of language learning in heterogeneous contexts remains on the political agenda.

Education Quality

Mapping the educational quality model that currently presides over the governance of Western European education systems is not an easy task. The strengthening of transnational mediatization and its legitimization via comparison (Kim, 2020) are helping to shape a technocratic approach that considerably reframes the idea of educational quality.

In this sense, the parameters of excellence, educational achievement, and/or maximization of results move the current construct of quality away from the democratic idea of educational equality (Gortazar, 2019) and highlight the existence of two quality models: that which is present in international reports, and that which is regulated in school reforms.

The measures identified in high-quality education systems include providing greater resources to disadvantaged schools, acting on the identification of drop-out factors and strengthening teacher training policies. These are not always represented in the contextual reforms carried out by European governments, which remains an institutional contradiction (Özer, 2020).

Western Europe is currently debating whether to consolidate quality one-dimensionally, through external/internal evaluation models (England represents the largest laboratory in school performance), or to rethink the impact that these evaluations have at the political level and, as a consequence, the segregation that they generate in education (Zhao, 2020).

EQUALITY

The current educational agenda of international organizations has contributed to the fact that academic success also benefits from international and Western European educational equality policies. The conceptualization of equality in terms of academic achievement has been widely addressed in the literature on combatting early school drop-out (Calsamiglia & Loviglio, 2019; Choi et al., 2017).

In this sense, equality is included in the framework of the European strategy (2020 Goals) and in the UN's 2030 Agenda (Sustainable Development Goals), ranging from inclusion data that seek raise awareness of higher and university education amongst vulnerable groups and disabled people, who have not traditionally received these levels of education.

These policies generally represent a paradigm shift in the conceptualization of education. This is depicted in institutional inclusion projects such as the NET-NEET project – in which France, Italy, Spain, and Germany are participants – which is aimed at creating opportunities, through mobility, for young people with few qualifications.

CONCLUSION

The idea of *Europa Regina* remains a constant, many years after its first cartographic representation. The confluence of countries with great economic potential and decision-making legitimacy in global politics has made Western Europe a leading exponent of global governance.

In different areas of public policy, the European project of unity that began after the EU economic process has been expressed, not unambiguously, along joint lines of action by all member states, moving toward a model of transnational cooperation. The EU's prolific political agenda (the 2020 goals and the 2030 Agenda), combined with its representation on an international level, have helped to unify the positions of countries such as England, Germany, France, Italy, and Spain, which have significant structural and organizational differences, but which have managed to turn political institutions into a formal instrument in the fight against discrimination and in the enactment of global citizenship.

Europe's role as an educational benchmark has been presented in a series of global reports (TALIS, PISA, etc.) that allow us to comprehend the paradigmatic shift of European education over time, depicting its present and future potential in terms of trends and the power of spreading educational reforms across other continents in the search for educational excellence.

We cannot end this chapter without noting that the impact of geopolitical alliances on the development of the European project has remained constant over time (Matarranz et al., 2020). At this time, in the context of a global pandemic, it is a moral imperative to safeguard the European solidarity project whose future, in the words of Krastev (2020), is at stake. It is therefore up to the Europe of institutions and civil society to articulate scenarios and mechanisms that will enable a future of shared responsibility to be channeled, reaching beyond the metamorphosis and isolation that reductionist discourse on the global–local dimension may lead to.

REFERENCES

Adoumié, V. (Dir.) (2013). *Géographie de l'Europe* [*Geography of Europe*]. Hachette Livre.
Azcárate, M. V., & Sánchez, Z. J. (2013). *Geografía de Europa* [*Geography of Europe*]. UNED.
Blanchenay, P., & Burns, T. (2016). Policy experimentation in complex education systems. In T. Burns & F. Köster (Eds.), *Governing education in a complex world* (pp. 161–186). OECD Publishing. Retrieved June 15, 2020, from http://dx.doi.org/101787/9789264255364-10-en/

Bowers, A. (2020). *Examining a congruency-typology model of leadership for learning using two-level latent class analysis with TALIS 2018*. OECD Education Working Papers, 219. OECD. Retrieved June 15, 2020, from http://doi.org/10.1787/c963073b-en/

Calsamiglia, C., & Loviglio, A. (2019). Grading on a curve: When having good peers is not good. *Economics of Education Review, 73*, 1–21.

Campani, G., & Pajnik, M. (2017). Democracy, post-democracy and the populist challenge. In G. Lazaridis & G. Campani (Eds.), *Understanding the populist shift: Othering in a Europe in crisis* (pp. 179–196). Routledge.

Choi, A., Gil, M., Mediavilla, M., & Valbuena, J. (2017). The evolution of educational inequalities in Spain: Dynamic evidence from repeated cross-sections. *Social Indicators Research, 138*, 1–20.

Cone, L., & Brøgger, K. (2020). Soft privatisation: Mapping an emerging field of European education governance. *Globalisation, Societies and Education, 18*(4), 374–390.

Cowen, R. (2001). Globalisation, educational myths in late modernity and reflections on virtue. In L. M. Lázaro & M. J. Martínez-Usarralde (Eds.), *Estudios de Educación Comparada [Studies in Comparative Education]* (pp. 11–40). Universitat de València.

Delanty, G. (2006). La idea de una Europa cosmopolita: De la importancia cultural de la europeización [The idea of a cosmopolitan Europe: Of cultural importance Of Europeanization]. *Recerca, Revista de Pensament i Anàlisi, 6*, 85–108.

Delanty, G. (2011). Dilemmas of secularism: Europe, religion and the problem of pluralism. In G. Delanty, R. Wodak, & P. Jones (Eds.), *Identity, belonging and migration* (pp. 78–97). Liverpool University Press. Retrieved June 15, 2020, from http://doi.org/10.5949/UPO9781846314537.005/

Diez-Hochleitner, R. (1994). No existe nada tan realista como la utopía. [There is nothing as realistic as utopia]. In N. Rosensohn (Ed.), *Horizontes de Europa 2020: Los albores de un nuevo Renacimiento [Horizons of Europe 2020: The dawn of a new Renaissance]* (pp. 15–17). Fundación BBV.

EFE. (2020). *El inglés, especie protegida en la UE tras el Brexit [English, protected Species in UE behind the Brexit]*. Retrieved April 7, 2020, from https://www.eldiario.es/internacional/ingles-especie-protegida-ue-brexit_1_1071166.html/

Egido, I. (2020). El acceso a la formación docente inicial en Europa: políticas e investigación [Access to initial teacher training in Europe: Policies and research]. *Revista Española de Educación Comparada, 35*, 197–211. Retrieved April 7, 2020, from http://doi.org/10.5944/reec.35.2020.24192/

Espejo, B., & Lázaro, L. (2014). Political change and education reform: Teacher training institutions in Italy. In R. Verdugo (Ed.), *Educational reform in Europe. History, culture and ideology* (pp. 63–94). Infoagepub.

Europarlament. (s.d.). *The Directorate-General for translation*. Retrieved April 7, 2020, from https://ec.europa.eu/info/departments/translation/

European Commission. (2016). *Eurobarometer 66. First results*. Directorate General Communication.

European Commission. (2019). Communication from the commission to the european parliament, the council, the european economic and social committee and the committee of the regions empty. The European Pillar of Social Rights Action 2020, https://ec.europa.eu/transparency/regdoc/rep/1/2019/ES/COM-2019-22-F1-ES-MA IN-PART -1.PDF

European Union. (s.d.). *Languages in EU*. Retrieved April 7, 2020, from https://europa.eu/european-union/about-eu/eu-languages_es/

European Union and GlobalStats. (2019). *Living in the EU: Demography*. Retrieved April 7, 2020, from http://www.globalstat.eu/

Francesco, F., & Guaschino, E. (2020). Reframing knowledge: A comparison of OECD and World Bank discourse on public governance reform. *Policy and Society, 39*(1), 113–128. Retrieved June 15, 2020, from http://doi:10.1080/14494035.2019.1609391/

Fundación Alternativas & Ebert-Stifung, S. (2019). *El estado de la Unión Europea: El Parlamento Europeo ante unas elecciones trascendentales [The state of the European Union: The European Parliament before a transcendental elections]*. Lua.

García-Ruiz, M. J. (2012). La universidad postmoderna y la nueva creación del conocimiento [The postmodern university and the new knowledge production]. *Educación XXI: Revista de la Facultad de Educación, 15*(1), 179–193.

Gortazar, L. (2019). ¿Favorece el sistema educativo español la igualdad de oportunidades? [Does the Spanish educational system favor equal opportunities?] FEDEA, *Estudios sobre la Economía Española* no. 2019-17. FEDEA.

Guirao, F. (Ed.). (2019). ¿*Una Unión Europea en crisis? Reflexiones para un debate urgente [A European Union in crisis? Reflections for an urgent discussion]*. Catarata.

Hall, D., & Gunter, H. (2016). England. The liberal state: Permanent instability in the European educational NPM laboratory. In H. Gunter et al. (Eds.), *New public management and the reform of education: European lessons for policy and practice* (pp. 39–54). Routledge.

Hodgson, A., & Spours, K. (2020). Young people and transitions in upper secondary education in England: The influence of policy on the 'Local Opportunity Landscape'. In K. Brunila & L. Lundahl (Eds.), *Youth on the move: Tendencies and tensions in youth policies and practices* (pp. 127–147). Helsinki University Press.

Jones, K., Harcher, R., Hirtt, N., Innes, R., Johsua, S., Klausenitzer, J., & Gracian, C. B. (2009). *La escuela en Europa Occidental. El nuevo orden y sus adversarios [The school in Western Europe. The new order and its adversaries]*. Germania.

Kim, J. (2020). Problematizing global educational governance of OECD PISA: Student achievement, categorization, and social inclusion and exclusion. *Educational Philosophy and Theory, 52*(14), 1483–1492. https://doi.org/10.1080/00131857.2020.1732928

Koerrenz, R., Blichmann, A., & Engelmann, S. (2018). *Alternative schooling and new education: European concepts and theories*. Springer International Publishing.

Krastev, I. (2020). *Is it tomorrow yet?: Paradoxes of the pandemic*. Allen Lane.

Le Monde Diplómatique. (2012). *Nuevas potencias emergentes [New emergency powers]*. Fundación Mondiplo-UNED.

Lingard, B., Martino, W., Rezai-Rasht, G., & Sellar, S. (2016). *Globalizing educational accountabilities*. Routledge. https://doi.org/10.4324/9781315885131/ Accessed 3 April 2020.

López-Palomeque, F., & Plaza, J. I. (2020). Europa. Aproximación geográfica, conceptos e ideas [Europe. Geographical approximation, concepts and ideas]. In F. López-Palomeque & J. I. Plaza (Eds.), *Geografía de Europa. Estructuras, procesos y dinámicas territoriales [Geography of Europe. Structures, processes and territorial dynamics]* (pp. 19–69). Tirant Lo Blanch.

Lundahl, L., & Brunila, K. (2020). Epilogue: Silences and challenges. In K. Brunila & L. Lundahl (Eds.), *Youth on the move: Tendencies and tensions in youth policies and practices* (pp. 185–190). Helsinki University Press. Retrieved April 17, 2020, from https://doi.org/10.33134/HUP-3-10/

Martínez-Usarralde, M. J. (2001). Los sistemas de Formación Profesional europeos a examen: desafíos, innovaciones y perspectivas de cambio para un entorno cambiante [The European Vocational Training systems under review: challenges, innovations and change perspectives for a changing environment]. *Revista Española de Pedagogía, 59*(219), 311–330.

Matarranz, M., Valle, J. M., & Manso, J. (2020). After 2020… Towards an European education area in 2025. *Revista Española de Educación Comparada, 36*, 98–128.

Medne, A., Lapina, I., & Zeps, A. (2020). Sustainability of a university's quality system: Adaptation of the EFQM excellence model. *International Journal of Quality and Service Sciences, 12*(1), 29–43.

Mikulec, B. (2017). Impact of the Europeanisation of education: Qualifications frameworks in Europe. *European Educational Research Journal, 16*(4), 455–473.

Moreno, L. (2019). El futuro del Modelo Social Europeo [The future of European Social Model]. En C. Ares & L. Bouza (Eds.), *Política de la Unión Europea. Crisis y continuidad [Policy of European Union. Crisis and continuity]* (pp. 291–306). Centro de Investigaciones Sociológicas.

Naumann, I. K., & Crouch, C. (2020). Rescaling education policy: Central–local relations and the politics of scale in England and Sweden. *Policy & Politics, 48*(4), 583–601. https://doi.org/10.1 332/030557320X15835195302535

Nóvoa, A. (2010). Governing without governing: The formation of a European educational space. In M. W. Apple et al. (Eds.), *The Routledge international handbook of the sociology of education* (pp. 264–273). Routledge.

OECD. (2015). *School governance, assessments and accountability*. OECD. http://www.oecd.org/pisa/keyfindings/ Accessed 17 April 2020.

OECD. (2019a). *International migration outlook*. OECD.

OECD. (2019b). *TALIS 2018 Results (Volume I): Teachers and school leaders as lifelong learners.* OECD Publishing.

Özer, M. (2020). What does PISA tell us about performance of education systems? *Bartın University Journal of Faculty of Education, 9*(2), 217–228.

Pashby, K., da Costa, M., Stein, S., & Andreotti, V. (2020). A meta-review of typologies of global citizenship education. *Comparative Education, 56*(2), 144–164.

Pew Research. (2019). A closer look at how religious restrictions have risen around the world. *Center,* July 15.

Popov, N., & Genova, T. (2019). Comparative education in Eastern and Central Europe. In C. C. Wolhuter & A. W. Wiseman (Eds.), *Comparative and international education: Survey of an infinite field.* International Perspectives on Education and Society (Vol. 36, pp. 119–135). Emerald Publishing Limited.

Prskawetz, A., Fent, T., Barthel, W., Crespo-Cuaresma, J., Lindh, T., Malmberg, B., & Halvarsson M. (2007). *The relationship between demographic change and economic growth in the EU.* Institut Für Demographie.

Sánchez, M. R., & Díaz, V. (2017). The future of welfare state in Europe. *Index de Enfermería, 26*(3), 190–194. Retrieved April 17, 2020, from http://scielo.isciii.es/scielo.php?script=sci_arttext&pid=S1132-12962017000200015&lng=es&tlng=en/

Valle, J. (2006). *La Unión Europea y su política educativa. [European Union and its educational policy].* Ministerio de Educación.

Zainuddin, Z., & Perera, C. J. (2019). Exploring students' competence, autonomy and relatedness in the flipped classroom pedagogical model. *Journal of Further and Higher Education, 43*(1), 115–126. http:/doi:10.1080/0309877X.2017.1356916/ Accessed 17 April 2020.

Zhao, Y. (2020). Two decades of havoc: A synthesis of criticism against PISA. *Journal of Educational Change, 21*, 245–266.

BALTIC COUNTRIES: FROM POST-SOCIALIST TO NEW-LIBERAL EDUCATION?

Irina Maslo

ABSTRACT

This chapter offers a survey of education development in the Baltic region and the dynamics of global forces in the three Baltic states' contexts. First, a brief overview of the incoming new-liberal global trend that impacted the education in the Post-Socialist European region will be provided, followed by a discussion of similarities and differences in the development of education in Baltic states as co-shaped by contextual contours of the post-socialist region at whole. It shows that the contextual social and cultural realities of Estonia-Latvia-Lithuania not only have a powerful mediating role on the impact of global forces but are in their own right an agency in shaping the education response of Post-socialist societies of this region. Second, the knowledge of the interrelationship between education and societal cultural contexts in the Baltic region will be explained, stressing the lack of research on informal settlements or the informal economy and its intersection with education. The International Comparative Education research agenda will not only be of significance for the Baltic states but to the entire world. Many aspects of the contextual architecture of the region are becoming increasingly evident world-wide tending the neo-liberalism in education as distinct from liberalism insofar as it does not advocate market-economic policy but instead is highly constructivist and approve a strong state to bring reforms in every aspect of society transforming the education and teaching labor market.

Keywords: Comparative and International Education; the Baltic states; globalization; economic growth; well-being; Transformation of education

World Education Patterns in the Global North:
The Ebb of Global Forces and the Flow of Contextual Imperatives
International Perspectives on Education and Society, Volume 43A, 85–103
Copyright © 2022 by Emerald Publishing Limited
All rights of reproduction in any form reserved
ISSN: 1479-3679/doi:10.1108/S1479-36792022000043A007

Followed the post-socialist liberal individual pedagogy, the new-liberal ideas of a human being as self-directed, self-organized, and collective agent (Apple, 1999) take place word wide transforming the education in the context of Globalisation of Education and Societies. As Susan L. Robertson (2007) in her paper "Remaking the World": Neo-liberalism and the Transformation of Education and Teachers' Labour states: "few disagree that the globalisation of a neoliberal utopia, like continental drift" (Bourdieu, 1998, p. 1), has become hegemonic. In doing so, "its promoters have remade the world, including the world of education. Out with the collective and welfare; in with the individual and freedom" (Robertson, 2007, p. 2).

The new knowledge production related to national and regional economies, committee education providers to the efficient and effective creation of "the new breed of entrepreneurs and innovators; the value-driven minds who will spearhead the battle for global markets and consumers" (Robertson, 2007, p. 2). It seems now evident that the current global situation let us rethink this last three decades of education development paradigm shifts in global and regional societal and cultural contexts.

Emphasizing Wolhuter' and Wiseman' (2019) regional variations and comparative aspects, this chapter offers a survey of education development in Baltic states, and the dynamics of global forces and the Latvian, Estonian, and Lithuanian context. This is followed first by an overview of the incoming tide of global forces impinging on education in the post-socialist period, followed by a discussion of education developments in Estonia, Latvia, and Lithuania as co-shaped by contextual contours of regional context of Baltic states.

REGIONAL CONTEXT

Geography

The Baltic states is a geopolitical term, typically used to group three sovereign states in Northern Europe on the eastern coast of the Baltic Sea. The Baltic states most shortened to the Baltics is the placement of the republics of Estonia, Latvia, and Lithuania, which became constituent republics of the former Soviet Union in 1940, regaining their independence in 1991 before joining the European Union (EU) in 2004. The Baltic states are bounded on the west and north by the Baltic Sea, which gives the region its name, on the east by Russia, on the southeast by Belarus, and on the southwest by Poland and Russia.

The territory of the smallest Baltic state, Estonia, exceeds that of Denmark, the Netherlands or Switzerland. If the Baltic states were a single country, its combined area would comprise 175,000 km^2 and rank ninth among the member states of the European Union (Puur et al., 2019).

The Baltic states display major similarities in terms of their geography and size, but also some differences in geographical bounding to their neighboring countries where Latvia has a central place, Estonia – the west and Lithuania the east position. They related, Estonia has geographically bound accordingly to Scandinavian in the west, but Lithuania – to Poland in the east of the Baltic.

Demography

Estonians, Latvians, and Lithuanians are linguistically diverse peoples. Estonians speak a Finno-Ugric language akin to Finnish, while Latvian and Lithuanian are the only surviving strands of the Baltic family of Indo-European languages. However, the Baltic countries are sparsely populated. In the EU context, only Sweden and Finland possess lower population density (Puur et al., 2019).

Demographic processes of the Baltic states are evolving over a long time. In the early 1990s, Lithuania had a relatively homogeneous ethnic composition with 80% of Lithuanians. The remaining 20% came (almost in half) from the East Slavs (Russians, Belarusians, and Ukrainians) and Poles. In Estonia, the main nation was about 60%, the East Slavs – 35%, the other 5% were other ethnic groups. In terms of ethnic composition, the most heterogeneous situation was and still is in Latvia (Table 1).

At the End of 2019, Baltics is home of 1,907 thousand people in Latvia, 1,326 thousand people in Estonia, and 2,760 thousand people in Lithuania. The largest relative reductions in population size over the period between 2019 and 2050, with losses of 22% is expected in Latvia, while those in Lithuania and Estonia could decline by 17% and 13%, respectively (United Nations, 2019).

Politics

The politics of Baltic states have similarities and differences affected by different history, traditions and customs. Allan Puur et al. (2019) provide a detailed analysis of historical development of politics in Baltic states:

> During the Northern Crusades, the countries that later became modern Estonia and Latvia were conquered by German and Danish conquerors colonized and gradually insured the indigenous population. On the contrary, the Lithuanians founded their political unit, which entered into a dynastic alliance with neighbouring Poland in 1386. This alliance with Poland led to the gradual Polonization of the Lithuanian nobility, although they retained a strong sense of identity. At the beginning of the 17th century, wars between Sweden and Poland-Lithuania were fought for control of the region. The conflict ended in 1629 when most of the territory of Livonia was transferred to Sweden, except Latgale in south-eastern Latvia, which remained under Polish rule. (Puur et al., 2019, p. 33)

Table 1. Main Population by Nationality in Latvia at the Beginning of the Year (CSB, 2020a).

	1935	1989	2000	2011	2019
Latvians	1,467,035	1,387,757	1,370,703	1,255,785	1 196 578
Russians	168,266	905,515	703,243	556,434	478 667
Belarusians	26,803	97,150	119,702	73,781	61 429
Ukrainians	1,844	92,101	63,644	49,134	43 069
Poles	48,637	60,416	59,505	47,201	38 821
Lithuanians	22,843	34,630	33,430	26,924	22 344
Jews	93,370	22,897	10,385	6,495	4 567
Roma	3,839	7,044	8,205	6,643	4 983
Germans	62,116	3,783	3,465	3,127	2,554
Estonians	6,928	3,312	2,652	2,085	1 625

Each nation develops its traditions, customs, and political behavior. *Latvia and Estonia* are parliamentary republics. *Lithuania* has a semi-presidential but parliamentary-inclined system.

ECONOMY

Since renewed independence in 1991 and transition from a centrally planned to a market economy, *Lithuania* has substantially raised the well-being of its citizens. Thanks to a market-friendly environment the country grew faster than most OECD countries over the past 10 years (OECD, 2018a). According to the OECD (2019) surveys, *Estonia* continues to perform well, and growing incomes support well-being (OECD, 2019a). *Latvia* enjoys strong economic growth (OECD, 2019b).

After joining the European Union in 2004, the Baltic states experienced a sharp economic rise. Unfortunately, for the rapid development of Latvia longevity was not destined because it was based on the wrong foundations – freely available and cheap foreign capital was used not for investment in economic development, but mainly for simple purposes for consumption (Eiropas Komisija, 2013). The shadow economy in Latvia reached 24.2% in 2018. The extent of the shadow economy in Lithuania was 18.7%m increased by 0.5%, and in Estonia – 16.7%, decreased by1.5% (Putniņš & Sauka, 2018).

The analysis by Aurélien Poissonier (2017) shows that the Baltic countries form a closely but slightly different economic space. Estonia is the most advanced of the three countries. On the contrary, Lithuania is more resistant to general crises. The analysis shows that "investments to stimulate potential growth in one of the Baltic states will benefit the entire territory in the long-term perspective" (Poissonnier, 2017, p. 9).

SOCIAL SYSTEM
Main Features of the Social System

The main conspicuous features of the social system of the Baltic seats are citizenship and minorities issues taking into account the differences in the social status of citizens and minorities in three Baltic states (Agarin, 2018; Hogan-Brun et al., 2007). A next feature is the social stratification of poor, affluent people, and the middle class, and, also, the labor migration what affects the primary social grouping, that is the family.

Citizenship

Lithuania was the first of Baltic states what adopted a citizenship law in December 1991. The right to naturalize was granted to all citizens of Lithuania, their descendants, citizens of the Lithuanian SSR and people born in Lithuania. *In Estonia,* in February 1992, the parliament effectively renewed the 1938 Citizenship Act. In 1995, a new citizenship law was passed, which allowed naturalization of persons who had lived in Estonia for five years, had legal sources of income, spoke Estonian, knew the constitution and took an oath of allegiance. In 1998, changes were made to the law, which gave the right to acquire citizenship to children born in Estonia whose parents are stateless. *In Latvia,* the first law defining citizenship of 1991 was adopted in August 1994 providing Latvian citizenship automatically to citizens of Latvia before 1940 and their descendants. In 1998, a new citizenship law was adopted in Latvia abolishing the "window" system and gave the right to acquire citizenship to non-citizen children born in Latvia.

Minorities

The linguistic diversity impacts social system in the Baltic states. Besides the Russian-speaking minorities, each of the Baltic countries has also one other significant minority. *In Estonia,* it is Võro, a linguistically closely related group to Estonians. *In Latvia,* it is Latgalians, closely related to Latvians. *In Lithuania,* it is the Polish minority. Urban minorities of fairly recent origin, the other minorities are largely rural and native in their territories (Lazdiņa & Marten, 2019). Minority communities are unevenly distributed across the Baltic states' regions.

In Estonia, the Russian minority is concentrated in one region – 73% of the population of Ida-Viru County (north-eastern region) is formed by the Russian-speaking community while in Tallinn, the capital, they constitute (37%).

In Latvia and Lithuania, the historical minorities are rather scattered across the country. In Latvia, the Russian ethnic group is concentrated in the biggest cities – Daugavpils (52%), Rezekne (47%), Riga (40%), and Liepaja (32%) (49). In Lithuania, Visaginas (52%), Klaipeda (28%), and Vilnius (14%) have the biggest share of the Russian minority. The Polish minority is concentrated in Vilnius (52%) and Šalčininkai district (78%) in the southeast of Lithuania (Mägi & Siarova, 2014).

Poor and Affluent People, and the Middle Class

All three countries get closer to the Western middle-class income standard. Estonian and Latvian middle-class have become relatively better-off. Income inequality in the Baltic was higher than in the Western European countries in 2016. Estonia has the most equal income distribution among the Baltic countries (Swedbank, 2018).

Urbanizing of Baltic States

As the economy develops, more and more people are choosing to live in the city. Although the proportion of people living in cities *in Latvia* decreased from 40% to 24% as a result of the World War I, urbanization continued during the years of independence. At the end of the 1930s, Latvia had the highest proportion of urban residents in the Baltic states – 35% of the population lived in cities, while *in Estonia* – 33%, but *in Lithuania* – only 23% (Ekonomiskā vide, 2018). The fastest urbanizing population is in Latvia (Ekonomiskā vide, 2018). In 2019, 632,614 thousand of Latvian population lived in Riga (CSB, 2020b).

Religion and World- and Life-view

The religious landscape in Lithuania, Latvia, and Estonia is very different. An important cultural border arises in the Baltic in the sixteenth century. The cultural division between the Lutheran north and the Catholic south has become a permanent feature of the Baltic region. The Reformation quickly spread to the -territory of modern Estonia and Latvia. Although Protestantism (in the form of Calvinism) gained some supporters in Lithuania, the southern part of the Baltic region remained Catholic (Puur et al., 2019). The number of Orthodox Christians is logically connected with Russian and other Slavic ethnic groups. A third of the total population of ethnic Russian and other Slavic people's lives in Latvia play a rather large role in society.

The Latvian-speaking population is almost equally divided between Lutherans and Catholics. The stable and conservative influence of the Catholic Church throughout history has been supported in its way by Lutherans representing Western Christianity. The Western liberal, individualistic, pragmatic, and consumer philosophy, with its attendant value system, has taken root in the Baltic region (Nisbett, 2003). Human Rights are also taking root, especially among those who enjoyed the benefit of new-liberal holistically inclusive education.

Compared to the other two Baltic countries, Estonia presents a unique picture because it attracts attention to the non-religious and religiously indefinite part of the population, which is quite large up to 70.69%. In Estonia, the Russian-speaking population defines themselves as part of the Orthodox Church. However, the most important and largest confession for Estonians is Lutheranism (Cusack, 2019).

THE INCOMING TIDE OF GLOBAL TRENDS

The reorganization of international production (Letto-Gillies, 2007), technological transformations (Frey & Osborne, 2017), the expansion of trade and globalization (M. R. Surugiu & C. Surugiu, 2015), and greater global interdependence (Marshall, 2015) have affected all three Baltic states. The aging of population and migration contribute to diversifying the demographic, cultural, linguistic, ethnic and religious makeup of Baltics, a specially in Latvia and Latvia's cities, suburbs and rural communities (Desjardins, 2019; Grzymala-Kazlowska & Phillimore, 2018). In this context, the provision of skills that would enable near social exclusion people to overcome challenges in including themselves in local, regional, and national contexts, could be helped with adequate holistically inclusive new-liberal education policies.

AGING OF POPULATION

Latvia faces one of the fastest declines in its working-age population among OECD countries due to aging and migration. The demographical crisis affects the Baltic countries differently. The population of Latvia and Lithuania decreased last year, while in Estonia it increased. Recently, Statistics Estonia (2019) published detailed data showing the expense of achieving this result, found out that Estonia largely grew its population at the expense of immigrants, including from Latvia (Table 2).

In turn, the return of Estonians from abroad plays a secondary role. Despite the documented low rates of immigration in 2013 to these countries (0.7% in Lithuania, 0.4% in Latvia and 0.3% in Estonia), which due to incomplete statistical data are expected to be higher, the number of immigrants in Estonia and Lithuania shows a slight increase since 2004 except Latvia, where the number of immigrants has been decreasing since 2018. Finland (26%), Russia (23%), and Ukraine (8%) are the major countries of origin of immigrants in Estonia, while in Lithuania, most immigrants are coming from Russia (25%), Belarus (16%), and Ukraine (13%). In Latvia, most immigrants come from Russia (42%), Ukraine (7%), and Uzbekistan (6%) (UNHCR, 2014).

Rising of Multilingualism

On the rise of multilingualism, the highest proportions of multilingual speakers are in Luxembourg, Belgium, Denmark, in the Netherlands, Sweden, Slovenia, Slovakia, Finland, as well as in the Baltic states. In Latvia, this indicator is 54.9% (one of the highest levels of foreign language knowledge in Europe in 2009). Lithuania and Latvia also have the lowest proportion of the population who do not know anyone foreign language. In Latvia, they are 2.5%. In the Baltic states, both English and German are used more by Estonians and Lithuanians, that is, about 40% respondents, however, French is slightly more popular among the Latvian population, they are 2% (1% in Lithuania and Estonia), the second place is held by the Russian (LETA, 2009).

Rising of Religious Migration

On the rise of religious migration, there are about 10,000 Muslims who are active participants in the local communities' life in Latvia. There are 7,000 Muslims in Lithuania which history of Muslims began with a group of soldiers and governors

Table 2. Non-EU Foreign-born Share of Population in %.

Country	Foreign-born Population by Country of Birth
Estonia	13.1
Latvia	11.3
Lithuania	3.9

Source: Eurostat (2018).

sent by the Crimean khans for assistance 630 years ago. Estonia has one of the smallest Muslim communities in Europe. According to the census of 2011, the number of people who profess Islam was 1,508 and around 5,000 Muslims is reported in 2017 in Estonia (Insamer, 2017). As relatively new European Member states, the three Baltic countries are among the few EU countries with negative migration rates.

Skill Shortages

According to the Education and training monitor report 2019, *in Estonia* the skills the challenge is insignificant imbalances in aligning skills supply to labor demand. Existing data suggest that there is a shortage of cognitive and other transversal skills (OECD, 2019b). To address these challenges, the 2019 country-specific recommendations call on Estonia to address skills shortages and foster innovation by improving the capacity and labor market relevance of the education and training system (Council of the European Union, 2019).

In Lithuania, skills mismatch and over-qualification are widespread among tertiary graduates. Recent tertiary graduates have a high employment rate (90.4% vs 85.5% at EU level in 2018), but at the beginning of their career, they tend to work in less qualified jobs because they lack job-relevant skills: "The quality of tertiary programmes may benefit from a regular framework for anticipating and monitoring skills demand and from enhanced cooperation between businesses and universities" (DG EAC, 2019, p. 178).

In Latvia, the skill mismatch is not reported. However, several occupations have been identified as a high mismatch for Latvia.

Development of Education in Baltic States

The Baltic states are often grouped, but the significant differences among they are reflected in education policy. Education reforms have therefore been a priority of each country since regaining independence (McGuinness, 2015). According Aims C. Jr. McGuinness (2015), education reforms in the Baltic states is best understood in terms of phases, beginning in the late 1980s.

First, each country's reforms can be traced in initiatives since 1987 undertaken in the spirit of the *perestroika* during which each country experienced unprecedented grassroots engagement of educators in exploring new possibilities.

Second, in the 1990–1992 period, while all three countries re-established independence and established the initial legal framework for education.

Third, the 1995–1996 period brought a temporary pause in the positive developments. Each country attempted to shape new state policies to provide a degree of order to the previously largely decentralized and often fragmented reforms.

Fourth, in the 1997–1998 period, all three countries experienced their strongest periods of economic revitalization and growth since 1991. The laws on education first enacted in 1991–1992 were either replaced or amended significantly to reflect an increased maturity in each country's education reforms.

Fifth, in the late 1998, the Russian economic crisis, beginning with the devaluation of the double slowed economic growth as well as the pace of education reform of the previous two years in all three countries (McGuinness, 2015).

Reformulating the McGuinness (2015) periodization phases in the Pre–Post-Socialist Education and the Post-Socialist Liberal Education extending with the phase of education reforms toward the new-liberal education in the Baltic states, let to make a more detailed analysis.

PRE–POST-SOCIALIST EDUCATION IN THE BALTIC STATES

Until the middle of 1990s, there were two parallel system of schools with Russian as the language of instruction in Baltics. Thus, the major part of the population of Baltic states was educated in an education system whose goal was the development of the society and an individual as a harmoniously developed person. The function of the education was upbringing, educating, and developing personalities. This approach was significantly different reflected in education policy of Estonia, Lithuania, and Latvia depend on the collective memory on the educational practice of this time-span.

Similarities

In Lithuania and Latvia by the time of *perestroika,* Russian progressive thought in education had started to diverge from the paradigm of ideologist-upbringing followed the most progressive ideas of Pestalozzi, Komenský, and Piaget, emphasized "collaborative pedagogy" between teachers and students and the importance of seeing the pupil as an individual who is an agent of his/her learning and development. Vygotsky's theories, what were displeased suppressed in Stalin's regime emphasized upon the central role of the teacher (Godon et al., 2004).

Differences

In Estonia, *perestroika* was characterized by socialist humanistic educational goals, as Silvia Kera (1996) reports, considered all people as "nation of learners," emphasizing everyone's freedom to learn shaping the socialist attitudes: "Education followed the principles of Soviet patriotism, the communist attitude toward work as a matter of honour, fame and heroism, collectivism, socialist humanism and consciousness" (Kera, 1996, p. 32). Baltic states followed "the philosophical, educational and psychological approaches in the articulation of the holistic development of the individual and theories of differentiated and modular teaching received considerable attention (Godon et al., 2004).

POST-SOCIALIST LIBERAL EDUCATION IN THE BALTIC STATES

Period of Re-establishing Independence

In Estonia, the Education Act of 1992 affirmed the principles of comprehensive schools, legalized private education and allowed four-year post-secondary schools ("technicums") to apply for the status of vocational higher education institutions similar as in other two Baltic states (OECD, 2016).

In Latvia, the specialization of education was introduced (humanitarian, natural sciences, etc.). The set of subjects changed, but the changes do not affect the educational process itself. In the 1991/1992 school year, a single curriculum was introduced in schools. During the academic year, a block or module of natural science subjects became optional.

In Lithuania, the Education Act of 1991 provided for changes in the objectives, content and structure of education. It underlined the need for individuals to know and understand the principles of a democratic pluralistic society, to accept humanism and tolerance as basic values in life, to develop skills for independent decision-making and to acquire professional skills: "the education system is based on European cultural values: the absolute value of the individual, solidarity, innate equality among human beings, freedom of conscience, tolerance and democratic social relations" (Word Data on Education, 2007, p. 2).

Period of Economic Revitalization and Growth

In Latvia, a working group of Latvian and foreign specialists was convened in 1995, which developed a 10-year comprehensive Latvian language acquisition program for social integration. The introduction of a completely new subject, Latvian as a Second Language (LAT2), was very useful for this strategy. Learning a second language differs from learning a foreign language in that it is a language learned in a language environment with all the needs that exist in normal language use. It was a revolution that instead of the usual grammatical paradigms, classical literature and folk songs, descriptions of the use of pop groups, microwave ovens and fax machines appeared in books and curricula, and much attention was paid to speech development and listening exercises. In-service teacher training had to focus on the teacher moving away from monologue to the activity in which the student is the center, to group and pair work, to a project approach (Priedite, 2002). In 1998, four models of minority education programs were developed, which determined the proportion of subjects in Latvian, bilingual and/or minority languages. Each school could choose one or more of these models, or develop its curriculum (fifth model) (LR MFA, 2018).

In Estonia, the new curriculum, which came into force in 1996, was seen as an instrument for building a democratic, dynamic, information-based society, turning toward Europe and supporting the establishment of a market economy. The new curriculum emphasized problem-solving, democratic decision-making, critical thinking, and an awareness of personal responsibility. A key objective was to facilitate students' ability to motivate, reflect, and manage their learning. Estonia turned to Finland to learn about building a more effective education system (OECD, 2016).

In Lithuania, the establishment of an education system, covering formal and non-formal education in an expanded network of public and private educational institutions, the evaluation of the reform results and the revision of the educational structure, curricula, and textbooks tacked place in 1997–2002. The 10-year (4+6+2) compulsory basic education has been introduced during 1998–2000 and one year of pre-primary education free of charge in 2002 (Word Data on Education, 2007).

Period of a Strong Commitment to New Education Reforms

Opposite to the evident interconnection of educational reforms and economic growth in the development of all three Post-socialist Baltic states described above, only the Estonian economy has grown nearly tenfold since 2002. An important policy lesson from Estonia is that these outcomes are not random, but rather a result of a national education strategy to support a high-tech, high-skill, high-wage economy, and contributed to the country's high PISA ranking in each of the subject domains in the past three rounds of PISA 2006, 2009, and 2012: "This is a remarkable result compared to western European countries given their much more well-developed education systems and more disposable financial resources throughout the 1990s and early 2000s" (Delaney & Kraeme, 2020).

THE FEATURES OF THE TWENTY-FIRST CENTURY EDUCATION IN THE BALTIC STATES

Education Objectives

In the Baltic states, new-liberal tendencies are evident in educational objectives. *In Estonia*, the focus is on the ability and willingness of citizens to have a positive impact on society. The concept of active and responsible citizens is introduced in national basic and second level education curricula "in which it is named as one of the democratic competences to be achieved, aiming for students to become active and responsible members of society" (Kersh & Toiviainen, 2017, p. 12).

In Latvia, the concept of an "active and responsible citizen" plays an important role in the policy document Sustainable Development Strategy of Latvia until 2030, which calls that "in 2030 Latvia will be a thriving country of active and responsible citizens" (Kilis, 2010, p. 11).

In Lithuania, the concept of "active citizen" is not explicitly used in the Lithuanian Development Strategy "Lithuania 2030" but citizens are described as being

> proactive, enterprising, trusting their fellow-citizens, creative in their solutions and ready to take risks. Ideally, citizens would assume responsibility not only for themselves but also for others and society, with a strong feeling of national ownership. The image of the citizen as an active and responsible actor, demonstrating "growing civic maturity" is connected with an ideology claiming that the government must reduce areas of intervention, thus enabling citizens and communities to take responsibility into their hands. (Kersh & Toiviainen, 2017, p. 13)

Lithuania's progress strategy is a visible example of a new-liberal policy in action (Kersh & Toiviainen, 2017).

Organization and Administration

In Lithuania, the *Seimas* forms the national education policy for every 10 years considering and approving the annual state budget and funds for municipal budgets. Another important function of the Seimas is also the establishing of the state universities. The Government, the MoES, and other ministries participate in the formation and implementation of the national education policy. The Government also establishes state colleges. Municipalities are responsible for the establishment of pre-schools and schools (Eurydice, 2019).

In Latvia, the Education system is administered at three levels – national, municipal, and institutional. The Parliament (*Saima*), the Cabinet of Ministers, and the MoES are the main decision-making bodies at a national level. The schools are independent in developing and implementing educational programs, staff hiring, and school management. The higher education institutions are autonomous regarding the organizational procedure, implementation of the study process, internal rules and regulations, hiring and discharge of academic and technical personnel and distribution of allocated funding (Eurydice, 2017).

The Estonian education system is decentralized. The division of responsibility between the state, local government and schools is clearly defined. Provision of education is supervised by the state. Local governments have the obligation to provide every child with the possibility to attend a pre-school institution and compulsory school with the possibility to study in the school of residence. The vast majority of pre-school institutions and general education schools are municipal schools. Vocational schools are mostly state owned and universities are institutions in public law. A half of institutions of professional higher education are state owned and the other half are institutions in private law. Financing of educational institutions depends on the ownership of the institution. (Eurydice, 2018).

EDUCATION SYSTEM AND ITS STRUCTURE

With some differences, all three Baltic countries have similar Educational Systems regulated by European Qualification Framework (EQF) as the bridge between national qualifications systems (Eurostat, 2018). The core of the EQF is its eight reference levels defined in terms of knowledge, skills and autonomy-responsibility as learning outcomes of pre-primary (Level 0), basic, secondary, upper secondary (Levels 1–3), and upper secondary vocational education (Level 4). The short cycle developed by the Joint Quality Initiative as part of the Bologna process corresponds to the learning outcomes for EQF level 5. The descriptors for the first, second, and third cycle correspond respectively to the learning outcomes for EQF levels 6–8.

The educational systems of Baltic states differ in a duration of primary and secondary education: "6 years' primary education + 5, 6 or 7 years' secondary education in Estonia and Latvia, and 4 years' primary education + 8 or 9 years' secondary education in Lithuania" (Popov, 2012, pp. 32–33). Latvia does not have the adult education law/act so as Estonia and Lithuania. So too, according to McGuinness (2015), the High education degrees in Latvia has to be revised:

> The narrow Soviet degree structure gave to an award structure that is not only more flexible but also consistent with Western models and rising expectations of the Bologna Joint Declaration for common structures across Europe and the world. (McGuinness, 2015, p. 13)

CURRICULUM

Responding to the need for new solutions in a rapidly changing world, all three Baltic countries are in reforming process of all educational level curricula in the framework of OECD Learning Framework 2030 which defines the knowledge, skills, attitudes, and values that learners need to fulfill their potential and contribute to the well-being of their communities and the planet. The OECD 2030 Learning Framework provides a vision and a set of underpinning principles for the future of education systems. It focuses on well-being for 2030 at the individual and societal levels and provides a holistic vision of learning. It is designed to show policy-makers how these knowledge, skills, competencies, and values could be embedded in existing curricula rather than by creating new subject areas (OECD, 2018b).

LEARNERS

Student agency for 2030 "is rooted in the belief that students have the ability and the will to influence positively their own lives and the world around them. Student agency is defined as the capacity to set a goal, reflect and act responsibly to effect change" (OECD, 2018a, 2018b).

However, the challenges are evident. In all three Baltic states, young men are more likely than young women to lack an upper secondary qualification, while regional differences in enrollment levels for 20–29 year-olds are relatively low in Estonia, Latvia, and Lithuania. Latvia also has the highest ratio between the highest and lowest enrollment rates at the subnational level for this age group.

Across countries, the highest employment premiums for tertiary-educated learners over those with upper secondary or post-secondary non-tertiary education are in Lithuania and Estonia. The largest shares (more than 45%) of adults participating in non-formal distance learning are in Lithuania (OECD, 2019c).

TEACHERS

As TALIS (2018) reports, the average teacher in Baltic states is over age 48 by the OECD age average around 44. The largest gender differences in the teaching profession are observed especially in Estonia (41% of male teachers vs 69% of female teachers) and Latvia (55% vs 76%). A significant gap is found in favor of novice teachers in Latvia (OECD, 2019d, chapter 2). Job security is the most cited factor by teachers in Latvia by 93% of teachers (OECD, 2019d, chapter 3).

Estonia has recently reformed the initial teacher education system to make the work-based teacher education a mandatory element by aligning teacher education programs to national competency standards in 2013. There are seven competency areas defined in the Estonian teacher standards, each having "activity parameters" as follows: teachers' tasks in an area; knowledge required to perform those tasks; and evaluation methods used to measure the acquisition of the competencies (OECD, 2019d).

Work-based Education

The development of workplace learning (WBL) in initial vocational training (VET) is one of the national policy priorities in Baltic states. The Baltic Apprenticeship Alliance (BAfA) started the implantation of WBL in VET in 2015. In the five-year collaboration between the education ministries and other stakeholders in Latvia, Lithuania and Estonia, common approaches to WBL and WBL mentor training were developed and tested in cooperation with companies, schools and students. Finland joined the Baltic states in the testing a professional development model for WBL mentors. The Baltic education ministries have agreed on a common competence profile for WBL tutors, including core knowledge, skills and competences for working with apprentices (Cedefop, 2020).

Teaching and Learning

Richard Nisbett's (2003) research explores ways of teaching and learning that are in tune with the cultural context of Western and Eastern countries and allows us to understand the development of pedagogy in the Baltic states. The using of knowledge and resources of the Western individual and Eastern personalized collaborative learning is drawing on socialist experience, post-socialist liberal and new-liberal values of the politics of Europeanization and post-socialist transformations in Baltic countries (Lindstrom, 2014). The TALIS 2018 study examines the extent to which teachers engage in related activities to support student learning:

> Blended learning seeks to use the potential of new technology to offer more individualised teaching and direct instruction. Gamification includes the pedagogical core of gaming and the benefits of playful environments for student engagement and well-being. Computational thinking intersects mathematics, ICTs and digital literacy looking at ICTs as a platform for developing problem-solving reasoning in students. Experiential learning refers to approaches where learners are directly into contact with the realities being studied. Embodied learning refers to pedagogical approaches that focus on the non-mental factors involved in learning and that signal the importance of the body and feelings. (TALIS, 2018, chapter. 4)

The extent to which teachers and schools can innovate in their methods of teaching and working together depends on the teachers' self-efficiency in classroom management; instruction; and student engagement. Only Estonia between some other countries and economies shows in TALIS 2018 a positive change in the reported self-efficacy of teachers in classroom management between 2013 and 2018 (TALIS, 2018).

Languages of Instruction

In all Baltic states, schools' language of instruction is national state language (Estonian, Latvian, or Lithuanian). The share of instruction in the state language and minority language in bilingual schools differs across the Baltic states. In Latvia and Estonia, the 60/40 model is used which means that a minimum of 60% of the curriculum at the gymnasium level must be taught in the state language, while in Lithuania schools are required to teach at least 45% of the secondary school curriculum in Lithuanian (Mägi & Siarova, 2014). Bringing forward the examples of successful practice toward greater inclusiveness to respond to the diverse needs of the learners, state-funded bilingual education in Latvia is implemented in seven minority languages of instruction – Russian, Polish, Jewish, Ukrainian, Estonian, Lithuanian, and Belarusian, which is more than in most European countries. Representatives of international organizations have repeatedly praised the reform of minority education implemented by Latvia. Latvia's experience in the field of minority education is of interest to both European Union member states and countries such as Georgia, Moldova, Kyrgyzstan, Tajikistan, and others (Mägi & Siarova, 2014). Thus, in Latvia, the transition to teaching in the state language at the secondary level in general education institutions with the 2019/2020 school year started moving from existing five minority education models to the new three minority primary education models and to the new model of bilingual education in grades 7–9, which envisages that not less than 80% of the study content is taught in the state language, including foreign languages. The government will continue to support state-funded basic education programs for minorities in seven languages which are mentioned above (LR MFA, 2018). English, German, French, and Scandinavian languages are popular languages of instruction in many public and private schools. In higher education is English as instruction language used in several programs or courses.

Education Quality

The analysis made according to Bergmann's (1996) four components of education quality, let to state that, despite the comparable educational policies in all three Baltic countries, there are visible distinguishes between the input quality, process quality, output quality, and product quality of education. At the state level, all three Baltic states have the Lifelong Learning strategies which guide the long-term developments. The national education standards guarantee the quality provision of education, laws and regulations establish the principles of education funding, state supervision and quality assessment (*indicators of input quality*). Estonia is creating the best of the world what is evident through the PISA results (*output quality and product quality indicators*), described above (OECD, 2016). Evidence on *quality of education process* remains the furthered research.

Equality

The universal dimensions of educational inequality, that is the trinity of gender, socio-economic descent and ethnic status, regional differences and others are mentioned in policy documents and implementation acts in all three Baltic states.

Gender equality in Estonia has improved at a faster pace than the average in the European Union. Lithuania is progressing toward gender equality at a slower pace than other member states (The Baltic Course, 2019). Segregation in education, poverty risks are named as greatest challenges to gender equality in Latvia. There are still professions in Latvia that are regarded as women's jobs, as the profession of teacher. In the future, such segregation can leave a negative impact on the labor market.

The dropout rate in Latvia's education system is also high. The number of boys dropping out of schools is higher than the number of girls who do not finish school. It is indicated that poverty risks in Latvia's society had increased since 2005. The risk of poverty is higher among women, especially single mothers. The European Gender Equality Index shows that the level of violence against women in Latvia is higher than in the EU on average (The Baltic Course, 2018).

In Latvia, a gradual transition to education in the Latvian as state language at the secondary school level started in the 2019/2020 school year. The Venice Commission recommends among others to return to the previous "bilingual approach" in play-based lessons applied to the whole period of pre-school education and to take the necessary legislative and other measures to ensure that state schools offer a minority education where is demand (Venice Commission, 2020).

CONCLUSION

The Baltic states provide excellent case studies of how states in Europe emerged from the policies and ideologies of the former Soviet Union to established new education policies and institutions appropriate for democracy and market economies (McGuinness, 2015). A survey of education development illustrates the dynamics of global forces in the three Baltic states contexts. The neighboring countries are very similar to each other in terms of their history, political systems, and structures, as well as the character and behaviors of their societies. However, young people in these countries continuously migrate to Western Europe and Scandinavia. The incoming new-liberal global trend, impacted the education in the Post-Socialist European region, demonstrate similarities and differences in the development of education in Baltic states as co-shaped by contextual contours of the post-socialist region at whole. It occurs that the contextual social and cultural realities of Baltic states not only have a powerful mediating role on the impact of global forces but are in their own right an agency in shaping the education response of Post-Socialist societies of this region. In the International Comparative Education research agenda, many aspects of the contextual architecture of the region are becoming increasingly evident world-wide tending the new-liberalism in education as distinct from liberalism insofar as it does not advocate market-economic policy but, instead, is highly constructivist and approve a strong state to bring reforms in every aspect of society transforming the education and teaching market-labor. Estonia has emerged as a top-performer on PISA, raising the question of how this former Soviet Republic created one of the strongest education systems in the world over the past 20 years. The innovative education reforms in Estonia highlight how changing an education system can contribute to the economic development and inclusive society of a country.

REFERENCES

Agarin, T. (2018). Nation-states into the national states: The impact of transformation on minority participation in the Baltic States. Intersection: East. *European Journal of Society and Politics*, *4*(3), 41–65. https://doi.org/10.17356/ieejsp.v3i4.393

Apple, M. W. (1999). Freire, neo-liberalism and education. *Discourse: Studies in the Cultural Politics of Education*, *20*(1), 5–20. https://doi.org/10.1080/0159630990200101

Bergmann, H. (1996). Quality of education and the demand for education – Evidence from developing countries. *International Review of Education*, *42*(6), 581–604. https://doi.org/10.1007/BF00601404

Bourdieu, P. (1998). Utopia of Endless Exploitation: The essence of neoliberalism, *Le Monde Diplomatique*, 12.

Cedefop. (2020, April 24). Latvia: The Baltic States develop common approaches to work-based learning. Retrieved August 22, 2020, from https://www.cedefop.europa.eu/en/news-and-press/news/latvia-baltic-states-develop-common-approaches-work-based-learning

Council of the European Union. (2019). Council Recommendation on the 2019 National Reform Programme of Estonia and delivering a Council opinion on the 2018 Stability Programme of Estonia. Publications Office of the European Union. http://data.consilium.europa.eu/doc/document/ST-10159-2019-INIT/en/pdf

CSB. (2020a). Main Population by Nationality in Latvia at the beginning of the Year. Retrieved from https://data.stat.gov.lv:443/sq/11862

CSB. (2020b). Population at the beginning of the year and population change and key vital statistics in regions, cities, towns and municipalities by Indicator, Territorial unit and Time period. Retrieved from https://data.stat.gov.lv:443/sq/11868

Cusack, C. M. (2019). Dynamics of religion: Past and present. In Ch. Bochinger & J. Rüpke (Eds.), *Proceedings of the XXI World Congress of the international association for the history of religions, Numen* (Vol. 66, no. 5–6, pp. 607–610). https://doi.org/10.1163/15685276-12341559

Delaney, A., & Kraeme, J. (2020, May 27). Global perspective: Estonia – A shining light in Eastern Europe. Retrieved August 2, 2020, from https://ncee.org/2014/05/global-perspectives-estonia-a-shining-light-in-eastern-europe/

Desjardins, J. (2019, February 15). Median age of population per continent. *Virtual Capitalist*. Retrieved August 2, 2020, from https://www.visualcapitalist.com/mapped-the-median-age-of-every-continent/

Directorate-General for Education, Youth, Sport and Culture [DG EAC]. (2019). *Education and training monitor*. Publications Office of the European Union.

Eiropas Komisija. (2013). Pētījums par ekonomisko un sociālo situāciju Baltijas valstīs: Latvija. Eiropas Ekonomikas un sociālo lietu komiteja, Brussele. https://www.eesc.europa.eu/resources/docs/qe-30-12-151-lv-c.pdf

Ekonomiskā vide. (2018, Novembris 26). "Trīs māsas" Eiropas kronī jeb pirmie neatkarības gadi. Latvijai 100. Retrieved August 2, 2020, from https://www.seb.lv/info/ekonomiska-vide/tris-masas-eiropas-kroni-jeb-pirmie-neatkaribas-gadi

Eurydice. (2017, October 9). Lithuania: Administration and Governance at Central and/or Regional Level. Retrieved August 2, 2020, from https://eacea.ec.europa.eu/national-policies/eurydice/

Eurydice. (2018, December 10). Estonia: Administration and Governance at Central and/or Regional Level. Retrieved August 2, 2020, from https://eacea.ec.europa.eu/national-policies/eurydice

Eurydice. (2019, January 2). Lithuania: Administration and governance at central and/or regional level. Retrieved August 2, 2020, from https://eacea.ec.europa.eu/national-policies/eurydice/

Eurostat. (2018, January 1). Foreign-born population by country of birth. European Commission. Retrieved June 2, 2020, from https://ec.europa.eu/eurostat/en/

Frey, C. B., & Osborne, M. A. (2017). The future of employment: How susceptible are jobs to computerisation? *Technological Forecasting and Social Change, 114*, 254–280. https://doi.org/10.1016/j.techfore.2016.08.019.

Godon, R., Jucevičiene, P., & Kodeljac, Z. (2004). Philosophy of education in post-Soviet societies of Eastern Europe. *Comparative Education, 40*(4), 559–569. https://doi.org/10.1080/0305006042000284547

Letto-Gillies, G.. (2007). Theories of international production: A critical perspective. *Critical Perspectives on International Business, 3*(3), 196–210. https://doi.org/10.1108/17422040710774987

Grzymala-Kazlowska, A., & Phillimore, J. (2018). Introduction: Rethinking integration. New perspectives on adaptation and settlement in the era of super-diversity. *Journal of Ethnic and Migration Studies, 4*(2), 179–196. https://doi.org/10.1080/1369183X.2017.1341706

Hogan-Brun, G., Ozolins, U., Ramonienė, M., & Mart Rannut, M. (2008). Language politics and practices in the Baltic States. *Current Issues in Language Planning, 8*(4), 469–631. https://doi.org/10.2167/cilp124.0

Insamer. (2017, May 22). Baltic Muslims. Retrieved August 2, 2020, from https://insamer.com/en/baltic-muslims_1119.html

Kera, S. (1996). *Education in Estonia: Historical overview up to 1991*. Estonian Ministry of Education.

Kersh, N., & Toiviainen, H. (2017). Broad research on adult education in the EU. Project report (EduMAP). https://www.researchgate.net/publication/326826771

Kilis, R. (2010). Sustainable development strategy of Latvia until 2030. Saima of the Republic of Latvia.

Lazdiņa, S., & Marten, H. F. (2019). Multilingualism, language contact and majority-minority relations in contemporary Estonia, Latvia and Lithuania. In *Multilingualism in the Baltic States* (pp. 1–25). Palgrave Macmillan.

LETA. (2009, Septembris 24). Baltijas valstīs viens no augstākajiem svešvalodu zināšanu līmeņiem. Retrieved August 2, 2020, from https://www.tvnet.lv/4935706/

Lindstrom, N. (2014). *The politics of Europeanization and post-socialist transformations*. Springer.

Mägi, E., & Siarova, H. E. (2014). Migrant education opportunities in the Baltic States: Strong dependence on the level of school preparedness. Praxis Center for Policy Studies. http://www.praxis.ee/wp-content/uploads/2014/11/Migrant-education-opportunities-in-the-Baltic-States.pdf

Marshall, T. (2015). Prisoners of geography: Ten maps that tell you everything you need to know about global politics. Elliot & Thompson.

McGuinness, A. J. (2015). Reforms in the Baltics. *International Higher Education*, 25, 183–203. https://doi.org/10.6017/ihe.2001.25.6951

Ministry of Foreign Affairs of the Republic of Latvia [LR MFA]. (2018, June 18) Minority education in Latvia. Retrieved July 5, 2020, from https://www.mfa.gov.lv/arpolitika/sabiedribas-integracija-latvija/mazakumtautibu-izglitiba-latvija

Nisbett, R. (2003). *The geography of thought: How Westerners and Easterns think differently, and why*. The Free Press.

OECD. (2016). *PIZA 2015 high performance: Estonia*. OECD Publishing.

OECD. (2018a). *OECD Economic Surveys: Lithuania 2018*. OECD Publishing.

OECD. (2018b). *The Future of Education and Skills 2030*. OECD Publishing.

OECD. (2019a). *OECD Economic Surveys: Estonia 2019*. OECD Publishing.

OECD. (2019b). *OECD Economic Surveys: Latvia 2019*. OECD Publishing.

OECD. (2019c). *Education at a Glance 2019: OECD indicators*. OECD Publishing. https://doi.org/10.1787/f8d7880d-en

OECD. (2019d). *TALIS 2018 Results (Volume I): Teachers and school leaders as lifelong learners*. OECD Publishing. https://doi.org/10.1787/1d0bc92a-en

Putniņš, T., & Sauka, A. (2018). Shadow economy index for the Baltic countries 2009–2017, SSE Riga. https://www.sseriga.edu/shadow-economy-index-baltic-countries

Poissonnier, A. (2017). The Baltics: Three countries, one economy? *European Commission*. https://ec.europa.eu/info/sites/info/files/eb024_en.pdf

Popov. N. (2012). Structures of school systems worldwide: A comparative study. In N. Popov, C. Wolhuter, B. Leutwyler, G. Hilton, J. Ogunleye, & P. A. Almeida (Eds.), *International perspectives on education* (11th ed., pp. 32–33). Bulgarian Comparative Education Society. https://files.eric.ed.gov/fulltext/ED567040.pdf

Priedite. A. (2002, Decembris n.d.). Latviešu valodas apguve – cīņa ar mītiem, stereotipiem un aizspri-edumiem. *Jaunā gaita, 4*(231), 400. http://zagarins.net/JG/jg231/JG231_Priedite.htm

Puur, A., Klesment, M., & Sakkeus, L. (2019). A turbulent political history and the legacy of state social-ism in the Baltic countries. In D. Hess & T. Tammaru (Eds.), *Housing estates in the Baltic Countries.* The Urban Book Series. Springer. https://link.springer.com/chapter/10.1007/978-3-030-23392-1_2

Robertson, S. L. (2007). Remaking the world: Neo-liberalism and the transformation of education and teachers' labour. In L. Weis & M. Compton (Eds.), *The global assault on teachers, teaching and their unions.* Palgrave Macmillan.

Surugiu, M. R., & Surugiu, C. (2015). International trade, globalization and economic interdependence between European countries: Implications for businesses and marketing framework. *Procedia Economics and Finance, 32*, 131–138. https://doi.org/0.1016/S2212-5671(15)01374-X

Statistics Estonia. (2019). The population of Estonia increased last year 2019. Retrieved June 12, 2020, from https://www.stat.ee/population

Swedbank. (2018). *Middle class in the Baltics.* Swedbank.

The Baltic Course. (2018, April 26). Analytics, education and science, EU – Baltic States, Latvia, Legislation, Society. Retrieved August 2, 2020, from http://www.baltic-course.com/eng/analytics/

The Baltic Course. (2019, October 15). Analytics, Estonia, Latvia, Lithuania, Society. Retrieved August 2, 2020, from http://www.baltic-course.com/eng/analytics/

The UN Refugee Agency [UNHCR]. (2014). *Asylum trends: First half of 2014. Levels and trends in industrialized countries.* The UN Refugee Agency.

United Nations. (2019). *Population division: World population prospects 2019.* United Nations. Department of Economic and Social Affairs.

Venice Commission. (2020, June 18). *Latvia – Opinion on the recent amendments to the legislation on education in minority languages.* European Commission.

Wolhuter, C. C., & Wiseman, A. W. (Eds.). (2019). *Comparative and international education: Survey of an infinite field.* Emerald Publishing Limited.

Word Data on Education. (2007, July n.d.). *Lithuania* (6th ed.). International Bureau of Education. UNESCO.

MENTORING OF MARGINALIZED ROMA STUDENTS – RESOURCE OF ACADEMIC SUCCESS AND RESILIENCE

Edina Kovács, Hedviga Haficova, Tatiana Dubayova, Tímea Ceglédi, Katalin Godó and Martin Kaleja

ABSTRACT

The aim of our research is to examine network of support persons of the students from marginalized Roma communities in Czech Republic, Hungary, and Slovak Republic. By conducting a qualitative analysis of the examples of good practice, that is, students who have managed to successfully study at a university despite their difficult family backgrounds, we have surveyed the type of support the students received during their studies and the persons who supported them at individual education levels. In the research part, we also analyze the factors which had an impact on the development of their resilient personality and the sources of support which helped them overcome barriers during their studies. The primary support persons were the members of their nuclear families whose emotional, informational, instrumental, and appraisal support was particularly crucial at the primary school. At the next education levels, especially important for respondents was the emotional support they received in the form of encouragement and improvement of respondents' self-confidence. Teachers are mentioned in the narratives of our respondents as persons engaging in their support and education at the primary and the secondary school. Their supportive influence fades away at the university, which is a pity for our group of students because it is the university environment which is completely unknown to them and so they must rely on the help of peers. A good strategy applied particularly

World Education Patterns in the Global North:
The Ebb of Global Forces and the Flow of Contextual Imperatives
International Perspectives on Education and Society, Volume 43A, 105–125
ISSN: 1479-3679/doi:10.1108/S1479-36792022000043A008

in Hungary is the creation of support groups led by a lecturer-mentor for students coming from marginalized Roma communities which help them during the first days at university. School achievements of respondents were also influenced by other persons who helped them at all levels based on personal sympathies and the established relationships. At the beginning, such persons occur in their life narratives incidentally, but later respondents learned to actively build networks of support relationships as part of their resilient behavior.

Keywords: Roma; social disadvantages; resilience; mentoring; social acceptance; counseling

INTRODUCTION

Early school leaving is a major issue in the European countries. Within the European Union, there are more than four million people between the ages of 18 and 24 without qualification and not receiving any formal education. The average portion of early leavers in the European Union is 10%. Early school leaving is a particular risk for disadvantaged children. In the in Eastern-Middle Europe region, many of them are of Roma origin, which, in addition to economic differences, also means cultural differences. If a society wants to reduce the transmission of poverty and social disadvantage, must support these students during their education.

The aim of this study to examine network of support persons of the students from marginalized Roma communities in Czech Republic, Hungary, and Slovak Republic. By conducting a qualitative analysis of the examples of good practice, that is, students who have managed to successfully study at a university despite their difficult family backgrounds, we have surveyed the type of support the students received during their studies and the persons who supported them at individual education levels. We do not dare to generalize the status of support to all university students from marginalized Roma communities based on our results due to certain limits resulting from the size and heterogeneity of our sample and the research method. However, our results highlight the importance of formal and informal mentoring.

Global Trends

The issue we are examining is at the intersection of economic growth and minorities. The growing affluence in the world has gone hand in hand with the expansion of education. Nowadays, people from (poor, or socially disadvantaged) groups who previously had no access to education, especially higher education are also gaining access to it. Because they do not take their lead from their parents, they also have to deal with issues that are obvious to children of intellectual families of the third generation. In this category, young Roma people form a special group. As will be shown below, the situation of the Roma population is specific in Eastern-Middle Europe. Their assimilation had already begun in the eighteenth century, often speaking only the language of the majority society (not "Lovari" or "Boyash"). But for several reasons, their situation is in many ways similar to that of immigrants in other countries. So, it is a very important issue in in the Eastern-Middle Europe countries how to support their academic career, especially during the years of higher education.

Regional Context

The so-called "Visegrad Group" or "V4 Countries" are Czech Republic, Hungary, Poland, and Slovak Republic. All the four countries are member of the European Union since 2004. They have similar historical background and common cultural roots, so their cooperation is based on common interests within the all-European integration. All four countries belonged to the socialist system until 1990. The change of regime caused similar social and economic problems. Unemployment has risen, privatization has led to the enrichment of a few social strata, while others have become very impoverished. In the 30 years since then, not all the problems of equal opportunities and equity have been resolved.

One of these problems is inequality in education. The latest PISA results show that although in terms of class size disadvantaged schools are better off compared to advantaged schools in all four countries, in terms of not fully certified teachers disadvantaged schools are worse off compared to advantaged schools in Hungary, and there is no significant difference in the other three countries. Proportion of teachers with a qualification lower than a master's degree: disadvantaged schools are worse off compared to advantaged schools in Czech Republic, Hungary, and Slovak Republic, and the difference is not significant in Poland (OECD, 2019).

As we mentioned above, early school leaving is also a major issue in the European countries. The average portion of early leavers in the European Union is 10%: the V4 Countries have similar data (Hungary has the highest and Poland has the lowest ratio). It is a disadvantageous position for a person, and for the society early school leaving causes lower rates of economic growth, higher unemployment, and higher welfare and public health payments (Gitschthaler & Nairz-Wirth, 2018). In Hungary (and in many other countries), the early school leaving is related to family background, which plays a crucial role in the school performance. As results of Fehérvári (2015) show teachers think that families are responsible for school failures; only few of them see the chance that the school can compensate for those handicaps. Teachers' opinions are significantly related to the proportion of Roma students in a particular school. Those teachers think that school has no role in the failures who teach in a school with high proportion of Roma students.

That is why we need to mention the situation of the Roma population in Eastern-Middle Europe. The position of the Roma inhabitants is quite different in Eastern-Middle Europe and Western Europe. Intentions of assimilation, that had been present in the region of Middle Europe in the eighteenth century, were amplified in the Eastern region during the decades of socialism. After the mentioned change of regime, the Roma got to the loser groups of people in Hungary, Romania, Czech Republic, Slovak Republic, and Bulgaria: their situation in the areas of education and employment got like that of the western-European immigrants. However, it is true for all the European countries that there was a plausible intention for the help of social integration of the Roma through education, the political intention often broke in different – institutional and personal – forms of opposition and exclusion. In sum, the 10–15% of the population are Roma in the mentioned countries; we do not know the exact number, because many people do not declare themselves Roma at the time of the census due to prejudices (Brüggemann & Friedman, 2017; Ćurčić et al., 2013; Eurofound, 2017; FRA, 2014; Kertesi & Kézdi, 2013; Koulish, 2010; Messing, 2017; Pásztor et al., 2016; Szalai et al., 2010).

In the case of the Roma students, there are differences in scope and forms of settlement. They are overrepresented in villages, where their rate is above 50%, while it is around 20% in the cities. Their lifestyles are very mixed; there are families begging in the streets and migrating on the one end of the scale and wealthy businessmen are in the other end of the scale, which has an influence on the school career of the youngsters (Pusztai & Torkos, 2001). The Roma identity is formed in several ways, from the intentions of integrity to the strategy leading to the exclusion of the negative identity; however, the greater is the revulsion of the majority society, the smaller is the chance that the Roma person could create a positive identification for himself. If being in a "disadvantageous" state clearly stigmatizes then answers are also destructive, while if it goes together with the chance of mobility, then strategies for solutions are also about quest, undertaking identity and accommodation (Messing, 2017; Messing et al., 2010).

Aims and Types of Mentoring

The aim of our study was to explore the network of support persons of the students from marginalized Roma communities in Czech Republic, Hungary, and Slovak Republic. Children from socially disadvantaged environment are generally, with some deviations, defined in V4 countries as children living in an environment which, considering the social, family, economic and cultural conditions, insufficiently develops the mental, volitive, and emotional qualities of children or pupils; does not support their socialization; and does not offer them enough appropriate stimuli for the development of their personalities. These social disadvantages go hand in hand with other obstacles which children from such background must overcome if they wish to get out of it. A simple thing: in a segregated environment there are less shop, library, services, etc. – so the children see less signboard, which means less letter. In contrast, a middle-class child often knows the capital letters by the time they go to school. As is evident from the nature of the problem, the effects of social disadvantage are most efficiently compensated for by social support and individualized approach which also build up children's resilience. Many authors, such as Ghaith (2002), Demir and Leyendecker (2018), and Sommers et al. (2008) proved the support provided by parents and teachers to lead to better school results. But it also has an impact on other component of children's behavior at school. For example, it influences the willingness to learn, doing homework related to education, cognitive autonomy, socially more friendly behavior, adaptation skills, as well as the health-related quality of life (Bacikova & Berinsterova, 2017; Demir & Leyendecker, 2018; Demaray & Malecki, 2002; Sommers et al., 2008).

Mentoring is essentially based on the philosophy of the so-called pedagogical optimism claiming that a pupil may achieve much more if we create proper conditions for his or her development. Therefore, one of the mentors' important roles is to create a safe space for self-exploration by the mentored individual. In that space, the mentored person may satisfy his or her individual needs through guidance and think about options, learn how to assess them, and is encouraged to make them happen (Hobson, 2012; Leake et al., 2011). Mullen (2012) lays emphasis on the psychosocial function which also includes social acceptance, counseling, and role behavior. Mentor discharges this function by being an active listener to the mentored person, giving advice and social support, stimulating the development of the mentored individual, and building his or her self-assessment and self-confidence.

Brumovská and Seidlová Málková (2010) list the following forms of formal mentoring that may be identified at schools:

Classical mentoring: This form applies to the cooperation of a more experienced mentor who provides guidance and support to a less experienced colleague.

Peer mentoring: This form takes place within one generation of children and adolescents; their age is not the same, but their age difference is not significant. However, recommended is the presence of an adult expert playing a supportive role for the child–mentor.

Intergenerational mentoring: This mentoring combines two generations with a significant age difference; mentor is usually over 55 years old and the mentee is a child or an adolescent.

E-mentoring: An electronic form of mentoring making use of e-mail, chat, skype, etc.

The position of a mentor is held by diverse individuals differing in age, completed education, qualification, opinions and attitudes to the world, and the prospects or quality of life. The general scheme describing the actors contains the following features of their obvious, identified, or generally perceived profile.

The profiles of mentors usually cover certain experience, knowledge, skills, willingness, interest, orientation, competence, or other potential which brought them to this position, and which makes them able to meet the objectives of the planned and implemented activities.

On the other hand, the descriptions of the mentee, that is of the second player being the object of help within mentoring, usually make use of two categories of features. The first one comprises the following: absence, lower level of certain or some entity or several entities listed in the mentor1s characteristics. In addition, the description of mentees may also involve the second category specific for certain assumption, disposition for the attainment of the goals set. That assumption usually is a matter of reflection of those who implement the phenomenon, that is, of the players, who supported (whether with finance or personnel or otherwise materially) the mentoring actions.

The individual providing mentoring support may be a volunteer or a profes-sional; however, important for the success of mentoring is the relationship created between the mentor and the mentee. If the relationship is built spontaneously without any external input, we speak of informal mentoring (our findings show that even the cleaning lady, or a neighbor, or a classmate's parent may become the important person). This type of relationship evolves based on one´s preferences and sympathies. It is quite frequent, and no special education is required for it. If the relationship is established based on a request of a third party (organization, school, etc.), the mentoring becomes formal. This relationship is built on men-tor's professionalism, mentor is entrusted with that function and carries it out within employment and receives wages or other compensation for this work. Peer mentoring is a specific form of formal mentoring. A more knowledgeable pupil may be asked to help another pupil. It also comprises professionalization associ-ated with education in the mentoring area. Brumovská and Seidlová Málková (2010) consider such a relationship to be of good quality if it meets the follow-ing criteria: regularity, resistance and durability, confidence, and empathy. This publication focuses on formal mentoring which takes place at school and is pro-vided by a professional. The above information concerning the phases or styles may also apply to the informal mentoring. However, mentor should know the background of the mentee (the individual who is the addressee of the mentoring activities). Mentor knows where the mentee lives, which factors played a role in mentees ontogenetic development and in what manner. Mentor understands and perceives differently, assesses, and approaches all kinds and even accidental mat-ters and phenomena which concern the content of the relevant mentorship.

Mentoring Programs in Slovak Republic, Czech Republic, and Hungary

Early school leaving is a serious issue in Slovak Republic, as we mentioned before. In the academic year 2019/2020, primary schools reported 30,450 pupils from socially disadvantaged background. In the same academic year, only 518 students were reported by secondary schools. This huge difference might be explained by an alarming number of children from disadvantaged background dropping out of the education system as soon as they complete the primary school. Mentoring as a form of support to students from socially disadvantaged background taking place mainly within programmes implemented by non-governmental organiza-tions or by way of state-funded projects.

In accordance with Article 4e(1) of Act No. 597/2003 Coll. on financing pri-mary schools, secondary schools and school facilities as amended, the Ministry of Education, Science, Research, and Sport may provide an allowance for the improvement of the conditions for education of pupils from socially disadvan-taged background to the founder of primary schools for pupils who are not edu-cated in a special class or by way of integration. The Article 4e(7) of the above Act provides that the allowance1 is provided for:

(a) staff costs of a teaching assistant for pupils from socially disadvantaged background, or for a social pedagog;

(b) procurement of didactic equipment and teaching aids;
(c) participation of pupils in activities under Article 30(7) of Act No. 245/2008 Coll. on education and on amendments and supplements to certain laws (primary schools may organize trips, excursions, language courses, sports events, school trips, and other activities based on prior informed consent and agreement with pupil's legal guardian);
(d) education of pupils in specialized classes;
(e) preventing transmission of an infectious disease;
(f) bonuses pay for work with pupils from socially disadvantaged background;
(g) procurement of the necessary teaching aids for pupils on top of the subsidy for a school supply kit provided under special legislation.

Formal mentoring has been so far provided mainly by non-profit organizations in Slovakia, although they are often supported by means of projects funded by governmental and regional institutions. The largest and oldest organizations which are known for engaging in mentoring of pupils include the *Roma Education Fund, Divé maky (Wild Poppies), ETP Slovakia* and *Človek v ohrození (People in Need)* organizations.

Roma Education Fund based in Prešov is a branch of the foreign *Roma Education Fund – Roma Oktatási Alap (REF)* which was founded within the *Decade of Roma Inclusion* in 2005. Its main objective is to help reduce the differences in school performance between Roma and non-Roma children through programmes supporting high-quality education. The Fund focuses mainly on the scholarship program for Roma secondary school pupils, aiming to reduce the number of pupils who drop out of school before passing the final school-leaving exams (Brüggemann & Friedman, 2017; Ćurčić et al., 2013).

Divé maky organization was found in 2005 as a program of the *PRO DONUM* civil association. In 2008, it started operating independently as a civil association and is currently a non-governmental non-profit organization. Its projects focus on talented Roma children, and development of young leaders who would become role models for children from the Roma environment. Children are financially supported by donors. The support takes the form of scholarships for pupils for at least one school year and donors donate amounts to specific children necessary for their studies and development of their talents.

ETP Slovakia (Centre for Sustainable Development) operates at the local, regional, national, and European level. It is a non-profit counseling and educational organization which was founded in 1992 by a US Agency for International Development as a direct follow-up of the *Environmental Education for Central and Eastern Europe* project. ETP became an independent entity in 1995. In recent years, it has focused on helping people living in extreme poverty and experiencing social exclusion in Slovak Roma ghettos. This organization was the first to engage in the so-called e-mentoring and started providing support by means of electronic media.

Človek v ohrození is a non-governmental and non-profit organization established in 1999 which helps people affected by all kinds of circumstances which deprive them of their human dignity and freedom. They help people from all around the world who are affected by the consequences of war, victims of natural disasters who live in the grasp of authoritarian regimes, or those who are caught in crisis situations in Slovakia. They help the people pushed to the margins of the society due to poverty to find their way back. They also engage in educational activities to help build Slovakia as an open, tolerant, and supportive society.

There is a scholarship program, the *Roma Memorial University Scholarship*. The aim of the program is to help create a sufficiently large group of Roma university graduates who would be self-confident and proud of their identity and would have academic and social skills. The assumption is that Roma individuals who acquire qualification in their field of expertise and maintain strong ties with the Roma community would support its development and inclusion in the mainstream society. The program intends to help them with their studies at universities in their home country or abroad and lends support throughout the studies until they successfully graduate. Scholarships are granted for one academic year. Students may renew their applications and apply for scholarship every year. The scholarship should cover the costs associated with their studies, such as the cost of textbooks, exam fees, and partially also their living expenses. Support may also be provided to distance students. However, this option only applies to postgraduate students. *Scholarships for Secondary School Roma Pupils* was an REF program which aimed to help get over adverse life situations and motivate pupils to reach as good school results as possible, successfully complete their studies, and continue into a higher-level education. Scholarships were intended for Roma pupils of secondary schools (completed with a school-leaving exam). The project distinguished the role of the mentor from that of the tutor. Mentors get involved in pupil's wider environment; they cooperate with many specialists. A tutor is perceived as a specialist addressing pupil's poor results in a selected subject. Tutor is a pedagog, a specialized worker who provides tutelage to the relevant pupil. The project was funded by individual donors, foundations, and corporate partnerships (all posted on their web site).

They also implemented a specific project called *Support of Roma Pupils of Secondary Pedagogical Schools in Slovakia* which aimed to increase the number of Roma teachers at Slovak kindergartens. The assumption within this project was that a higher number of Roma teachers at kindergartens would result in higher numbers of Roma children attending kindergartens, making them better prepared for primary schools. The financial support was the same as the support in the previous project.

In the Czech Republic, mentoring support is mostly elaborated within project activities of third-sector organizations. However, the institution primarily focusing on the improvement of mentoring quality (in general) in the Czech Republic, opening new development opportunities for employees, raising awareness about the importance of mentoring in Czech companies, and setting standards for mentoring in the Czech setting is the Czech Mentoring Association (*Česká asociácia mentoringu*). It is clear from its focus that they do not take mentoring as a general support method only, but they also plan to work with it in the context of the demographic, cultural and legislative peculiarities.

Roma Education Fund supports Czech students of Roma origin pursuing first or second degrees with the *Roma Memorial University Scholarship Program*. Financial support is provided based on students' academic achievement. The scholarship should cover expenses associated with the studies, for example, the cost of textbooks, exam fees, and partially the cost of living.

Slovo 21, z. s. is a non-governmental non-profit organization operating since 1999. They focus on the overall improvement of the social status of Roma living in the Czech Republic. A substantial part of their efforts is also targeted at the integration of foreign nationals into Czech society (*Slovo 21*, online 2017). Within their projects, they organize professional fellowships for future Roma professionals, support women groups dealing in the status of Roma women in family and community, develop their self-confidence and self-respect, women's rights, and engage in healthy lifestyle awareness-raising campaigns, or social and legal issues. The concept of one *Slovo 21* project titled *Dža dureder* (*Go on*) focused on the support of Roma primary school pupils. It aimed to tutor these pupils and prepare them for secondary school and counted on direct participation on the part of the school, teachers, and the parents of pupils. Other professionals engaging in educational activities relating to those pupils could join it as well. The key activities of the project included:

- tutoring on top of the curriculum of the relevant school's education program;
- support of the general knowledge and development of individual skills of pupils (the so-called mentoring); and
- support of professional teaching skills of teachers and teaching assistants.

The project deliverables went directly to pupils educated at the relevant primary schools in Prague and Bruntál. The students at these schools were Roma. More importantly, they were under significant influence of social exclusion, which affected their life strategies, world views, and attitudes, as well as the methods of communication and fulfillment of their needs. As a process, education created opportunities for the cultivation of personality; it opened perspectives and allowed to see the world differently. Therefore, we considered participation of students' parents to be important and reflected critically and objectively on the professional pedagogical work with these students.

In Hungary in average, the 10% of the children are socially disadvantaged but in the most disadvantaged regions their ratio is nearly 25% (KSH, 2016). There are two national programs which are available for cumulatively disadvantaged students. They are not just for Roma children but many of them take part in these programs (they are mentioned as a special target group) and get graduation degree.

The "Útravaló" (*On the Road*) Scholarship Program started in 2005. It is organized by the Hungarian Government; in the current structure, it means the Ministry of Human Capacities. The program has a primary school part so-called "Road to Secondary School." The target groups are 7th and 8th grade students. There is also having a secondary school part so-called "Road to Graduation." The target groups of this subprogram are 9–12th grade students. The Scholarship

Program provides personal mentoring (usually by a teacher) and scholarships to disadvantaged Roma students to prevent early school leaving and build and strengthen their path to further education. Students are enrolled in the program based on their social status (low income, live in small villages or towns, etc.), but the amount of the scholarship depends on the academic performance of the given year. The total amount is 30–60 EUR/month. The mentors also get some financial support for their work (cc. 30 EUR/month).

The first "Tanoda" (*Foundation School*) was founded in 1993. It was mentioned officially in the Public Education Act in 2003. The number of "Tanoda"s has increased significantly since 2004, when the first EU-funded call for proposals was launched. There are 280 "Tanoda"s in Hungary nowadays. The aim of "Tanoda" is to compensate disadvantages and support academic success. The programs work after school time, during the afternoons and weekends. Forms of mentoring are personal and group too. Mentors are mostly teachers but can be other professionals (e.g., trainers, social workers) and they work voluntarily. It targets disadvantaged and Roma youth. They are run by NGOs and students participate on a voluntary basis in these programs. The financial source of this program is the European Cohesion Fund the organizer the Ministry of Human Capacities. There are various target groups that depends on the given Region and NGO: primary school and secondary school students.

The *Let's Teach for Hungary Mentor Program* has started in 2019. This is a national program organized by the Hungarian Government. It works with seven universities (University of Debrecen, University of Miskolc, University of Nyíregyháza, University of Pécs, Eötvös Lóránd University, Eszterházy Károly University, John von Neuman University) and above 70 elementary schools in agglomeration of the universities. The university students had a special course during the autumn semester. They start their mentoring work in February 2020. They get scholarship for their work (about 80 EUR per month). Mentoring is mostly personal, but one mentor has 3–4 mentee, so it is possible to meet in small groups too. The target group of the program is primary school 7th grade students; they receive a university student as a mentor who helps their further education (Godó et al., 2021).

There are programs in higher education for Roma students in Hungary. The "Láthatatlan Kollégium" (*Invisible College*) (founded in 1998) and Wlislocki Henrik College (founded in 2001) were the first Roma Colleges for Advanced Studies. The Act CCIV (about National Higher Education, 2011) ordained the build of a national network of denominational Roma Colleges for Advanced Studies. There are currently 11 Roma colleges nationwide. The organizer is the Hungarian Government and works together with the Church which takes part in the operation of these colleges. Approximately 350 Roma students have graduated so far from the beginning. The basic elements include: a dormitory, a community building, support from a tutor and/or mentor, scholarships, professional support, religious education, self-knowledge, Roma identity empowerment, and social responsibility for society (Cserti-Csapó, 2019). These Roma Colleges are similar to other Advanced Colleges in Higher Education in that they also support the talented students with their own research. But the topics always connect to Roma people (their social status, their living conditions, their family values, their culture, etc.).

An important aim of Roma Colleges for Advanced Studies is creating a cosy environment through various trainings and team building activities. There is also a cultural module which contains Roma cultural history and basic romological knowledge. Institutions of Christian Roma Colleges for Advanced Studies emphasize Christian values, but religious affiliation is not an exclusion criterion. It is more important that the students be open, inclusive, and tolerant, and set an example for others. As these are Roma colleges, most of the ethnic group is in favor of the Roma, but disadvantage is also an aspect of admission, so there are some non-Roma students in these colleges. There is a personal mentor for each student in Roma Colleges for Advanced Studies, who helps them with their studies. Mostly, this is a university lecturer who is linked in some way to the field of study the given Roma college student is studying. The mentor and the mentee develop a plan for each semester together. They set aims in connection with academic achievement and other important competences, and at the end of the semester they jointly review what has been achieved.

Another higher educational mentoring program is the "Student Councils National Mentoring Program." There was a similar program between 2013 and 2017, the current one started in 2018. This is running at every university in Hungary, organized by the Student Councils and the Government. It is for first-year college students who feel that higher education is unknown and full of challenges. Disadvantaged students with low social status will get a letter along with the admission notice, which says that they can participate voluntarily in this university mentoring program. In the frame of this program, they get a mentor (preferably from the same faculty or program) who will help them with every part of university life: administration of dormitory, scholarship, higher education study system, etc. Older students can show how to proceed in these matters. Mentors also get fee; the amount depends on the number of their mentees.

Research Methods and Sampling

The aim of our research was to identify the support the respondents had at different education levels. We also wanted to identify the support lacked and would appreciate to have received at individual education levels.

We investigated students who can be characterized by academic resilience. According to the broad definition of resilience, it is "the capacity of a system to adapt successfully to disturbances that threaten the viability, function, or development of the system" (Masten, 2019, p. 101). In the OECD PISA test, those are considered resilient who, based on their social background, are in an unfavorable position yet have received a high point score on the test. Life path studies considered someone resilient if and when he could successfully complete their school career despite the fact that based on social features, we could not make it probable (Ceglédi, 2012).

The data were collected in May and June 2019. First, we administered an anamnestic questionnaire to respondents to survey the basic biographic data. Respondents then replied to questions in a structured interview made in writing based on uniform questions and instructions. They entered their replies in a template in a word document we prepared in advance. The full-version template with questions is contained in Annex I. Within the third step, students were asked to join a focus group created based on the selected aspects relating to the support at individual education levels. Whereas some students could not come in person for various reasons, only their written testimony was included in analyses. Students were first informed of the intentions of the interview and could refuse to take part in the research study at any time without giving reason. One student used this option.

The number of respondents included in the research study is in line with the principles of qualitative research work. Twelve students were approached, but only 10 provided complete data and life narratives. The final sample consists of these 10 students. Considering the international aspect of the project, the research sample contains university students who can already be successful. The sampling criteria were as follows:

• Student is of Roma origin and identifies himself or herself with this ethnic minority.
• Low socioeconomic status of the student's family typical for low education level of parents, low income and/or unemployment of parents.
• Student must be at least in the second year of university studies.

Students were asked to take part in the research study directly by the research team members based on previous personal contact. Approached were those who have already openly identified with the Roma ethnic minority. Respondents were 21–48 years old, they were mostly internal students, two respondents aged 36 and 48 years were external students (Table 1). Out of the total number of 10 respondents, 4 were female and 6 males. Two already had their own families. Six of them went to a pre-school facility, one did not, and three respondents did not provide this information.

The qualitative data were analyzed in line with the standard process in the following sequence of steps (Skutil & Zikl, 2011): transcription – segmentation

Table 1. Research Sample Characteristics.

Respondent	Identification of the Respondent	Country	Sex	Age	Year of University Studies	Current Family Status
Respondent 1	F-SK1	Slovakia	Female	21	2	Single
Respondent 2	M-SK2	Slovakia	Male	21	2	Single
Respondent 3	F-SK3	Slovakia	Female	21	3	Married
Respondent 4	M-SK4	Slovakia	Male	36	4	Single
Respondent 5	M-SK5	Slovakia	Male	48	4	Married
Respondent 6	F-CZ6	Czech Republic	Female	24	2	Single
Respondent 7	F-HU7	Hungary	Female	25	4	Single
Respondent 8	M-HU8	Hungary	Male	26	4	Single
Respondent 9	M-HU9	Hungary	Male	24	4	Single
Respondent 10	M-HU10	Hungary	Male	24	4	Single

Source: Our original data.

– coding – note taking – looking for correlations between categories – graphic representation – structuring – interpretation.

Results: Support Persons in Public Education

We found several barriers to academic success. One of them was poverty (F-HU7, M-HU9) and lack of money. These difficulties posed a serious challenge at certain stages, for example, they included lack of appropriate school supplies and environment, such as buying a file jacket for a seminar thesis, having no computer to file an application, no opportunity to enroll in language courses to improve language skills, no room to learn at home (M-SK2, F-SK3). School supplies sometimes were provided with the help of support persons, for example, the school cleaner. Studying at home took place in the hall, basement or in the attic, etc. Students tried to cope with the subsistence issues by engaging in temporary jobs; social scholarships helped as well. The life narratives contain an important moment when the respondents identified the risk factors and looked for solutions. They did not give up. The support persons and forms of support are summarized in Table 2.

I still learn in the hall outside the door or sometimes in the basement. At home, I have never had any room to learn. [M-SK2]

My mom and grandma told me that I had only one chance to get out (of poverty), and that I should learn as much as possible, so I do not have to live on benefits like them.[F-HU7]

Although not all respondents provided a detailed description of the family structure, we gained insight into the stable family structure of all but one respondent. The role of the mother was more significant in educational attainments, but some respondents, and particularly the males, also mention their fathers in connection with important moments. One respondent grew up in a foster home. In one case, there was a divorce. At that time, the respondent was left to his own devices as to what to do about his further education, because the event had a financial impact on the family. An interesting moment occurred in one of the interviews when it became clear that the mother–child relationship was also established between one respondent and the school cleaner who supported him as if she was his mother. Generally, the parent–child relationship is an important foundation stone in life and influences the relationships children will be able to build with support persons. Another typical feature is that in addition to parents, respondents also received support from other family members, like older siblings, grandparents.

Due to the social background, it may happen that the children's talents will not develop to the fullest as they otherwise would, because the family makes a bad school choice. We met families which expected children to head toward an occupation not requiring education going higher than the education the previous generations in the family completed (cook, baker). In one case, this pressure exerted by the family translated into the wish of the child-respondent, and the child identified with the choice. In the second case, the school choice matched the respondent's educational attainments. These situations required an intervention of a support person who would stand out of the family circle and would be able to assess the respondent impartially. But there also were parents who supported children in attaining higher education.

Table 2. Support and Support Persons During the Primary and Secondary School.

Respondent	Support Person	Brief Description of Support	Summary
F-SK1	Mother Sister Kindergarten teacher Father Martin (priest)	Support informal, coming from family, that is continuous. Also emphasized the kindergarten teacher who was very supportive and provided information about education. The priest provided her with informal support. The older sister was the role model, support person in the emotional and informational area.	Due to a very strong informal system of support and quite good financial situation, the respondent was not short on material support.
M-SK2	Mother School cleaner at the primary school Class teacher at the secondary school History teacher	In addition to the mother's emotional support, the informational support was also provided by the school cleaner who served as a link with the institution. Teachers at secondary schools provide particularly the appraisal support.	There is no relationship between the support persons; the respondent gathers the necessary mentoring capacities on his own. He desperately needed financial support at the secondary school and must take on a job during university studies.
F-SK3	Mother who was also a teaching assistant Class teacher at the primary school	Her situation was unique, because her mother could provide her with informational support, which is very important. She faced race-based exclusion at the secondary school and had to change school.	Mother has been a support person as well, although there was no formal mentorship. At the secondary school, she particularly lacked the appraisal support.
M-SK4	Teacher at the primary school Class teacher	Support at the primary school was usually informal and included appraisal and partially also emotional support. He did not come across mentorship during secondary school.	Identified the lacking continuous mentorship and informational support as a drawback. Generally, he did not have bad experience, which did him good. But he partially takes it as good luck.
M-SK5	Mother, Father Class teacher at the primary school	Family support was continuous. Informal support only available at the primary school, the first year at the secondary school made difficult by one racist teacher.	He lacked a lot of continuous formal mentorship, both financially and informationally.

F-CZ6	Mother Grandma Class teacher at the secondary school English teacher	The emotional support from the family was constant, but the informational support at the secondary school was not sufficient anymore.	The respondent lacked formal support; it was difficult for her to choose the right school due to lack of information.
F-HU7	Mother, Grandma Class teacher at the primary school Class teacher at the secondary school	Family support was continuous, support from persons at school regular. Both were informal. She lacked formal mentorship. Informal support provided by the class teacher.	No link between the family and the institution. Family (mother and grandma) provided emotional support; material deprivation was a huge problem for the respondent.
M-HU8	Father Kindergarten class teacher	The respondent only mentions support by family, father an important role model. Except emotional support, he lacked all other support dimensions.	He lacked guidance at school, seemed to be accidental. Surveyed information about higher-level education on his own (e.g., from books, Internet).
M-HU9	Cousin Class teacher at the primary school	Teacher at the primary school provided important informational and partially also appraisal support.	No link between the family and the institution. Family and the warmth of home did not provide the necessary support. The respondent felt a great need for a formal mentor.
M-HU10	Class teacher at the primary school Geography teacher Caregiver at the secondary school Advocate for Children's Rights in the foster home	Support provided regularly and on an informal basis. Formal mentoring lacking completely. At the secondary school, emotional support was also provided by the Advocate for Children's Rights.	He grew up in a foster home, so there was no support from family. During studies, he happened to find informal mentors.

Source: Our original data.

I wanted to be a cook, or to go to a military high school. My father did not allow me to, he told me to continue my studies at the general secondary school.[M-SK5]

Starting a family in early adulthood is one of the risk factors of Roma families. Career is therefore taken as a competitive activity to starting one´s own family. F-SK3 decided for education instead of becoming a wife and a mother, a life path usually expected from women in her community. She did not find much understanding among her family members and her decision was constantly called into doubt. In addition to the Roma origin and difficult living conditions, being female thus seems to be an additional disadvantage in the narratives analyzed. Nevertheless, the gender-related aspect played a role in the decision-making about the educational path only in one respondent.

I was perceived by my neighbourhood as the one who preferred career (study) to a child. Nobody asked me how I was doing at school, all my neighbours were only curious why we didn't have children yet. [F-SK3]

Results: Experiences in Higher Education

Higher education is that area where family support is almost eliminated. Lower educated parents were not able to advise their children; it only may have been an older sibling already in higher education who could support the respondent. The results of a recent Hungarian research[1] show that 78% of students who are struggling to make progress in their studies, and who are one or two semesters behind, do not ask their teachers for help, even with academic issues. According to this research, the majority of those with the highest rates of struggling students have parents with a secondary education. For this reason, it is likely that less advantaged students are less likely to ask support (Table 3).

Based on their experiences in higher education, we put the 10 respondents in three groups: the first one contains those who could rely on their families, friends and, to some extent, even on university classmates also during their university studies. Three respondents belong in this group: F-CZ6, F-SK3, and M-SK4. They had mixed feelings at the beginning of their university education and faced

Table 3.   Proportion of Students Asking Advice from a Lecturer
(Chi-Square Test, $p \leq 0.05$).

Paths of Progress	Students, Ask Advice from a Lecturer, If They Become Insecure About Their Studies		Total
	Yes	No	
Corrective (change their specialization)	33.1%	66.9%	100.0%
Delay	22.3%	77.7%	100.0%
Average/expected	33.7%	66.3%	100.0%
Total	32.0%	68.0%	100.0%

Source: PERSIST (2019), see also: Godó (2021, p. 59).

difficulties and did not know what was going on. But in the end, they have positive memories of their studies.

In fact, I did not know how it was going on at the university and I was quite uncomfortable, but it helped me that before the semester S. University organized for students of first classes activities and help us to communicate together. We obtain there a lot of knowledges, we could ask, to know the town of the University, and each other. [F-CZ6]

The second group includes those who, probably based on their previous experience, also found informal mentors during their university years among their university teachers (M-SK2, M-SK5, F-SK1). They are those who have been supported by an older sibling, who could help them with practical information too. They experienced their university beginnings more positively than the members of the first group; they took it as an important milestone after all the efforts they had made. They seem to have received emotional, informational and appraisal support, but two of them hinted they would have appreciated the financial support they needed. One of them (M-SK5) received a scholarship from the Roma Education Fund for some time and assessed it as a great help.

I was ready for what awaited me because I could watch my sister's university studies again. I was a little worried if the combination of fields (she has 2 specializations) would not be too difficult for me. [F-SK1]

The third group covers those who were included in the formal mentoring process during their university years: F-HU7, M-HU8, M-HU9, and M-HU10 received support from teachers and Roma colleagues from universities, and therefore they do not feel like they need more support for their studies and administrative matters. They are students from Hungary where Roma students at specialized schools receive scholarships which are higher than usual university scholarships in Hungary and range from EUR 100 to EUR 170 a month. Therefore, these students did not say they needed material/financial support during their studies. But it is important to notice that they also did not know what to expect at the beginning, but the community of Advanced Roma Colleges helped them to settle in.

I was not nearly ready. Earlier I never had learnt a lot so I thought if I started to learn it would be a smooth goose. But I had to struggle instead. [M-HU8]

The features of support during tertiary education are summed up in Table 4. Most respondents decided to apply to university on their own. Their families have supported them in their decision. The only exception is M-HU10 who grew up in a foster home and who was supported by the Advocate for Children's Rights. Having received no formal mentorship at secondary schools, this means that the respondents were basically left to stand on their own, and they applied to university based on their own decision, will, and skills. This is also the reason why the beginnings of their university life were not only a positive experience for a half of respondents. It was difficult for them to cope with the initial expectations, requirements, and assignments. It is also evident that formal support and mentorship are of exceptional importance in this period. Those who receive formal mentorship support basically do not have any other requirements.

Table 4.   Respondents' Support in Higher Education.

Respondent	Support Persons at Applying to University	Feelings at the Beginning of University Studies	Support Persons During University Studies	Support they Would Appreciate During University Studies
F-SK1	Mother	It was even better than she expected. Her sister is still her role model.	Family, group members.	–
M-SK2	Decided on his own	Beginnings were very good, he knew he was learning for himself.	Several university lecturers and a very good friend.	Financial support, especially because Roma are disadvantaged on the labor market.
F-SK3	Partner (future husband)	In the end, she believes it was a good decision although she faced prejudice.	Husband and mother.	–
M-SK4	Decided on his own	Perceived the beginnings as a chaos and change in his life.	Friend, group members.	Professional mentor who would motivate and help him.
M-SK5	Decided on his own	It was a conscious choice, he was getting ready and started studying with good feelings.	Class-mates, instructor.	Mentor who would help him to move forward; financial support.
F-CZ6	Family Friends	It was strange, but the icebreaker "camp" for the first-grade students helped.	Fiancé, he studied similar study program.	Help with seminar and academic papers.
F-HU7	Family	Was ready, studied all available materials.	Teachers of core subjects, mentors.	–
M-HU8	Decided on his own.	He was not ready, it was harder than he expected.	Caregiver.	Financial support.
M-HU9	Decided on his own	He was sure he wanted to study at a university, but was afraid of the unknown environment.	Two older class-mates in the same study program, especially in the administrative matters.	–
M-HU10	Advocate for Children's Rights Teacher at the primary school	He knew that his life would change, and he would become a role model.	University teachers, peers	–

Source: Our original data.

CONCLUSIONS

We do not dare to generalize the status of support to all university students from marginalized Roma communities based on our results due to certain limits resulting from the size and heterogeneity of our sample and the research method. However, we assume that a higher number of respondents would only confirm these results and would not change them substantially. We believe that we managed to capture all areas of support and types which are tied with individual education levels. The retrograde view of the past events may be distorted by the unreliability of human memory and by the actual condition of the respondent. Nevertheless, the strong side of the research study is the identification of support persons who had very similar features despite geographical distance. Identification of the types of support and needs of students at individual education levels is crucial for the selection of efficient methods of support, which may then be used in preparation and development of support programmes for children from marginalized Roma communities to break the cycle of the so-called inter-generational transmission of poverty.

The results highlight the importance of institutional mentoring. It can be seen to what extent the network of Roma Advanced Colleges in Hungary has been able to compensate for the difficulties in higher education, where family support is really limited. This is also a reminder of the need for formal mentoring at the previous education levels, for those who cannot find an informal mentor – unlike our respondents.

Social and economic disadvantage and marginalization may have different characteristics in other geographical areas and in other societies. Sometimes the members of the disadvantaged communities can be refugees, sometimes they can be part of a national minority. But if a society wants to reduce the transmission of poverty and social disadvantage, mentoring, both formal and informal, can be a good way to do this.

NOTES

1. PERSIST research, $N=1034$, carried out by CHERD Hungary, University of Debrecen.
The large-sample PERSIST student database of the 2019 quantitative research was created by the CHERD-Hungary research center, which conducted research in Hungary and in Slovakia, Romania, Ukraine and Serbia from neighboring countries. A total of 2,199 people were interviewed, of which the Hungarian sample was 1034 ($N=1034$).

REFERENCES

Agasisti, T., Avvisati, F., Borgonovi, F., & Longobardi, S. (2018). *Academic resilience: What schools and countries do to help disadvantaged students succeed in PISA*. OECD.
Bacikova, M., & Berinsterova, M. (2017). Changes in teachers' social support and cognitive autonomy of primary school pupils. *Edukacia, 2*(1), 8–16.
Brüggemann, C., & Friedman, E. (2017). The decade of Roma Inclusion: Origins, actors, and legacies. *European Education, 49*(1), 1–9.
Brumovská, T., & Seidlová Málková, G. (2010). *Mentoring*. Portál.

Ceglédi, T. (2012). Reziliens életutak, avagy A hátrányok ellenére sikeresen kibontakozó iskolai karrier. *Szociológiai Szemle, 22*(2), 85–110.

Csert-Csapó, T. (2019). Az uniós roma oktatáspolitika – magyar tanulságok. [Roma education policy in the EU – Hungarian facts] *Educatio, 28*(1), 58–74.

Ćurčić, S., Miscovic, M., Plaut, S., & Ceobanu, C. (2013). Inclusion, integration or perpetual exclusion? A critical examination of the decade of Roma Inclusion, 2005–2015. *European Educational Research Journal, 13*(3), 257–267.

Demaray, M. K., & Malecki, C. K. (2002). Critical levels of perceived social support associated with student adjustment. *School Psychology Quarterly, 17*(3), 213–241.

Demir, M., & Leyendecker, B. (2018). School-related social support is associated with school engagement, self-competence and health related quality of life (HRQoL) in Turkish immigrant students. *Frontiers in Education, 3*(art. 83), 1–10. https://www.frontiersin.org/articles/10.3389/feduc.2018.00083/full

Eurofound. (2017). *Social mobility in the EU*. Publications Office of the European Union.

Fehérvári, A. (2015). A hátrányos helyzetű tanulók oktatásának változása, 2006–2014. [Changes in the education of disadvantaged students] In A. Fehérvári & G. Tomasz (Eds.), *Kudarcok és megoldások. Iskolai hátrányok, lemorzsolódás, problémakezelés* (pp. 31–52). Oktatáskutató és Fejlesztő Intézet.

FRA. (2014). *Education: the situation of Roma in 11 EU member state*. European Union Agency for Fundamental Rights.

Ghaith, G. M. (2002). The relationship between cooperative learning, perception of social support, and academic achievement. *System, 30*(3), 263–273.

Gitschthaler, M., & Nairz-Wirth, E. (2018). The individual and economic costs of early school leaving. In L. Van Praag, W. Nouwen, R. Van Caudenberg, N. Clycq & C. Timmerman (Eds.), *Comparative perspectives on early school leaving in the European Union* (pp. 59–73). Routledge.

Godó, K., Ceglédi, T., Dabney-Fekete, & Ilona Dóra. (2021). Resilient teacher candidates as mentors. The Let's Teach for Hungary Mentor Program as a resource of individual and community empowerment. Conference presentation. A társadalomtudományok 30 éve a Partiumban. Nagyvárad/Oradea (Romania). 26.03.2021. (online)

Godó, K. (2021). Lecturer relationships. In G. Pusztai & F. Szigeti (Eds.), *Progress and drop-out risk in higher education* (pp. 57–59). CHERD Research Report. Kapitális Nyomdaipari Kft.

Hobson, A. J. (2012). Fostering face-to-face mentoring and coaching. In S. J. Fletcher & C. A. Mullen (Eds.), *Mentoring and coaching in education* (pp. 59–73). SAGE Publication, Inc.

Kertesi, G., & Kézdi, G. (2013). *School segregation, school choice, and educational policies in 100 Hungarian towns*. Roma Education Fund.

Koulish, R. (2010). Hungarian Roma attitudes on minority rights: The symbolic violence of ethnic identification. *Europe-Asia Studies, 57*(2), 311–326.

KSH [Central Statistics Office]. (2016). Gyermekesély [Chances for Children] https://www.ksh.hu/docs/hun/xftp/stattukor/gyermekvedelem14.pdf

Leake, D. W., Burgstahler, S., & Izzo, M. V. (2011). Promoting transition success for culturally and linquistically diverse students with disabilities: The value of mentoring. *Creative Education, 2*(2), 121–129.

Masten, A. S. (2019). Resilience from a developmental systems perspective. *World Psychiatry, 18*(1), 101–102.

Messing, V. (2017). Differentiation in the making: Consequences of school segregation of Roma in the Czech Republic, Hungary, and Slovakia. *European Education, 49*(1), 89–103.

Messing, V., Neményi, M., & Júlia, S., with Contributions from Szász, Anna. (2010). Ethnic differences in education in Hungary: Survey report. In *EDUMIGROM Survey studies*. Center for Policy Studies.

Mullen, C. A. (2012). Mentoring: An overview. In S. J. Fletcher & C. A. Mullen (Eds.), *Mentoring and coaching in education* (pp. 7–23). SAGE Publication.

OECD. (2019). *PISA 2018 Results (Volume II). Where All Students Can Succeed*, PISA. Paris: OECD Publishing. https://doi.org/10.1787/b5fd1b8f-en

Pásztor, I. Z., Pénzes, J., Tátrai, P., & Pálóczi, Á. (2016). The number and spatial distribution of the Roma population in Hungary – In the light of different approaches. Folia geographica, Acta facultatis studiorum humanitatis et naturae *Universitatis Prešoviensis*, *58*(2), 5–21.

Pusztai, G., & Torkos, K. (2001). *Roma gyermekkor a Partium területén.* (*Roma Childhood in the Partium*). *Educatio*, *3*, 584–594.

Skutil, M., Zikl, P. a kol. (2011). *Pedagogický a speciálně pedagogický slovník.* Praha: Grada Publishing.

Sommers, Ch. L., Owens, D., & Piliawsky, M. (2008). Individual and social factors related to urban African American adolescents' school performance. *High School Journal*, *91*(3), 1–11.

Szalai, J., Messing, V., & Neményi, M. (2010). Ethnic and social differences in education in a comparative perspective. In *EDUMIGROM comparative papers* (pp. 1–23). Central European University, Center for Policy Studies.

EDUCATION IN SOUTH-EAST EUROPE FROM THE PERSPECTIVE OF THE EUROPEANIZATION PROCESS

Klara Skubic Ermenc

ABSTRACT

This chapter aims to present the development of education in the South-East European (SEE) countries, which took place under strong influence of the European Union (EU) education policy. This is examined irrespective of the different relationships these countries have with the EU. Some of these are Member States, and others are candidate or partner countries. The chapter opens with the explanation of the concept of SEE, and it is processed with a discussion on the concept of Europeanization in the education field. The concept refers to the process of forming a common education policy in the EU. This is also transferred to non-EU European countries. The third subchapter synthetizes and evaluates the main characteristics and challenges of the education in the SEE countries from the perspective of common European policy goals.

Keywords: South-East Europe; Europeanization of education; comparative and international education; education system development; The Balkans; Policy transfer

World Education Patterns in the Global North:
The Ebb of Global Forces and the Flow of Contextual Imperatives
International Perspectives on Education and Society, Volume 43A, 127–148
Copyright © 2022 by Emerald Publishing Limited
All rights of reproduction in any form reserved
ISSN: 1479-3679/doi:10.1108/S1479-36792022000043A009

INTRODUCTION

In 1999, the UN special reporter for the right to education published a report on the state of affairs in South-East Europe (SEE). She rightfully stated that SEE, and particularly the Balkan peninsula, was:

> One of the world's most complex areas in terms of ethnicity, language and religion. Nation states mean less, generally speaking, than ethnic allegiances that cross borders: there are Albanians in Macedonia, Macedonians in Bulgaria, and Serbs in Croatia – the mix is often uneasy and in recent times it has been explosive (e.g. Kosovo, Bosnia). (Tomasevski, 1999, p. 1)

In the last decade of the twentieth century, the collapse of the Communist regimes, the introduction of the free market economy, and the disintegration of Yugoslavia have tremendously affected a large amount of the region. At the same time – particularly after 2000 – the globalization and Europeanization processes intensified and global education reform (Sahlberg, 2016) emerged: Education in Europe and globally began to follow the same agenda, bringing education systems closer together, for "better or worse" so to speak. Comparative education teaches us that no matter how intense global tendencies are, what happens on local level depends on complex contextual characteristics. For deeper understanding of education in the countries located in SEE the geopolitical history is of particular importance, and indicates that the region is marked with extreme diversity: here was the division between Eastern and the Western Roman Empire, later also the division between the Austro-Hungarian and Ottoman Empires. Furthermore, Yugoslavia was neither entirely Eastern nor Western country, and it was highly decentralized and diverse in itself. Albania was isolated until the late 1980s, Bulgaria and Romania were part of the Eastern bloc, and Greece with Cyprus to Western (Tomasevski, 1999). Comparing histories and contemporary developments in education within the area would be an overwhelming scientific endeavor. This endeavor would demand a close collaboration of many researchers, and it proceeded over the course of many years. The aim of this chapter is more humble. It presents contemporary SSE country-related developments, all of which are tightly linked to the process of Europeanization of education in the EU in its partner countries. The concept of Europeanization forms the framework of this analysis.

This chapter is divided into three parts. The first part discusses the concept of SEE. The second part provides an explanation of the Europeanization process. The third part synthetizes and evaluates the main characteristics and challenges of education in the SEE, particularly from the perspective of common European policy goals.

SEE: AN UNCLEAR CONCEPT

The usage of the term SEE has increased following the fall of the Berlin wall. This event caused the disappearance of the post-World War II divisions between Eastern and Western Bloc European countries. It seems that its usage reflects the desire to find a politically neutral (geographical) term. In the naming of a politically and economically unstable, unsettled part of Europe, it was vital that the name be agreeable and accepted by all the referred countries.

According to the United Nations Group of Experts on Geographical Names (UNGEGN) – whose goal is to encourage geographical names standardization – SEE is part of the East Central and South-East Europe (ECSEE) Division. The East Central and South-East Europe (ECSEE) Division is one of the 23 UNGEGN Divisions. Its countries belong to three geographical regions: *Southern Europe* (Albania, Bosnia and Herzegovina, Croatia, Greece, Montenegro, Serbia, Slovenia, and North Macedonia), *Eastern Europe* (Bulgaria, Czech Republic, Georgia, Hungary, Poland, Romania, Slovakia, and Ukraine), and *Western Asia* (Cyprus and Turkey). Some of the countries are active in more divisions (UNGEGN Divisions, n.d.).

Notwithstanding, different UN offices or commissions use the term SEE countries to denote a selected list of these countries. This most often consists of Albania, Bosnia and Herzegovina, Montenegro, North Macedonia, and Serbia, as well as Kosovo (e.g., UN Office on Drugs and Crime, under United Nations Security Council Resolution 1244); this list may also take the form of Albania, Bosnia and Herzegovina, Bulgaria, Croatia, Greece, Montenegro, Romania, Serbia, and North Macedonia (e.g., The United Nations Economic Commission for Europe, UNECE, n.d.). Similarly, the World Bank (n.d.) includes all former Yugoslavian countries (Bosnia and Herzegovina, Croatia, Montenegro, Serbia with Kosovo, and North Macedonia – excluding Slovenia) and Albania.

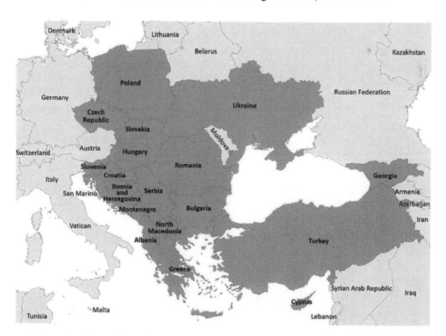

Picture 1. East Central and SEE Division. *Source*: UNGEN. East Central and South-East Europe Division. (n.d.). http://ecseed.zrc-sazu.si/.

It seems that the term SEE countries is associated either with aid recipient countries or countries included in various development programs. These programs often target economic, safety, cultural, educational, and other policies in developing countries. As such, the term cannot be viewed neutrally; in comparative education particularly, there is a risk that such conceptualization may link it to the idea of modernization (Welch, 2007). This is a particular challenge since all these countries are, according to the world-system theory (Arnove, 2009), semi-peripheral – or even peripheral – countries (Chase-Dunn & Hall, 1997).

SEE Countries Vis-á-Vis the European Union

Some of the SEE countries are members of the European Union (the EU); among them Cyprus, Greece, and Slovenia also belong to the Eurozone and are therefore categorized as inner-periphery (Bartlett & Prica, 2016). Those which are not part of the Eurozone (Croatia, Bulgaria, Romania) are categorized as outer-periphery. Neighboring countries of the Western Balkans are categorized as super periphery. Regardless of their status within or *vis-á-vis* the EU, they all are non-core countries. All of these countries are dependent on the powers which have culturally and historically supported or ruled them (e.g., the role of Russia in Serbia, France in Romania, or the importance of Germany in regards to Slovenia).

As part of the European continent, the SEE countries are in some way or another linked with or dependent on the EU, including their education policies. Considering their relations with the EU, the SEE countries – which will be analyzed in this chapter – can be divided into four groups:

1. The first group consists of the EU member states: Bulgaria, Croatia, Cyprus, Greece, Romania, and Slovenia. Among them, only Greece is an "old" Member State, having been a part of the group since 1981. Cyprus and Slovenia have been members since 2004, Bulgaria and Romania since 2007, and Croatia since 2013.
2. The second group consists of countries which fall under the EU enlargement policy (EU Enlargement, n.d.) and can be subdivided into two groups:

   a. Candidate countries: Albania, Republic of North Macedonia, Montenegro, Serbia, Turkey
   b. Potential candidates: Bosnia and Herzegovina and Kosovo.

3. The third group falls under the neighborhood policy: Albania.

THE EUROPEANIZATION OF EDUCATION: WHO CREATES THE AGENDA AND HOW IS IT TRANSMITTED?

Education in the EU is one of the policy areas regulated by the Treaty of Lisbon (n.d.). The competence over education is limited and is associated with the principle of subsidiarity. This implies that the Union has "competence to carry out actions to support, coordinate or supplement the actions of the Member States" (Art. 2E). Article 3b explains in more detail:

> Under the principle of subsidiarity, in areas which do not fall within its exclusive competence, the Union shall act only if and insofar as the objectives of the proposed action cannot be sufficiently achieved by the Member States, either at central level or at regional and local level, but can rather, by reason of the scale or effects of the proposed action, be better achieved at Union level.

The EU is not in a position to lay down the rules on education, training, and youth policy, however these arrangements do not prevent the EU from taking a very active role in the development of European education. On the contrary, the EU plays a unique and important role as a coordinator, facilitator, and advisor. It encourages cooperation between Member States and supplements their action. This is the reason why the concept of Europeanization of education emerged.

The concept of Europeanization first appeared in the 1980s in political studies literature, and it achieved greater recognition in the 1990s, particularly in the field of European studies (Mikulec & Ermenc, 2016; Nordin, 2014; Ongur, 2010). Europeanization represents the process of forming the EU (Lawn & Grek, 2012); it is a political and network-based phenomenon as well as a specific element of globalization. It reflects the complexity of processes that include transnational flows and networks of people, ideas, and practices across Europe; these processes involve European, national, and local actors (Castells, 2010; Mikulec, 2019). It also refers to the process of successful integration of candidate countries for EU membership and the adoption of "European standards" in various fields (Verger, 2014). For example, when the former Communist countries of Central and Eastern Europe were preparing to join the EU in 2004 and 2007, they were required to accept various EU demands. Something similar was asked of Turkey, which was expected to adopt European standards in various fields (Rahigh-Aghsan, 2011). The same is also true for Serbia (Ermenc & Spasenović, 2011). These countries are "expected to converge towards the EU model, rather than the EU and the neighboring countries mutually adjusting to each other" (Langgein & Börzel, 2013, p. 572).

Many authors identify the Lisbon Strategy as a key turning point in the Europeanization of education (Alexiadou, 2014; Ertl, 2006; Lawn & Grek, 2012; Nóvoa, 2010; Pépin, 2007). Through it, the EU set itself a strategic objective for the coming decade: "to become the most competitive and dynamic knowledge-based economy in the world capable of sustainable economic growth with more and better jobs and greater social cohesion" (European Council, 2000, para. 5). The Strategy identified lifelong learning as a key factor of the future economic and social development of the EU. A consequence of this has been a greater connection of education policy with economic, social, and employment policy; it has also brought on more cooperation in the field of education (Fredriksson, 2003; Pépin, 2007; Rasmussen, 2014; Mikulec, 2019). It has conceptualized education as part of social, labor market, and general economic policy, and not as an independent "teleological" policy field (Dale, 2009, p. 38).

The first step in the implementation of the Lisbon Strategy was the Council decision on common objectives for future EU policy development in the education and training field (European Commission, 2001). The second step was a document adopted the following year, known as "Education and Training 2010" (Council of the European Union, 2002). After the end of the 10-year period, the Commission defined a strategy for the development of education and training for the next 10-year period (2010–2020) known as "ET 2020" (Council of the European Union, 2009). The latter was a part of the broader context of the "Europe 2020" strategy (European Commission, 2010), with which the Commission responded to the growing economic crisis in Europe in 2010. In 2020, the Commission adopted another strategic document, "Communication form the Commission to the European Parliament, the Council, the European Economic and Social Committee and the Committee of the Regions on achieving the European Education Area by 2015" (European Commission, 2020). The document expresses the Commission's commitment to make European Education Area (the EEA) a reality by 2025. The EEA is defined along six dimensions, each including means and milestones: (1) quality, (2) inclusion and gender equality, (3) green and digital transitions, (4) teachers and trainers, (5) higher education, and (6) geopolitical dimensions (European Commission, 2020, p. 5).

The EU "exports" its education policy to its partner countries, and education has become a part of the EU foreign policy (La Rosa, 2014). In the case of higher education, the EU promotes EU-like reforms in neighboring countries; following the World Bank, the European Commission is the world's second-largest multilateral funding body for education, and their funds are not free of conditions: "In the field of higher education there is a clear persuasion towards convergence with the Bologna principles and the European higher education reform agenda." (La Rosa, p. 7). La Rosa reiterated Rutkowski's concept of global "soft convergence," meaning influencing and converging policy agendas in such a way that the local, national, and global dimensions converge into the recognition of a similar policy. In the field of education, full convergence is not possible due to the fact that education is very much connected with cultural aspects and local realities that are usually difficult to ignore or homogenize. Yet, the recipient countries increasingly subscribe to international standards and benchmarks (La Rosa, 2014).

Similarly, the EU exports its education agenda to non-EU member SEE countries within the field of vocational education. For almost 25 years, it achieved this through The European Training Foundation (ETF, n.d.), and this entailed the EU agency supporting countries surrounding the European Union to reform their education, training, and labor market systems. The Agency cooperates with governments, business, and social partners in 29 countries, including Albania, Bosnia and Hercegovina, Serbia, Kosovo, Turkey, Montenegro, and North Macedonia. In 2010, inspired by the Copenhagen process (see Chapter: Upper secondary and vocational education), the ETF launched what is known as the Torino process. The Torino process is defined as "a participatory process leading to an evidence-based analysis of the vocational education and training (VET) policies in a country" (Torino Process, n.d.). It is carried out in every participating country every two years; this provides the stakeholders with the analysis of their

VET system's state of development with the priorities for the future. The process is claimed to be based on broad and open participation, as well as on the idea of countries' ownership; it is guided, however, toward similar understanding of the role of VET in society and similar goals (Milovanovitch, 2019). As Bartlett and Pagliarello (2016) pointed out, the policy is transferred by "policy entrepreneurs," who are

> individuals or institutions with access, time and resources in a specific policy sector that aim to build consensus and coalitions around certain issues [...]. They set the policy agenda, frame the policy issues, and identify and create policy venues. As agents for policy change, they promote policy issues and ideas to policy communities, aiming to gain acceptability for a policy. (2016, p. 307)

It is further explained that policy entrepreneur in the Western Balkans is the EU, and it influences domestic policies through the enlargement process and international donors with special expertise in VET policy, as well as business councils, international donor agencies from Germany, Luxembourg, Austria, Switzerland, and others. These have supported VET reform by funding school projects, modernizing the curricula, preparing students to enter the labor market, etc. They also indicate that the EU – which has played an important role of policy entrepreneur – has also played a role in asserting the principle of inclusive education. This idea, however, is rarely transmitted to the Western Balkans.

EDUCATION SYSTEMS IN SEE COUNTRIES AND MAIN POLICY DEVELOPMENTS

As previously mentioned, education systems in SSE countries are diverse, making it impossible to describe them as one entity. Yet, due to the aforementioned process of Europeanization, the education systems of the SEE countries inside and outside the EU follow similar goals and priorities. This inevitably brings them closer together. The following subchapters are aimed to capture some basic characteristics of the individual systems, particularly from the perspective of the common priorities, targets, and goals. The "ET 2020" defined several targets to be achieved at the European level by 2020. Among them, at least 95% of children were expected to participate in early childhood education. Fewer than 15% of 15-year-olds were expected to be under-skilled in reading, mathematics, and science. The rate of early leavers from education and training aged 18–24 (with, at most, lower secondary education and who were not in further education) was expected be below 10%.

Early Childhood Education and Care

Access

Quality early childhood education and care (ECEC) is considered to be on the main cornerstones of the education system. Many studies indicate that early inclusion in ECEC positively influences children's development and learning,

Table 1.   The Inclusion of Children Age 4 and Above in ECEC.

Children in ECEC (age 4 and over)	Albania	Bulgaria	Croatia	Cyprus	Greece	North Macedonia	Romania	Serbia	Slovenia	Turkey
Benchmark: 95%The EU Average: 95.4%	81 %[a]	83.9%[b]	82.8%	92.0%	81.5%	39.5%	89.6 %	68.6%	92.1%	54.7%

[a]For Albania, see OECD (2020a).
[b]For other countries, see European Commission/EACEA/Eurydice (2019).

improves the equality of the education system, and is particularly advantageous for vulnerable children (Hočevar & Šebart, 2018). These are the reasons why the EU places ECEC among its main priorities in the education field. This is also why it is seen as the cornerstone for building a greater amount of improved equitable education systems. (Education, Audiovisual and Culture Executive Agency, 2014). Access and quality are the two main ECEC issues facing policymakers in European countries at present. Table 1 indicates that none of the SEE countries has reached the EU benchmark on inclusion of children in ECEC, but a large difference can be noticed among the countries. On one part of the continuum, there are Cyprus and Slovenia (with around 92%), and on the other part of the continuum is North Macedonia with less than 40%.

Most European countries have committed themselves to providing an ECEC place for all children, either by establishing a legal entitlement to ECEC (e.g., in Slovenia) or by making attendance compulsory for at least the last pre-primary year. The last year or two of pre-primary education is compulsory in Bulgaria, Greece, Croatia, Cyprus, and Serbia.

Organization
The most common form of ECEC structure in Europe – *the split system* – structures ECEC services according to the age of the children. Provision is delivered in separate settings for younger and older children, and the age break is usually around three years old. The responsibility for ECEC governance, regulation, and funding are divided between different authorities. Educational guidelines normally apply only to provision for older children. The requirements for staff qualifications also usually differ depending on the type of provision. Moreover, conditions of access may vary greatly. A legal entitlement usually applies to older children and not to younger ones. Among the SEE countries the split system is less common compared to the rest of Europe; it is in operation in Albania, Cyprus, and – to some extent – also in Greece, Romania, and Bulgaria.

In contrast, in *unitary systems*, ECEC provision for all pre-school aged children is organized in a single phase and delivered in settings catering for the whole age range. There is no break or transfer between institutions until children start primary school. The ministry of education is responsible for ECEC governance, regulation, and funding. All care and education for young children is considered to be part of "early education" services, and educational guidelines cover the entire ECEC phase. Unitary settings have a single management team running provision for children of all ages, and the same level of staff qualification (i.e., usually tertiary level) is required for working with the entire age range. Furthermore, a legal entitlement to ECEC, or free ECEC, is often granted from a very early age in unitary systems. This type of system prevails in most of the Baltic countries, but also in most of the former Yugoslavian countries; the systems are entirely integrated in Bosnia and Herzegovina, Croatia, and Slovenia, and to some extent integrated in Serbia and North Macedonia (European Commission/EACEA/Eurydice, 2019, p. 17).

Educational Staff
Educational staff working with older children are usually required to have a bachelor's degree as a minimum qualification. Educational staff are employed in all settings for older children and in two-thirds of ECEC settings for younger children. This is also the case for the majority of the SEE countries. A bachelor's degree is required for the entire ECEC phase in Bosnia and Herzegovina, Croatia, Montenegro, Slovenia, Greece, Cyprus, and Bulgaria; a bachelor's degree is required only for children aged 3 and over in Albania, North Macedonia, Serbia, and Turkey (European Commission/EACEA/Eurydice, 2019, p. 14).

Learning Objectives
Countries set learning objectives related to children's progress and development. The effectiveness of the teaching and learning process largely determines the quality of ECEC. Therefore, all European countries – including the SEE countries – issue official educational guidelines to help settings improve their provision. However, in some countries, such guidelines are restricted to settings for children over three years old (Albania, Greece, Cyprus, Bulgaria); in the rest, the guidelines cover the entire ECEC phase (European Commission/EACEA/Eurydice, 2019, p. 17). All European countries list learning objectives referring to personal, emotional, and social development, as well as language and communication skills for older, and some also for younger, children. For both groups of children, most countries stress health education, physical development, the development of artistic skills, and understanding of the world. Literacy, numerical, and logical reasoning, as well as adaptation to school life, are more often directed toward older children.

Disadvantaged Children
Disadvantaged children have lower ECEC participation rates, even though most countries offer means-tested financial support to parents. In Europe, one in four children under the age of 6 is at risk of poverty or social exclusion and may need specific measures to support their educational needs. Almost one in two

children in Bulgaria (51.4%) and Romania (47.4%) is at risk of poverty or social exclusion. Among the EU Member States, Greece and Croatia have considerably higher rates than the EU average. The situation is even more complex in non-EU SEE countries, where attendance tends to be much lower in general. In Turkey (OECD, 2020b), only 5% of children under the age of 5 attend *crèches* or day-care centers; in Bosnia and Herzegovina, around 13% (Camović & Hodžić, 2017) attend, and in Serbia 14.5% attend.

Increasing the participation in ECEC of children from disadvantaged backgrounds is one the main priorities of European ECEC policy. Support measures for disadvantaged children exist in most European countries, and language development is often the main focus in order to reach those children who potentially have learning difficulties as a result of their background; most education systems use cultural and/or linguistic criteria to target the groups most at risk, but socio-economic and geographic criteria are also considered important in many European countries (European Commission/EACEA/ Eurydice/Eurostat, 2019). In non-EU SEE countries, support measures such as attendance under preferential terms are also in place; this issue, however, is very often tackled by the support of international organizations, such as UNICEF (Camović & Hodžić, 2017) and domestic NGOs, such as the Red Cross (Novović, 2017).

Primary and Compulsory Education

Organization
Three different organizational models for compulsory education can be distin-guished across Europe: Single structure education, primary education followed by a period of integrated secondary education, and primary education followed by differentiated secondary education (Education, Audiovisual and Culture Executive Agency, 2012). In SEE countries, the following two models can be found:

1. The most common model is *single structure education* (primary and lower sec-ondary education combined), found in countries such as Albania, Croatia, Bosnia and Herzegovina, Bulgaria, Montenegro, Serbia, and Slovenia (that is comparable to Scandinavian countries). In these countries, compulsory gen-eral education is provided in single-structure schools with no transition neces-sary between primary and lower secondary levels. Single structure education is a legacy from the socialist times; it was believed that long, unified basic (folk) school was the cornerstone of an equitable education.
2. *Primary education* (ISCED 1) followed by a period of *integrated secondary education* (ISCED 2) corresponding to a 'common core' of provision in coun-tries is adopted in countries such as Greece, Romania, and Turkey (that is comparable to Francophone countries). After primary education, all students follow the same common core curriculum during lower secondary education (i.e., up to 15 or 16 years of age).

Compulsory Education

In most SEE countries – as compared to other EU countries – compulsory education lasts for a minimum of nine years (i.e., Albania, Bosnia and Herzegovina, Croatia, Montenegro, Serbia, and Slovenia). However, in some of these countries, this period totals 10 years or more, such as Cyprus (10), Greece and Romania (11), Turkey (12), and North Macedonia (13). Compulsory education starts in most countries at primary level (i.e., usually for six-year-olds). In Bulgaria, Greece, Croatia, Cyprus, and Serbia, compulsory education is extended to pre-primary level and children are obliged to take part in pre-primary education programs. These programs are primarily designed to introduce very young children to a school-type environment. In Romania, compulsory education is extended to part of the upper secondary education; in North Macedonia and Turkey, it covers full upper secondary education level as well.

Curriculum

Regarding curriculum, the European Commission mainly supports the introduction of competence-based curricula. In particular, the concept of "key competences" is adopted, which is defined as knowledge, skills, and attitudes needed by all for personal fulfillment and development, employability, social inclusion, and active citizenship. In 2006, the European Parliament and the Council adopted the Recommendation on Key Competences for Lifelong Learning. It provided a common European reference framework on key competences for policymakers, education and training providers, the social partners, and learners themselves. In May 2018, revised Recommendation (European Commission, 2018) was adopted. Eight key competences were defined: Literacy; Languages; Science, technology, engineering and mathematics (STEM); Digital; Personal, social and learning; Civic; Entrepreneurship; Cultural awareness and expression. In 2009, the Council adopted a benchmark related to basic skills, which aimed to reduce the rate of 15-year-olds underachieving in the subjects of reading, mathematics, and science to less than 15% by 2020. In spite of the fact that some EU countries – including Slovenia as the only SEE country – are among the top performers in the study of PISA (OECD, 2016), underachievement (i.e., performing below level 2 in the PISA test) continues to be a serious challenge across Europe.

The concept of key competences has also been transferred to non-EU SEE countries. Albania was assessed by the OCED (2020a), which found that its introduction of a competency-based curriculum contributed to improvement across key education indicators. This, however, failed to prevent a large share of Albanian students from leaving school without mastering basic competencies. Similarly, other countries among the Western Balkans are seen as countries which – despite the introduction of competence-based curricula – still face tremendous challenges in students' achievements (OECD, 2020c). One of the several obstacles preventing these countries from success is supposedly inefficient teaching methods:

In Western Balkans, teacher practices are largely traditional and centered around the teacher (e.g., delivering a lecture to the whole class), with less emphasis on individualized, adaptive instruction (which is associated with higher student outcomes) compared to international benchmarks. (OECD, 2020c, p. 12)

Quality

The issues of the quality and equity of education systems in the SEE countries are complex. First and foremost, conclusions on quality are often solely based on the PISA results, which offer a very limited picture (Gaber et al., 2012). Many of the SEE countries have long traditions of public education, dating back to the late eighteenth century (e.g., those that were part of the Austro-Hungarian Empire, including Croatia, Slovenia, and part of Serbia), but have historically built on Herbart's concepts of knowledge and teaching; this differs enormously from prevailing contemporary constructivist and pragmatic concepts (Ermenc et al., 2013). It is arguable whether modern concepts do indeed bring about more quality. On the other hand, it is true that economic problems, political turbulences, and wars prevented the development of educational theory as well as the practice and policies in some of the SEE countries. Thus, a negative impact was seen on the quality as well as the equity of education systems.

Table 2 summarizes the data from the PISA 2018 study on the shares of students who were under-skilled in reading and mathematics. The underachievement is a general problem in Europe. Slovenia, however, is the only country among those SEE countries whose results were above the EU average. Croatia came close to the average, while the situation was particularly difficult for Kosovo.

Table 2.   The Shares of Under Achievers in Reading and Mathematics (PISA 2018).

The EU Benchmark: below 15%	Albania	Bosnia and Herzegovina	Bulgaria	Croatia	Cyprus	Greece	Kosovo
The EU Average: 21.7% (reading) 22.4% (mathematics)	52.2% "[a] 42.2%	53.72% " 57.85	47.1%**[b] 44.4%	21.6%** 31.2%	43.7%** 36.9%	30.5%**	78.7% " 76.6%

Montenegro	North Macedonia	Romania	Serbia	Slovenia	Turkey
44.4% " 46.2%	55.1% " 60.2%	40.8%**	37.7% " 39.7%	17.9% ** 16.4%	26.1% " 36.7%

[a]Data marked with " were obtained from: OECD (2019).
[b]Data marked with ** were obtained from: PISA 2018 AND THE EU (2019).

Equity

Judging from the PISA 2018 result, students from disadvantaged backgrounds performed lower than more advantaged students. Interestingly, better performing countries (i.e., Slovenia, Greece, and Turkey) are less equitable compared to worse performing countries (i.e., Albania, North Macedonia, Bosnia and Herzegovina, Serbia, and Kosovo) (PISA 2018, n.d.). Romania is the only SEE country which performs relatively poor in both aspects, while Croatia is the only SEE country which is above the OECD average on equity and close to the OECD average in quality. The explanation of the phenomenon is not straightforward. It potentially indicates that low performing countries provide equally poor education to all students. It might also be taken into consideration that these countries are former socialist countries where equitable education and society was on the pillars of the socialist societies. However, one can also agree with Halász (2015), who stated that these countries had aimed to improve equity by structural reforms neglecting the everyday pedagogical practice, of which Slovenia was a good case (Cankar et al., 2017).

Teachers

Most countries in Europe require a master's degree as the minimum entry qualification for becoming a primary and lower secondary teacher, and this usually takes five years to complete. Among the SEE countries, master's degree is required in Croatia, Slovenia, Albania, Montenegro, and Serbia. In other SEE countries, a bachelor's degree suffices. This difference, however, does not necessarily indicate the difference in quantity and quality of initial teacher education; in Bulgaria, Greece, Cyprus, Bosnia and Herzegovina, and Turkey, the initial teacher training takes between four and five years, but it is classified as bachelor level training (European Commission/EACEA/Eurydice, 2021).

The latest study on teachers in Europe (European Commission/EACEA/Eurydice, 2021) reports that many education systems are facing a vocational crisis of the teaching profession. Many countries are suffering from shortages while some are experiencing an oversupply of teachers. The aging of teachers is considered to be a challenge in more than half of the education systems. Among younger teachers, an increasing number are working on temporary contracts of less than one year. There is also general dissatisfaction among teachers with their salaries.

As far as teacher shortages are concerned, some countries need particularly to attract teachers to specific geographical areas or subject-specific studies. In Bulgaria, for instance, teachers in mathematics, physics and astronomy, computer science, and information technology receive higher salary as well as transport and rental allowances if they teach within specific regions. In Serbia, the education ministry supports students enrolled in ITE programs with scholarships. In Turkey, on the other hand, they face a surplus, since many new faculties have been established over the last 20 years; every year, 100,000 people graduate from these faculties (European Commission/EACEA/Eurydice, 2021, pp. 30–31).

In many European countries, the majority of teachers currently employed are in the highest age groups. At the EU level, the latest Eurostat data indicates that almost 40% of lower secondary teachers are 50 years old or above, and less than 20% are below 35 years old. In Greece, this rate rises to more than half of lower secondary; in Bulgaria, the share of this age group is between 40% and 50%, above 35% in North Macedonia, and only 5% of the teacher population in Turkey (European Commission/EACEA/Eurydice, 2021, p. 32).

School Autonomy

Although school autonomy has apparently become more widespread among the EU Member States, this has been the result of a gradual process of implementation which began in the 1980s and expanded during the 1990s. In SEE countries, which were either socialist/communist (Albania, Bulgaria, Romania, and former Yugoslavia) or experienced military regimes (Greece), the idea of school autonomy is much more contemporary; it was brought about by democratization processes. To some extent, the only exception was Yugoslavia, which was a federative state with many competences transmitted to the republics in the area of education. Today, schools in SEE countries have decision-making powers in the area of teaching and learning. In a majority of countries, power is retained over particular aspects of managing human resources as well. Outside their role as members of the school governing body, teaching staff in almost all countries do not make decisions on human resource issues. However, they are generally involved – to varying degrees – in decisions on teaching and learning. Unfortunately, a lack of experience in this respect has resulted in a weak capacity for school planning. For instance, Albania (OECD, 2020a) has embarked on significant education reforms, such as the decentralization of school governance. Schools play an important role in hiring and dismissing teachers and selecting textbooks, but they lack discretionary financial resources. Thus, the capacity for school planning and self-evaluation remains weak.

Upper Secondary and Vocational Education

Participation

At the EU level, participation in upper secondary education (ISCED 3) increased to almost 80% at the age of 17. More than half of 18-year-olds – and around one quarter of 19-year-olds – were still registered in upper secondary education, but this participation rate subsequently fell to less than 12% by the age of 20. The data is available only for the members of the EU, and indicates (Table 3) that early leaving only represents a challenge for some SEE countries, while others achieve high international standards in this respect. This is not surprising, since former communist countries invested in human capital; this was due to the view of education was as a crucial instrument in the transformation of society and the modernization of the economy (Halász, 2015; Vujisić-Živković, 2015).

Table 3. Early School Leavers.[a]

The EU Benchmark: Below 10%	Bulgaria	Croatia	Greece	Cyprus	Romania	Slovenia
The EU Average: 10%	12.7%	3.3%	4.7%	7.8%	16.4%	4.2%

[a]*Source*: European Commission (2019). Education and Training Monitor 2019. Directorate-General for Education, Youth, Sport and Culture.

General and Vocational Education

At the EU-27 level between 2000 and 2009, the proportion of students in general education – as a percentage of all students at ISCED 3 – increased by 5.5 percentage points, reaching 50.4% in 2009 (European Commission/EACEA/Eurydice, 2018). According to the ratio between general and vocational upper secondary students, the SEE countries differed to a great extent due to very different historical and political contexts: in Cyprus and Greece the proportion of students in general upper secondary education was very high – between 60% and 70%. In contrast, high participation rates in vocational upper secondary education (i.e., more than 60%) were found in former Yugoslavian countries such as Slovenia, Croatia (Cedefop, 2019a), and Montenegro (ETF, 2020). Romania and Bulgaria were somewhere in between, with over 50% of students in vocational education (Cedefop, 2019b). High shares of students in VET can be explained from a political-historical perspective, since vocational and technical education was crucial for communist countries in that it was supposed to contribute to industry development (Halász, 2015; Walterová, 1994).

Vocational education and training is also one of the EU priorities. It is viewed as a key element of lifelong learning systems equipping people with knowledge, know-how, skills, and/or competences required on the labor market. VET systems in Europe can rely on a well-developed network of VET providers. They are based on governance structures with the involvement of social partners and different bodies. European cooperation on vocational education and training was launched in Copenhagen in 2002 and has been further enhanced thereof (i.e., the Copenhagen process). In 2015, the candidate countries, European Economic Area countries, EU social partners, the European Commission, and European VET providers agreed on a set of deliverables (i.e., Riga Conclusions) for the period of 2015–2020. Among them, work-based learning in all its forms was promoted, with special attention to apprenticeships. The European Alliance for Apprenticeships was established in 2013, and this mobilized EU Member States, European Free Trade Association and EU candidate countries, and over 230 stakeholders to engage in enhancing the supply, quality, and image of apprenticeships. Recently the mobility of apprentices has also been added to the objectives of the Alliance. In 2017, the European Apprentices Network was established to make sure that the voice of young apprentices was heard in discussions related to VET and apprenticeships. Throughout the process, emphasis was given to quality assurance mechanisms in VET, which were expected to establish continuous information and feedback loops within VET systems based on learning out-comes. A reference instrument called the European Quality Assurance Reference Framework (EQAVET) was designed to help EU countries promote and monitor the continuous improvement of their VET systems on the basis of commonly-agreed references. Moreover, it was also expected that key competences in VET curricula would be strengthened. Systematic approaches were initiated with the intention of developing initial and continuous professional development of VET teachers, trainers, and mentors in school- and work-based settings.

As mentioned, these goals and ideas were further exported to non-EU SEE countries via the European Training Foundation (ETF). Taking Montenegro and Serbia as examples, the ETF currently supports the country in the implementa-tion of the dual education system (ETF, 2020; Spasenović, 2021), which is "seen as an effective way of improving smooth and sustainable transition from school to work" (CEDEFOP, 2017, p. 20). Halász (2015) evaluates that vocational edu-cation in former communist countries was much more specialized; it often pro-duced obsolete skills and transmitted factual knowledge instead of preparing students for the creative use of knowledge. Since key competences and the use of knowledge are at the center of the European policy, these countries faced chal-lenges. Some of the local researchers (Spasenović, 2021) observed that contextual factors are not taken into consideration, which causes inefficient transfer of education policy.

Higher Education
The Bologna Process is a term that refers to an intergovernmental coopera-tion of 49 European countries in the field of higher education (EHEA, n.d.). The process includes the efforts of public authorities, universities, teachers, and students, together with stakeholder associations, employers, quality assurance agencies, international organizations, and institutions – including the European Commission. It guides the collective effort of improving the internationaliza-tion of higher education. The process was named by The Bologna Declaration, which was signed in 1999 by ministers responsible for higher education from 29 European countries. It set in motion a European cooperation process that has radically changed higher education. Reforms have affected countries within and beyond Europe, including all SEE countries. Higher education systems in Europe differ widely, and the EU strives to support Europeans to use qualifications from one country to apply for a job or a course in another. Increased compatibility between education systems makes it easier for students and job seekers to move within Europe. The main focus is the introduction of the three cycle system (bach-elor/master/doctorate), supported by strengthened quality assurance and easier recognition of qualifications and periods of study. The Bologna Process also sup-ports the modernization of education and training systems to make sure these meet the needs of a changing labor market.

The implementation of the reform is documented in regular reports that are called Communiqués. The last Communiqué was adopted in Rome in 2020. It built on the Paris Communiqué (2018), which called for an inclusive and innovative approach to learning and teaching, integrated transnational cooperation in higher education, research and innovation, and securing of a sustainable future for the planet through higher education. It also called for stronger, better support of under-represented and vulnerable groups, as well as promoting them to access and excel in higher education. The Rome Communiqué (EHEA Rome, 2020), adopted during the current COVID-19 pandemic, adopted a new vision which resounds the new European Commission's agenda (2019–2024), as well as the United Nations' Sustainable Development Goals; in this, members have committed to build an inclusive, innovative and interconnected European Higher Education Area by 2030 (EHEA Rome, 2020).

The latest Bologna Process Implementation Report (European Commission/ EACEA/Eurydice, 2020) provides a wide-ranging and detailed picture of how the EHEA has been moving forward. The Report indicates that the number of students in most countries is constantly increasing: "The largest percentage increase in the number of enrolled students between 2000 and 2017 took place in Turkey, with an increase of over 600%, followed by Cyprus (increase of over 300%) and Albania (increase of over 200%)" (European Commission/EACEA/ Eurydice, 2020, p. 19). Only a few countries experienced a decrease, including North Macedonia (33%); slight decreases were also recorded in Bulgaria and Slovenia. The period between 2005 and 2010 reveals a growth of more than 12% across the EHEA as a whole. For this period, Romania, Cyprus, Turkey, Albania, and Montenegro recorded increases above 30%. Between 2010 and 2015, Turkey recorded an increase of 71.8% in student numbers. In contrast, decreases in student numbers were apparent in about half of the EHEA countries, including four of the larger countries (i.e., France, Italy, Ukraine, and Poland). The Report lists several reasons for these trends: demographic changes (increases or decreases in the size of young population cohorts); the structure of the (higher) education systems (whether or not short-cycle tertiary programs exist, and whether part-time study is facilitated); country-specific characteristics, national policies aimed at increasing tertiary entry and completion rates, financing provided, changes in economic conditions; admissions rules and procedures etc. Dakowska and Harmsen (2015) drew attention to the fact that the higher education systems in post-communist countries underwent significant reforms, and these were significantly characterized by academic and economic liberalization:

> The restoration of university autonomy was one of the main objectives of and justifications for the reforms. However, the notion of autonomy encompasses a variety of realities, ranging from a Humbolditan commitment to collegiality and freedom of research to a marker orientation and financial autonomy" they rightfully claim. (Dakowska & Harmsen, 2015, p. 6).

The result of these processes were both the privatization and the massification of higher education. The share of students attending private higher education institutions soared to one-third in some countries (e.g., Romania), while others (e.g., Slovenia) remained minor. "Catching up with Europe" was the main justification for the reforms, but state funding was reduced and market mechanisms gained more ground. Reference to Humboldtian tradition was also strong in countries that experienced some university autonomy before the World War

II, particularly in some former Yugoslavian countries such as Croatia, Slovenia, and Serbia. In SEE countries, there was less contestation of the Bologna Process in comparison to Germany or Italy, but some assessments imply that this does not necessarily translate to full compliance with the rules and recommendations; it may even indicate a façade compliance (Dolowitz and Marsh, cited in Dakowska & Harmsen, 2015). A good example of such façade compliance is described by Protner et al. (2020), who came from countries of former Yugoslavia and both analyzed and compared the consequences of Bologna reform in the area of teacher education in these countries; clear proof emerged that, by implementing the Bologna Process, differences among countries and universities – and even among individual universities – increased significantly as a result of different interpretations of the Bologna declaration.

CONCLUSION

It can be undoubtedly concluded that the SEE countries follow the common European agenda in education. Moreover, their success is continuously being assessed by the international public along the lines of identical benchmarks and quality concepts. These place access to education, as well as a functionalist approach to education, at the forefront of this agenda. In order to become a Member State, gain funding, or be internationally recognized, national authorities strive to "catch up" with Europe. These authorities often put themselves (or get pushed) into a subordinate role. It seems that domestic expertise loses importance and support, in spite of the fact that – in its modern history – it has developed in constantly with world trends in education theory (Medveš, 2015; Vujisić-Živković, 2015). It is also important to mention the incredible achievements of some former socialist and communist countries after the World War II, specifically in the areas of illiteracy eradication, access to education from preschool to secondary, technical and higher education, girls' and women's education, education of rural youth, and education of minority ethnic communities (Halász, 2015; Miovska-Spaseva, 2015; OECD, 2003; Vujisić-Živković, 2015). Instead of imposition (Dale, 2009), a partner and emancipatory approach may have the potential to bring about more synergy of European – and even global – agenda and international expertise with national contexts. In this way, more productive support can be given to SEE for the quality and equity of their education systems to improve.

REFERENCES

Alexiadou, N. (2014). Policy learning and Europeanisation in education: The governance of a field and the transfer of knowledge. In A. Nordin & D. Sundberg (Eds.), *Transnational policy flows in European education: The making and governing of knowledge in the education policy field* (pp. 123–140). Symposium Books.

Arnove, R. (2009). World-systems analysis and comparative education in the age of globalization. In R. Cowen & A. M. Kazamias (Eds.), *International handbook of comparative education* (pp. 101–120). Springer.

Bartlett, W., & Pagliarello, M. C. (2016). Agenda-setting for VET policy in the Western Balkans: Employability versus social inclusion. *European Journal of Education*, *51*(3), 305–319. https://doi.org/10.1111/ejed.12182

Bartlett, W., & Prica, I. (2016). *Interdependence between core and peripheries of the European economy: Secular stagnation and growth in the Western Balkans*. LSE's 'Europe in Question' Discussion Paper Series. The London School of Economics and Political Science.

Camović, D., & Hodžić, L. (2017). An analysis of preschool education in Bosnia and Herzegovina: Fairness and equal opportunities for all children. *Sodobna pedagogika/Journal of Contemporary Educational Studies*, *68*(2), 154–170.

Cankar, G., Bren, M., & Zupanc, D. (2017). *Za večjo pravičnost šolskega sistema v Sloveniji. Analize povezav dosežkov učenk in učencev s socialnimi, kulturnimi, ekonomskimi in regionalnimi značilnostmi učenk in učencev, pridobljenimi prek podatkov Statističnega urada* RS. Državni izpitni center.

Castells, M. (2010). *The rise of the network society*. Blackwell Publishing Ltd.

Cedefop. (2019a). *Vocational education and training in Europe*. https://www.cedefop.europa.eu/sl/tools/vet-in-europe/systems/croatia

Cedefop. (2019b). Spotlight on VET. Romania. https://www.cedefop.europa.eu/files/8128_en.pdf

CEDEFOP. (2017). *Apprenticeship review: Slovenia. Putting apprenticeship on track in Slovenia*. Publications Office of the European Union. Thematic Country Reviews.

Chase-Dunn, C., & Hall, T. D. (1997). *Rise demise: Comparing world-systems*. Westview Press.

Council of the European Union. (2002). *Detailed work programme on the follow-up of the objectives of education and training systems in Europe*. [OJ C 142/1 of 14.6.2002].

Council of the European Union. (2009). *Council conclusions of 12 May 2009 on a strategic framework for European cooperation in education and training* ("ET 2020"). [OJ C 119/2 of 28.5.2009].

Dakowska, D., & Harmsen, R. (2015). Laboratories of reform? The Europeanization and internationalization of higher education in Central and Eastern Europe. *European Journal of Higher Education*, *5*(1), 4–17. https://doi.org/10.1080/21568235.977318

Dale, R. (2009). Contexts, constraints and resources in the development of European education space and European education policy. In R. Dale & S. Robertson (Eds.), *Globalisation and Europeanisation in education* (pp. 23–44). Symposium.

Education, Audiovisual and Culture Executive Agency. (2014). *Eurydice policy brief. Early childhood education and care*. https://doi.org/102797/52737

Education, Audiovisual and Culture Executive Agency. (2012). *Key data on education in Europe 2012*. https://doi.org/10.2797/77414

EHEA Rome. (2020). Rome Ministerial Communique. Retrieved June 3, 2021, from https://www.ehea.info/Upload/Rome_Ministerial_Communique.pdf

EHEA. (n.d.). *European Higher Education Area and Bologna process*. Retrieved June 3, 2021, from http://ehea.info/index.php

Ermenc, K. S., & Spasenović, V. (2011). Competitive managers of change at risk. In N. Popov, C. Wolhuter, M. Mihova, & J. Ogunleye (Eds.), *Comparative education. Teacher training, education policy, social inclusion, history of education* (pp. 219–228). Bureau for Educational Services.

Ermenc, K. S., Spasenović, V., Vujisić Živković, N., Vrcelj, S., & Popov, N. (2013). Comparative pedagogy in Slavonic South East European countries. In A. W. Wiseman & E. Anderson (Eds.), *Annual review of comparative and international education* 2013 (International perspectives on education and society (Vol. 20, 1st ed., pp. 191–218). Bingley [etc.]: Emerald.

Ertl, H. (2006). European Union policies in education and training: The Lisbon agenda as a turning point? *Comparative Education*, *42*, 5–27. http://dx.doi.org/10.1080/03050060500515652

ETF. (2020). Montenegro. Education, training and employment developments 2020. Country Fiche 2020 Montenegro Education Training and Employment Developments.pdf

ETF. (n.d.). *ETF. About*. Retrieved June 3, 2021, from https://www.etf.europa.eu/en/about

EU Enlargement. (n.d.). Retrieved June 3, 2021, from https://ec.europa.eu/info/policies/eu-enlargement_en

European Commission. (2018). *Developing KEY COMPETENCES for all throughout life*. https://ec.europa.eu/education/sites/education/files/document-library-docs/factsheet-key-competences-lifelong-learning_en.pdf

European Commission. (2001). *Report from the Commission: The concrete future objectives of education systems.* COM (2001) 59 final.

European Commission. (2010). Communication from the Commission. Europe 2020. A strategy for smart, sustainable and inclusive growth. COM(2010) 2020.

European Commission. (2019). *Education and Training Monitor 2019. Directorate-General for Education, Youth, Sport and Culture.*

European Commission. (2020). *Communication form the Commission to the European Parliament, the Council, the European Economic and Social Committee and the Committee of the Regions on achieving the European Education Area by 2015* (COM(2020) 625 final).

European Commission/EACEA/Eurydice. (2018). *Structural Indicators for Monitoring Education and Training Systems in Europe – 2018. Eurydice Report.* Luxembourg: Publications Office of the European Union.

European Commission/EACEA/Eurydice. (2019). *Key Data on Early Childhood Education and Care in Europe – 2019 Edition.Eurydice Report.* Publications Office of the European Union.

European Commission/EACEA/Eurydice. (2020). *The European Higher Education Area in 2020: Bologna Process Implementation Report.* Luxembourg: Publications Office of the European Union.

European Commission/EACEA/Eurydice. (2021). *Teachers in Europe: Careers, development and wellbeing. Eurydice report.* Publications Office of the European Union.

European Council. (2000). *Lisbon European Council 23 and 24 march 2000 presidency conclusions.* Retrieved May 30, 2015, from http://www.europarl.europa.eu/summits/lis1_en.htm

Fredriksson, U. (2003). Changes of education policies within the European Union in the light of globalisation. *European Educational Research Journal, 2,* 522–546. http://dx.doi.org/10.2304/eerj.2003.2.4.3

Gaber, S., Cankar, G., Marjanovič Umek, L., & Tašner, V. (2012) The danger of inadequate conceptualisation in PISA for education policy. *Compare, 42*(49), 647–663.

Halász, G. (2015). Education and social transformation in Central and Eastern Europe. *European Journal of Education, 50*(3), 350–371. https://doi.org/10.1111/ejed.12130

Hočevar, A., & Kovač Šebart, M. (2018). Concern for the effectiveness of preschool education or "soft engineering" of the workforce of the future? *Sodobna pedagogika, 69*(4), 152–176.

La Rosa, M. (2014). *EU: Education policies and third countries. Civilian Power or just foreign policy?* LUND University.

Langgein, J., & Börzel, T. A. (2013). Introduction: Explaining policy change in the European Union's eastern neighbourhood. *Europe-Asia Studies, 65*(4), 571–580. https://doi.org/10.1080/0966813 6.2013.766042

Lawn, M., & Grek, S. (2012). *Europeanizing education. Governing a new policy space.* Symposium Books Ltd.

Medveš, Z. (2015). Socialist pedagogy: Caught between the myth of the fairness of the unified school and cultural hegemony. *Journal of Contemporary Educational Studies, 66*(2), 14–41.

Mikulec, B., & Ermenc, K. S. (2016). Qualifications frameworks between global and European pressures and local responses. *SAGE Open, 6*(2), 1–10. https://doi.org/10.1177/2158244016644948

Milovanovitch, M. (2019). Reforming VET in Eastern Europe, Central Asia, Northern Africa and the Middle East: Patterns of risks and reform implementation. In B. E. Stalder & C. Nägele (Eds.), *Trends in vocational education and training research, Vol. II. Proceedings of the European Conference on Educational Research (ECER), Vocational Education and Training Network (VETNET)* (pp. 303–311). https://doi.org/10.5281/zenodo.3371543

Mikulec, B. (2019). *Evropeizacija izobraževanja. Izobraževanje odraslih med teorijo, evropsko in nacionalnimi politikamu ter prakso.* Znanstvena založba Filozofske fakultete Univerze v Ljubljani.

Miovska-Spaseva, S. (2015). Achievements and contradictions in the development of schooling and pedagogy in socialist Macedonia (1945–1990). *Journal of Contemporary Educational Studies, 66*(2), 114–128.

Nordin, A. (2014). Europeanisation in National Educational Reforms: Horizontal and vertical translations. In A. Nordin & D. Sundberg (Eds.), *Transnational policy flows in European education: The making and governing of knowledge in the education policy field* (pp. 141–158). Symposium Books.

Nóvoa, A. (2002). Ways of thinking about education in Europe. In A. Nóvoa & M. Lawn (Eds.), *Fabricating Europe. The formation of an education space* (pp. 131–155). Kluwer Academic Publisher.

Novović, T. L. (2017). The preschool educational system in Montenegro: Current state and prospects. *Sodobna pedagogika/Journal of Contemporary Educational Studies*, *68*(2), 172–189.

OECD. (2003). *Reviews of National Policies for Education: South Eastern Europe 2003: Volume 1: Albania, Bosnia-Herzegovina, Bulgaria, Croatia, Kosovo, Reviews of national policies for education*. OECD Publishing. https://doi.org/10.1787/9789264100725-en

OECD. (2019). *PISA 2018 Results (Volume I): What Students Know and Can Do*, PISA, OECD Publishing, Paris, https://doi.org/10.1787/5f07c754-en

OECD. (2016). *PISA 2015 Results (Volume I): Excellence and Equity in Education*, PISA. OECD Publishing. http://dx.doi.org/10.1787/9789264166490-en

OECD. (2020a). OECD Reviews of Evaluation and Assessment in Education: Albania. https://www.oecd-ilibrary.org/sites/7f73878b-en/index.html?itemId=/content/component/7f73878b-en#:~:text=Early%20childhood%20education&text=The%20net%20enrolment%20rate%20at,%25)%20and%20Montenegro%20(60%25).

OECD. (2020b). Turkey. Education policy outlook. Retrieved June 3, 2021, from https://www.oecd.org/education/highlightsturkey.htm

OECD. (2020c). Education in the Western Balkans: Findings from PISA. PISA, OECD Publishing. https://doi.org/10.1781/764847ff-en

Ongur, H. O. (2010). Towards a social identity for Europe? A social psychological approach to European identity studies. *Review of European Studies*, *2*(2), 133–143. http://dx.doi.org/10.5539/res.v2n2p133

Pépin, L. (2007). The history of EU cooperation in the field of education and training: How lifelong learning became a strategic objective. *European Journal of Education*, *42*, 121–132. http://dx.doi.org/10.1111/j.1465-3435.2007.00288.x

PISA 2018 and the EU. (2019). *Striving for social fairness through education*. Directorate-General for Education, Youth, Sport and Culture. Luxembourg: Publications Office of the European Union.

PISA 2018. (n.d.). Retrieved June 3, 2021, from https://www2.compareyourcountry.org/pisa/

Protner, E., Medveš, Z., Batinić, Š., Miovska Spaseva, S., Spasenović, V., Šušnjara, S., Radeka, I., Zorić, V., & Vujisić Živković, N. (2020). Usporedba razvoja obrazovanja učitelja u državama nekadašnje Jugoslavije. In E. Protner (Ed), *Razvoj i aktualne tendencije pedagogije i školstva na području nekadašnje Jugoslavije* (1st ed., pp. 13–31). University of Maribor Press, Faculty of Arts. https://doi.org/10.18690/978-961-286-320-3.2

Rahigh-Aghsan, A. (2011). Turkey's EU Quest and political cleavages under AKP. *Review of European Studies*, *3*(1), 43–53. http://dx.doi.org/10.5539/res.v3n1p43

Rasmussen, P. (2014). Adult learning policy in the European Commission. In M. Milana & J. Holford (Eds.), *Adult education policy and the European Union. Theoretical and methodological perspectives* (pp. 17–34). Sense Publishers.

Sahlberg, P. (2016). The global education reform movement and its impact on schooling. In K. Mundy, A. Green, B. Lingard & A. Verger (Eds.), *The handbook of global education policy* (pp. 374–384). John Wiley & Sons.

Spasenović, V. (2021). *Izobraževalna politika. Globalni in lokalni procesi*. Znanstvena založba Filozofske fakultete Univerze v Ljubljani.

The Treaty of Lisbon. (n.d.) Retrieved June 3, 2021, from http://www.europarl.europa.eu/factsheets/en/sheet/5/the-treaty-of-lisbon

The World Bank. (n.d.). *South East Europe Regular Economic Report*. Retrieved June 3, 2021, from https://www.worldbank.org/en/region/eca/publication/south-east-europe-regular-economic-report

Tomasevski, K. (1999). *The Right to Education. Preliminary Report submitted to the UN Commission on Human Rights.*

Torino Process. (n.d.). Retrieved June 3, 2021, from https://www.torinoprocess.eu/

UNECE. (n.d.). *South-Eastern Europe*. Retrieved June 3, 2021, from https://unece.org/south-eastern-europe

UNGEGN Divisions. (n.d.). *United Nations Group of Experts on Geographical Names*. Retrieved June 3, 2021, from https://unstats.un.org/unsd/ungegn/

Verger, A. (2014). Why do policy-makers adopt global education policies? Toward a research framework on the varying role of ideas in education reform. *Current Issues in Comparative Education, 16*(2), 14–29.

Vujisić-Živković, N. (2015). Constitutive discontinuity. Education and pedagogy in the socialistic Serbia (1945–1990). *Journal of Contemporary Educational Studies, 66*(2), 82–95.

Walterová, E. (1994). *Kurikulum. Proměny a trendy v mezinárodní perspektivě*. Masarykova Univerzita. Centrum pro další vzdělávání učitelů. Brno.

Welch, A. (2007). Technocracy, uncertainty, and ethics: Comparative education in an era of postmodernity and globalization. In A. F. Robert & T. C. Alberto (Eds.), *Comparative education. The dialectic of the global and the local* (pp. 21–46). Lanham: Rowman & Littlefield Publishers, Inc.

EDUCATION IN EAST ASIA: CHANGING SCHOOL EDUCATION IN CHINA, JAPAN, AND KOREA

Yuto Kitamura, Jing Liu and Moon Suk Hong

ABSTRACT

Despite children's academic excellence in East Asian countries, school education in this region faces a range of challenges to build inclusive and quality education for all. This chapter aims at examining how these challenges occur and what actions have been taken to deal with them. By focusing on China, Japan, and the Republic of Korea, the chapter first reviews reforms of school education since the 1990s in these countries. The subsequent sections then present educational disparity and a new mode of teaching and learning in these countries. It concludes by addressing that East Asian countries must explore more common ground for building a more collective sense and identity to share responsibility for building a resilient, inclusive and sustainable world through global citizenship education and education for sustainable development.

Keywords: Disparities; inequality; new mode of teaching and learning; competencies; curriculum; quality education

INTRODUCTION

This chapter discusses the current situation of school education in East Asia with a special focus on China, Japan, and Republic of Korea. It is widely known that children in these countries have maintained high levels of scholastic performance for many years, as attested to by their scores in PISA (OECD Program for International Student Assessment) and other similar international surveys, indicating the high quality of school education in those countries. However, despite

World Education Patterns in the Global North:
The Ebb of Global Forces and the Flow of Contextual Imperatives
International Perspectives on Education and Society, Volume 43A, 149–168
Copyright © 2022 by Yuto Kitamura, Jing Liu and Moon Suk Hong
Published under exclusive licence by Emerald Publishing Limited
ISSN: 1479-3679/doi:10.1108/S1479-36792022000043A010

their children's academic excellence, school education in those countries is facing a range of challenges. Many of these challenges are phenomena typically found in East Asia, with varied responses made by the respective countries in attempts to address them.

This chapter therefore examines such phenomena, notably two commonly observed in East Asia, presenting how they occur and what actions have been taken in response to them. The two phenomena are as follows: (1) disparity in education reflecting socioeconomic inequality and (2) the growing relevance of new modes of teaching and learning to develop the skills and abilities required for new times, which are often referred to as "twenty-first century skills" or "key competencies." Education in East Asia has undergone great transformation since the 1990s, in particular under the influence of globalization. Therefore, our analysis is mainly concerned with education since the 1990s.

As stated above, we will mainly discuss China, Japan, and Republic of Korea, but references will also be made on a more limited scale to Taiwan, Hong Kong and Macau as East Asian regions. The following sections give a brief review of status of school education in China, Japan, and South Korea since the 1990s. The subsequent sections then present educational disparity and new modes of learning and teaching these countries. It concludes by addressing similarities and differences of these countries in achieving inclusive and quality education for all toward 2030.

SCHOOL EDUCATION

China

With the start of the "Reform and Opening Up" for modernization since the 1980s, educational development in China opened a new chapter. Since then, "Efficiency first, give attention to equity" became the key principle of education reform in the following decades. On the one hand, the reform aims at pursuing educational efficiency to cultivate as many human resources as possible within short period for the country's construction. On the other hand, the reform gives concern on equity of schooling for all. In order to efficiently provide abundant human recourses to accommodate need for economic development, a key school system was reintroduced. With the start of this system in the 1950s, it distinguishes two development pathways of public schools in China. Compared with regular schools, key schools have more highly qualified teachers, better equipment, and much greater funding, as well as the number of better-performing students with better education transition (Liu, 2018). The system was officially abolished in 1997 with the increasing criticism on polarization of public school (Liu, 2018). However, with development of decades, those former key schools have already got strong attraction and deep influence on good performing students and affluent parents who have education aspiration (Zhang & Bray, 2017).

With a rapid economic reform, the Chinese government has taken actions to decentralize and marketize social policy and social welfare. With reposition of the role of government as facilitator in socioeconomic development, a government monopoly education system started to transform to a new system with collaboration between government and social forces. In terms of compulsory education, the government transferred the main financial responsibility to local governments. And they encouraged local government to operate public schools by attracting social fund. However, due to the imbalanced economic development, this policy widened educational financial disparities at local level. And it further caused imbalance in education development at local level. On the other hand, it left institutional loopholes for high-performing public schools to commercialize the limited access to quality education. With the rise of family income, public schools could sell the access to the affluent families to accommodate their demand for quality education. Consequently, this caused unprecedented competition for admission to high-performing public schools in urban China in the late 1990s. It intensified inequality in public school education in urban China. Moreover, it pushed a shift of the Chinese public education from a meritocracy-based education to a more parentocracy-based schooling (Liu, 2018).

The rapid economic development and urbanization also led to an unprecedented internal (rural to urban) migration in China. The population of internal migrants rapidly increased from 121 million in 2000 to 241 million in 2018 (National Statistic Bureau, 2019). There were around 19 million migrant children who were on move with their parents to urban China in 2017. The large number of migrant children flowing into urban areas generated a big demand for education in urban context. However, institutional barriers, such as household registration based public school admission, limited access to public schools in urban China for migrant children. On the other hand, it is estimated that there were 6.97 million children of left-behind in rural China in 2018 (Ministry of Civil Affairs, 2018). Education for these children faced various challenges, such as lack of quality education resources, limited number of teachers with rich teaching experiences, incomplete curriculum, and limited communication with parents. With the rise of concerns on education for left-behind children, the government has been taking initiatives to protect the rights of left-behind children and accommodate their education needs (UNESCO, 2019).

Entering the 1990s, the government started to promote reform for "Quality-oriented education," known as *sushi jiaoyu* in Chinese, to cultivate all-round developed human resources to best meet the new demand for construction of a socialist market economic system (Chinese Communist Party Central Committee, 1994). The reform gives emphasis on comprehensively fostering the development of all students with innovative spirit of daring to explore, the practical ability to solve problems And it aims at solving problems caused by the exam-oriented education which one-sidedly pursuing enrollment rate and increasing study workload of students (Tan, 2013). Moreover, to meet the demand for cultivating human resources to build a knowledge-based economy, the curriculum reform started in the late 1990s. It aimed at promoting a holistic development of all students in moral, intellectual, physical, esthetic and social aspects through diverse learning experiences (Tan, 2013). The effect of the reform was widely recognized by the *Shanghai Shock* in 2012 when students from the Shanghai bid the top of PISA ranking. Although there are critiques on the sampling and implementation of

PISA in China, there are increasing numbers of research analyzing how Shanghai succeeded through various educational initiatives.

In 2019, the Chinese government released *China Education Modernization 2035*. It aims at constructing a modernized education system of lifelong learning for all. It provides universal access to pre-school school with high quality, builds compulsory education with quality and balance, promotes universal access to upper secondary education, enhances service capacity of vocational education, improves competitiveness of higher education, provides inclusive education for disadvantaged children, and constructs a new pattern of education governance with participation of the whole society by 2035.

Japan

With continuous nation-wide endeavor since the mid-19 century, Japan has constructed an egalitarian school education system. In Japan, elementary school education was completely universalized at the beginning of the twentieth century, and the percentage of lower secondary school graduates going on to upper secondary school surpassed 90% during the first half of the 1970s. Today, the majority of the school-age population in Japan receive a total of 12 years' school education.[i]

School education has thus become ubiquitous among the Japanese population, and the country has come to enjoy an international reputation for the high quality of its basic education, as have other East Asian countries. Nevertheless, Japan's school education has also experienced various problems. They first became particularly conspicuous in the 1990s, as Japan's education experienced major transformation under the influence of globalization, the bursting of Japan's economic bubble,[ii] and the ensuing economic recession. Socioeconomic inequality accentuated by the economic downturn began to manifest itself clearly in children's educational environment and academic ability. Meanwhile, the increased number of university graduates led to an expansion of the white-collar population, resulting in shortages of unskilled workers in various industrial sectors. To address this problem, in the 1990s, Japan began actively accepting foreign nationals to make up for the shortage of low-wage workers. The children of these immigrants, referred to as "Newcomers,"[iii] found themselves in poor educational conditions, which came to be recognized as a serious social problem. The disparity in education and the educational environment for immigrant children are discussed in detail below.

During the 1990s, there was a shift in focus in the Japanese educational system from standardized curricula to those more adjusted to individual children and their needs. In line with this shift, upon the revision of the Course of Study (i.e., national curriculum) in 1998, educational reform resulted in a reduction of the number of lesson hours and curricular content, in an attempt to afford leeway to school life, which had become undeniably stressful and stifling for many students. The model of school education founded on this revised Course of Study came to be known as "*yutori* education," *yutori* being the Japanese word for "leeway." This educational policy triggered criticism from both experts and the general public, who were concerned that it might lower students' academic ability. Responding to such criticism, in the 2008 revision of the Course of Study (which is revised every decade or so), both lesson hours and educational contents were increased (Ichikawa, 2002).

The criticism of *yutori* education was partially provoked by the PISA results of 2003 and 2006. The declining trend of Japanese students' academic performance signaled by the test results was perceived by some as the "PISA shock." Japanese PISA scores began picking up again in 2009 and have remained since then at high levels. Furthermore, it was revealed that students who were taught under the revised 1998 *yutori* Course of Study from their first year of elementary school had begun to participate in PISA in or after 2009, not in 2006. This suggests that the criticism of *yutori* education following the PISA shock was not necessarily justified (Yamanouchi & Hara, 2010).

Since the 1990s, one component of educational reform has continued to capture great societal interest throughout educational levels, from primary to secondary to higher education: internationalization. In other words, many people began to believe that education must be "internationalized," or become more in tune with general international trends and practices, against the backdrop of advancing economic globalization and the increasing diversity of Japanese society, to enable students to acquire internationally employable skills and abilities. Following this way of thinking, many changes ensued (discussed in greater detail below), including the introduction of English lessons in selected primary schools, as opposed to the conventional practice of initiating students to English in lower secondary school, and the opening of English-medium courses at some universities. Needless to say, the internationalization of education cannot be realized solely through "Englishification," or an enlarged presence or active use of English in school. Noting this fact, some educational institutions attempted to introduce the instruction of other languages or internationalize their curricular contents. Nevertheless, the basic trend has been to view "internationalization" as some form of Englishification. Incidentally, this phenomenon is not limited to Japan but is observed across East Asia.

Republic of Korea

Over the past four decades, South Korea experienced rapid modernization, poverty reduction, and a notable democratization process, education in Korea had played a distinctive role in national development and acted as a critical driver for social changes. Today, Korean education at all levels – from elementary to higher/tertiary education – is universalized. Universalization of elementary school education was as early as the 1950s (91.1% of elementary enrollment in 1957) (Y. Kim, 2008). Since the end of the Korean War in 1953, the universalization of public schooling was fast and efficient. Numerous works of literature have recorded that a dramatic increase in elementary school enrollment rate during the post-war period. This increase in attendance was due to a combination of deliberate government policies and education enthusiasm of Korean families (famously known as education fever) (Y. Kim, 2008; Kwak, 2008). The introduction of the Six-Year Compulsory Education Completion Plan (1954–1959) emphasized cultivating "modern" and patriotic citizens which were largely supported by various national literacy and education campaigns. Post-war education policies also implemented the single-track education system with an emphasis on equal access to education and no discrimination on basis of status or class (Huh, 2009; Lee et al., 2006). Modern-day Education for All (EFA) like literacy campaign used that "accessibility strategy." The Double-shift school system, school support network, as well as active usage of humanitarian aid, and efficient education budget allocation were some of the factors that affected the fast-educational recovery in the post-colonial and war era (Huh, 2009; Oh, 1974).

Universalization in all levels of education continued. In the 1960s, a single-track educational system was established. The Korean Committee on Educational Planning planned 6–3–3–4 systems. This system greatly expanded educational opportunities for the "average person." It is rare to find literature that highlights the education funding mechanism based on national and local Acts in Post-War Korea. The *Local Tax Act* was the first act that was a value-added tax collected to fund education. The *Education Tax Act* also aimed at funding a plan to realize compulsory education. It is worthy to note that the *Local Education Subsidy Act* funds elementary and secondary education. These funding Acts significantly contributed to the universalization of Korean education institutionally possible (Y. Kim, 2008).

Implementation of the policy in 1974 marked an important turning point of equalization education policy. The policy was intended to reduce private tutoring, minimize the competition of high school entrance examinations and introduce the provision of balanced growth in the adolescent development stage. Introduction of *No Examination High School Admission Policy*, aimed to provide an equalized educational environment that covered a broad range of educational conditions for equalized educational benefits; and to reduce social conflict which resulted from private coaching and undesirable educational practices in secondary schools. Ultimately, the Ministry intended to eliminate the competition factor in high school admission. The "3 Bans" Policies in Korean Education was followed. The policy introduced (i) banning University organized entrance exams; (ii) banning donation admissions in universities; (iii) banning ranking high schools. Even in the 1970s, the name value of high school was largely prioritized in university entrance, leading to competition in enrolling in prestigious high schools. Various arguments and discussions on the effects of the equalization policy, whoever a very limited number of empirical studies to test the effects of the policy were conducted.

Regardless of various policy efforts with some dramatic measures, the educational conditions of the high schools were not completely equalized. Many favors such an equalization policy that can lead to lessen the burden of competition, normalization of the middle school curriculum, lessen the inequality of education, ranking schools cause decreased human capital development. At the same time, a significant portion of society has expressed constant concerns regarding Korean students' academic excellence and global competitiveness in education and student freedom in choosing schools.

Entering the 1990s, Korea enacted notable education reforms over the past 30 years as the county was rapidly changing into a post-industrialized and knowledge-based society. May 31 Educational Reforms in 1995 marked another critical turning point in Korea's education overhaul (Lee & Kim, 2016). The reform aimed to build a new education system centered on learners, diversity, specialization of education. This trend had arguably continued under the Kim Dae-Jung and Roh Moo-hyun presidency. Many argued that the New neoliberal paradigm in education was fully embraced in the May 31 Education Reform. Certainly, the main notions that drove South Korea's social change in the mid-1990s were "globalization" and "educational reform." In this period, globalization was considered a critical resource to build Korea's economic competitiveness, and both public and private schools and higher education institutions were tasked with enhancing the human resource capacity (Byoun et al., 2015). However, the internationalization of Korean HEIs has been controversial and many questions are still being raised by numerous scholars (Kim & Lee, 2019; Ko et al., 2019; Oh & Park, 2018). Some critics state that government-driven internationalization programs and policies were developed without considering the characteristics and contexts of the Korean education and other scholars criticize that this progress will continue to lag unless government policies fully integrate matters of quality (T. Shin, 2011; Van Damme, 2001). In this sense, Jeon, Hwang, and Hong (2021) argued that one may question whether the government policies foster "standardization" rather than "internationalization" of education.

In the 2000s, the Korean education system faces new challenges and reforms as a response to strong socio-political demands by the public for better equity in education as well as the need for an education system that can push scientific and technological innovation (Hong & Hwang, 2020). In response to the societal changes and demands, contemporary major education policies in Korea are mysteriously located somewhere between happiness, competency, and education justice paradigm. While Korea's population is decreasing, the former quantity-based approaches in Korea's education may turn toward more quality focused system. Currently, the Korean government emphasizes various equity measures such as the *Happy Education for All Students Policy, Raising Intelligent Learners for Society Initiatives, Education that Leaves No Child Behind* as well as *Korean Education that Harmonizes with the World Approach* (including enhancing Educational Competitiveness through International Cooperation, Global Citizenship Education, Expansion of education ODA). The success or failure of such a strong equity-focused education policy can be only evaluated in the future since the suggested policies are currently in the process of implementation (CIATE KOREA, 2019; Ministry of Education, 2020).

INEQUALITY IN EDUCATION

China

Educational inequality in China has been receiving continuous concern since the 1990s. With slogans of "Let part of people get rich first" and "Efficiency first," the Chinese economic development also follows the similar model which gives more development priorities and resources to the eastern part and the coast areas of the country. Accordingly, education sector in these areas also received more investment and more high-quality human resources. This caused an imbalance of educational development between the east and west part of China. Moreover, the key school system based on elitism concept further enlarged the imbalance between public schools in the same areas. Public schools in urban China have been institutionally stratified. There are gaps in terms of school infrastructure, teacher quality, and performance of students among schools in the same areas. And these caused fierce competition between schools and between families (Liu, 2018). Furthermore, with the marketization of public education, the limited quality education resources have become commercial goods for public schools and affluent families to exchange. In recent years, the affluent families are keen on sending children to after-school private tutoring in order to get their children well prepared for competition for admission to the limited high-performing schools (Zhang & Bray, 2017). The competition for the limited quality education resource is becoming more serious in recent decade. Research shows that there is an increasing number of parents who purchased the house in popular school districts in order to enroll their children to prestigious schools in these districts (L. Yang et al., 2018). On the other hand, it is difficult for the socially and economically disadvantaged groups to take part in such competition for quality education resources.

Educational inequality in China is also caused by household registration system (*hukou*). In China, admissions to public primary and junior high schools are based on principle of proximity. In principle, students can get free education at public primary and junior high schools which are located in the neighborhood where their *hukou* are registered. However, as there are gaps between schools in the same neighborhood, parents have to pay for extra fees or utilize their social capital to enroll their children to the schools with higher quality but locating in different neighborhood. Moreover, the *hukou* system excluded rural–urban migrant children from access to quality education in urban China. Although there is an increasing number of migrant children who could enter public primary schools and lower secondary schools, they still have to meet various requirements to enter upper secondary schools and take part in the national college entrance exam in the receiving areas. These requirements include *hukou* status of migrant families and their socioeconomic status. And these become barriers for migrant children to continue their post compulsory education in the receiving areas. Migrant children whose families cannot meet the requirements can only enter vocational education in the receiving areas. Those who want to go to upper secondary schools and universities have to return to hometown to continue their education.

Educational disparity in rural China is also receiving critical concerns in the past decades. A shrinking rural school system cannot fully accommodate educational needs from the local communities. With the decline of population in rural areas, the government promoted a school consolidation campaign to readjust the distribution of educational resources in rural areas for educational efficiency. By 2011, 40% of rural primary schools were closed. Moreover, the deterioration of education environment in rural areas led left-behind children in rural areas to a more difficult situation. The rural school consolidation had many negative impacts on students' safety, educational attainment, and physical and psychological development (UNESCO, 2019). Moreover, research show there are limited interaction between teachers and left-behind children in the classroom. And there are limited opportunities of extracurricular learning for these children (Han et al., 2017). In recent years, stakeholders have been taking various actions to support left-behind children's education and wellbeing. Beside the institutional guarantee of access to education for left-behind children, they also actively provided support for rural schools and teachers to enhance psychological education and mental care for these children (UNESCO, 2019).

Balancing educational development has become a key principle for eliminating educational inequality and improving education quality for all since the 2000s. Education resource sharing as a common approach has been widely adopted to enhance school collaboration and regional partnership for improving education quality for all (Liu, 2018). Local governments have introduced diverse models to promote school collaboration through sharing education resources among high-performing school and low-performing schools at the same level in the same district or in different districts. Moreover, they also adopted this approach to enhance collaboration between schools in urban and rural areas for school improvement. Research have shown positive effects of school collaboration on school improvement (Liang et al., 2016). It enlarged service of quality education and provided students more access to quality education resources. It also enhanced teacher training and empowered teachers and school managers in the low-performing schools. Nevertheless, there are concerns on the top-down initiative which may not generate sustainable motivation of stakeholders for the reform. Moreover, there is a risk of homogenizing schools in the same groups or alliances (Liu, 2018).

Japan

Following the bursting of the economic bubble in the early 1990s, Japanese society entered a long period of economic recession. Consequently, Japan's social structure was largely transformed. Up until the 1980s, the majority of people living in Japan constituted a huge middle class, giving rise to the expression "all 100 million people in the middle class" (Japan's total population at the time being roughly 100 million), describing a society that enjoyed great relative equality and stability. This subsequently changed to a state marked by great economic disparity due to the recession, which has seriously affected the education sector. Since the 1990s, many academic studies have been carried out, mainly in the domain of sociology, with a stance critical of disparity in education.

In the West, many researchers, including Pierre Bourdieu of France, have noted since the 1970s the accumulation of human capital by socioeconomically affluent households and the mechanism of intergenerational reproduction of this imbalance. The same phenomenon has never been absent in Japan, but it was only in the 1990s that Japanese society at large came to recognize the problem of educational disparity (particularly in terms of difference in academic performance) caused by socioeconomic inequality.

Research indicates phenomenon of disparity in education "double-hump camel academic ability" (or bipolarization of academic ability) during the 1990s. Research reveals that the students' academic ability declined as a whole, with an increasing percentage of low-scoring students (Kariya et al., 2002).[iv] Moreover, disparities were found to have widened over the period between students who engaged in proactive learning at school, spent long hours studying at home, and came from socioeconomically privileged families at the upper end, and students with opposite characteristics to the above at the lower end.

The same study shows the possibility of reducing the disparity in academic performance and learning situations between students in different social strata through appropriate educational interventions at school. Some such gap-filling measures include instruction focusing on students' motivation for learning and personalized instruction according to individual students' levels of scholastic comprehension. By conducting research at the same elementary and lower secondary schools in 2013, researchers (Shimizu et al., 2014) demonstrate that students' academic ability improved on the whole from 2001, accompanied by a narrowing of disparity in academic performance. The authors also found that students tend to have higher academic standards at schools equipped with abundant social capital, suggesting the existence of interpersonal networks in schools, households, and communities. Furthermore, at these schools, academic performance improved even among students with little or no extra-school learning experience (participation in "shadow education" in the form of lessons at an after-school cram or tutoring school).

Contrary to those research findings, recent studies by Matsuoka (2015, 2018) show that students from higher socioeconomic strata tend to have more accumulated shadow education, which is a major contributory factor to higher levels of academic ability. Matsuoka (2019) further maintains that differences in the family environment translate into various factors, including learning experience at and outside school, which greatly influence not only students' academic ability but also their actions, consciousness and expectation. This study, supported by abundant data, shows that "unequal" competition for educational credentials is forced upon children amid these disparities in education, which cannot be easily dispelled.

In addressing problems relating to disparity in education in Japan, it is also important to analyze them taking into account the increasing globalization and diversity of Japanese society. As mentioned above, in the 1990s, Japan began to experience shortages of unskilled workers as a result of the increase in the number of university graduates and hence white-collar workers, coupled with the effects of population aging and falling birth rates in more recent years. To facilitate the introduction of foreign workers into Japan, the Japanese government adopted several initiatives, including the revision of the Immigration Control and Refugee Recognition Act and the establishment of legal frameworks for migrant reception.[v] Under such circumstances, foreign workers, notably Latin Americans of Japanese descent and those from South and Southeast Asia, arrived in Japan. Many such workers have since been living in Japan on a long-term basis with their families. Education for their children has thus surfaced as a major social issue.

Miyajima (2014) explores problems and challenges facing such children, with a special focus on Newcomer children (defined above) among all types of children of foreign origin. Since the 1990s, when Newcomer foreign residents began to increase in Japan, national and local governments have adopted various policy measures to support their children's education. These measures are still far from sufficient. Miyajima points out inadequacies in the following three areas in particular: (1) acquisition of host-country language (Japanese) proficiency and basic academic skills, which are indispensable; (2) education for the maintenance and development of immigrants' mother tongues and cultures; and (3) environmental adjustment that promotes cross-cultural respect and understanding.

It is well known that obstacles in these areas have already led to a certain number of Newcomer children giving up on learning and even dropping out of school due to their inability to understand school lessons (Yamamoto, 2014). The real existence of children deprived of adequate educational opportunity cannot be overlooked, all the more so in Japan, which has succeeded in establishing an otherwise egalitarian educational system as described above. To correct this situation, various studies have been made, and administrative initiatives taken at national and local levels. Still, it should be emphasized here that these efforts have not yet proven sufficient or effective.

Republic of Korea

Inequality in the Korean education system has not only been "an educational matter," but it has also been the most heated debate in the socio-political arena. The state-driven Korean education equalization policy of the 1980s has experienced deterioration since the May 31 Education Reform which as result lead to a new phase of debates on inequality highlighted by dichotomized debates on equity *versus* excellence in education which has been going on since the 1990s. The fundamentals of the formal school system which is based on the concept of elitism further widened the imbalance between public and private schools. The past Stratification of public schools in urban Korea has not been erased, but with the introduction of various private schools, foreign language high schools and "autonomous high schools," these gaps have been further institutionally stratified. There are gaps in terms of school infrastructure, teacher quality, and student performance on a national level. The recent introduction of diversification of high school policies in Lee's administration between 2002 and 2006, intensified competition between schools and students throughout the first two decades of the 2000s. Ironically, having a strong egalitarian emphasis on the views on society as well as showing meritocratic ambitions for ones' family members' success and education, Korean education stakeholders including education enthusiastic family members have pushed Korea's recent education reform to focus on equity. Since Moon Jae-In's administration, the education policy direction took a dramatic turn toward the emphasis on education equity. *Free high school education, customized programs for students at risk, equal opportunity admission screening* as well as *reducing educational costs* for lower-income groups are some of the most notable policies implemented by Moon's Government.

As discussed earlier, high school education in Korea is not compulsory but is de facto universal with a 99.7% admission rate for middle school graduates (Ministry of Education, 2019). To increase the public role of secondary education and to ease the burden of education expenses for both students and parents, a free high school education system was implemented in stages, from the second semester of 2019. Free education is expected to expand to all grades until 2021. With free high school education, which supports admission fees, tuition fees, school operation expenses, and textbook costs for high school students, student – paying expenses of approximately KRW 4.8 million per student will be reduced over a period of three years. As a result, the government intended for all students, regardless of family background, region, income, or class, to have equal educational opportunities up to high school level (Ministry of Education, 2018, 2019). Since the mid-2000s, Korea society has been experiencing a widening a gap in income as a result, free high school education is expected to play a significant part in reducing educational gaps by ensuring equal opportunities for all students, regardless of family background, regions, or classes, and in fulfilling the national responsibility for education up to the secondary level (Ministry of Education, 2019). Furthermore, it is a notable change in the current government policy direction of as well as the meaningful social message that a people-oriented and inclusive education system has been placed at the core of the national education policy as it guarantees the basic right to education of all citizens as stipulated in the Constitution. Among various new policies, *Happy Education for All Students Policy* (including Free semester; Innovation School Model; The 2015 Revised Curriculum; Character Education) and *Education that Leaves No Child Behind* (such as Edu-Care Service, The Nuri Curriculum, Educational Support for Students with Disadvantaged Background, Prevention of School Drop-outs) are the most notable efforts.

Korea's modern education history has evolved around the issues of educational equity and excellence in academic achievement (Hong, 2020). Since the 2000s, new issues and agendas have emerged in Koreas education discourse, these include peace education, education equity and gender, democratic citizenship education, sustainability and education, global citizenship education, international development, and education are central new in the Korean education's normative arena. Much newer debates on education and social justice have opened up both new challenges and possibilities in Korean education. Taking into account the increasing globalization and diversity in Korean society, ethnicity, religion, identity, citizenship, and gender issues are newly energizing and challenging Korea's contemporary education.

NEW MODES OF TEACHING AND LEARNING

China

Since the 1990s, the term "Quality-oriented education" has become one of the mainstream educational discourses in China's education reforms. A new curriculum reform of basic education started in 2001. It aimed at transforming examination-oriented education to quality education to accommodate needs for education in the twenty-first century (Liu, 2020). Also, it gave emphasis on cultivating the critical thinking, creativity, and innovation skills which are necessary in the global market and the knowledge-based economy. There were four perspectives of the reform. In terms of the management system, a decentralized reform introduced a "three-level national-local-school curriculum management system" to encourage schools to be a key driver of the curriculum development and implementation. In terms of the curriculum content, it adopted a compulsory course named as "integrated practical activity" from primary to upper secondary levels to strengthen students' awareness of inquiry and innovation, encourage students to link knowledge and practices, and foster their sense of social responsibility. Moreover, the reform adopted elective course for students' holistic development. In terms of pedagogy, teachers are motivated to transfer a traditional "Talk and Chalk" teaching approach to a student-centered and collaborative approach. This transition gives emphasis on students' independence and autonomy. Besides, the reform advocates a holistic approach to encourage teachers to evaluate students beyond the scope of academic results (Tan, 2013). Nevertheless, researchers show concerns on the contradictions between "creativity and critical thinking" and the moral and patriotic education, and autonomy assigned to teachers and schools and the de-professionalization threatened by the established competency-based evaluation (Vickers & Zeng, 2017). In 2016, China released "Core Competencies for Student Development" to emphasize cultivation of holistic development of individual students with core competencies, including (1) learning to learn; (2) living in a healthy way; (3) taking responsibility as a citizen; (4) practice, creativity, and innovation; (5) knowledge of one's cultural heritage; and (6) scientific literacy. These aim at cultivating the all-round developed person and fostering human recourses to contribute national competitiveness and "comprehensive national strength" in the global competition (Zhao, 2020).

Moreover, the curriculum reform led to a new reform of *Gaokao*. The reform aims at enhancing connection between knowledge and practice. And it gives more focus on evaluating students' ability of analysis and problem-solving. Furthermore, the admission standard includes not only academic achievement but also non-cognitive achievements. Besides, the reform also provides more flexibility and choices for students to decide what they should learn. It also encourages schools and universities to take a more holistic approach to evaluate students. Notwithstanding, the reform brought new challenges to schools, universities, and education authorities. The elective subjects may limit students' participation in subjects which are commonly considered as difficult subjects in *Gaokao*. Moreover, the reform may cause more educational inequality in the under-developed areas. The demand for more investment in school facilities and human resources will become barriers for schools in the under-developed areas to actively promote the reform. And it may further lead to educational exclusion of students in disadvantaged status (Yuan, 2018).

Information and communication technology (ICT) education in China has become a key to fulfill China's Education Modernization. In the *China Education Modernization 2035*, the government promotes educational revolution by constructing integrated intelligent platform for teaching, management and service. Moreover, they encourage educational innovation for education resources sharing and co-construction. The promotion of ICT-based education in the under-developed areas have shown positive impact education resource sharing to enhance collaborative teaching to improve education equity in rural China (Z. Yang et al., 2018).

ICT provides an alternative approach to keep continuity of teaching and learning. Nation-wide networks of education resource sharing which are ICT-based
successfully enabled 280 million students and 17.31 million teachers at different
levels of education to achieve "Classes suspended but learning continues" in the
COVID-19 pandemic in 2020 (Ren, 2020).

Japan

In the 1980s, the Ad Hoc Council on Education compiled a report which emphasized the importance of nurturing students' creativity and individuality in school
education, and it became a major turning point of Japanese educational reforms.
The new direction of education thus proposed eventually gave rise to new concepts, such as the view on what constitutes academic ability in the present-day
context and the notion of "Zest for Living" as an educational goal, advocated
by the Ministry of Education, Culture, Sports, Science and Technology (MEXT)
since the 1990s. The new view on academic ability was presented in the revised
Course of Study of 1989: it champions students' will to learn proactively, rather
than passively absorbing knowledge, encouraging them to develop the ability
to think autonomously, make decisions, and express themselves, and to acquire
skills and abilities that enable individuals to better respond to changes in society
(Fujioka, 1996). Based on this new view, a shift was made to problem-solving-
type school lessons with greater emphasis on empirical practice such as experi-
ment and observation, so as to lead students to nurture their "Zest for Living"
expressed through the mobilization of their ability to identify problems and find
solutions autonomously, effective communication with others, critical thinking
involving observation from multiple viewpoints, and ability to collect, study and
screen various types of information (MEXT, 2001).

These new concepts constitute a space for coexistence between the learner-
centered view of education that cherishes and respects individual children, and
the neoliberal view of education advocating the development of internationally
competitive human resources in a knowledge-based economy. This encounter was
made possible by the common objectives of departing from the conventional passive mode of learning heavily focused on one-sided knowledge acquisition, and
creating new modes of teaching and learning. In other words, it can be said that
both sides recognize value in competences such as problem-solving, critical thinking, and proactive learning.

Based on such a view of learning, the most recent Course of Study (revised
edition of 2017/2018) upholds the goal of realizing "proactive, dialogic and deep
learning," and emphasizes the practice of active learning to achieve this goal.
In addition, the new Course of Study clearly demonstrates a policy of promoting Education for Sustainable Development (ESD). The document recommends
that exploratory learning and collaborative learning be actively implemented in
schools within the framework of ESD.

With regard to the implementation of these new modes of teaching and
learning, it is necessary to bear in that "learning capital" of students who are
from different socioeconomic background may influence their engagement and

performance in the new modes of learning (Kariya, 2010). In an educational context that attaches importance to proactive learning, students from a socioeconomically privileged background usually have a better chance of learning fully to their advantage. In general, students from a socioeconomically privileged background tends to be richer in "learning capital" than their peers from a less privileged background. In engaging in exploratory learning, it is important to have the personal experience of being frequently exposed to various societal topics in daily life and to diverse persons with different views and opinions. In other words, students from families that have the custom of discussing social, political, or economic issues on a daily basis are more likely to be able to easily adapt to the new style of learning. On the other hand, for students who have little or no such experience in their home environment, this mode of learning, which cannot be completed simply by studying from textbooks, can represent a huge burden. In other words, depending on the amount of "learning capital" that students have, their performance in exploratory learning can differ greatly. Therefore, promoting the new modes of teaching and learning with no consideration of individual students' backgrounds runs the risk of further widening the already existing disparity in education. In recent years, Japanese educational practitioners have begun to discuss this issue.

Republic of Korea

The much-hyped discussion regarding ICT in Korea's education is not new. By leveraging its competitive advantage in the field of Information Technology, Korea enthusiastically responded to the discourse of the Fourth Industrial Revolution. The ICT discourse in education has been so widespread that many believe it might potentially lead to "a fundamental shift" in the Korean education paradigm – the shift from conventional education to lifelong learning enabling learners to access all levels of education based on online content regardless of time and place. However, Hong and Hwang (2020) argued that the intensity, extensivity, and velocity of institutional and pedagogical shifts in Korean education practices have been somewhat disappointing, despite the advantages of having ICT friendly infrastructure at all levels of education. Surprisingly, it is not the technological applications in education, but the world pandemic – COVID-19 – that has pushed Korea's education institutions and actors to rethink the existing epistemological assumptions of contemporary education and learning in Korea.

Even before the pandemic hit the world, Korean education stakeholders showed enthusiasm toward establishing ICT education in primary and secondary schools, since 2015 the Korean government has identified and spread best practices through research and the operation of leading schools. Software education was expected to be conducted in all middle schools by 2020, with gradual application from 2018 according to the 2015 Revised Curriculum, and is provided in the fifth or sixth grade of all elementary schools in 2019 (Ministry of Education, 2019). Under the new policy, elementary school students are required to receive software education for at least 17 hours, and middle school students for 34 hours during three school years. High school provides software education with elective courses (51–119 hours) (Ministry of Education, 2019). Under COVID-19, both hardware and software of ICT in education innovations are undergoing. Despite ongoing concerns on equity issues in Korean education and its active technological adaptation and application, new pedagogical experimentations are occurring in all aspects of formal education.

Besides ICT in education, a student-centered education to support students' individual growth as well as professional development of teachers (i.e., The First-class Teacher Training and Education System, Continuous Teacher Competency Development Policy, Professional Development and Motivation of Teachers Imitative) have become one of the issues of Korean formal education. Currently, the Korean government operates the national-level curriculum in primary and secondary schools. The curriculum currently in use was fully revised in 2015 and will be fully applied on an annual basis by 2020. The new curriculum was revised to cultivate creative and convergence talents with both humanistic imagination and scientific and technological creativity. In particular, this new student-centered curriculum was designed to develop practical competencies for life in the future, presenting new core competencies for students to thrive in a future society. At the high school level, a variety of elective courses (93 courses) are offered in addition to the common courses, and the curriculum is designed to be customizable for students in consideration of students' careers and desires. This revised curriculum is designed to prevent the rigid operation of the national curriculum.

Another ambitious school reform that intends to inspire new ways of teaching and learning such as the expansion of *the Free Semester* and the *Innovative School Model*. There have been growing concerns and social demand for solutions to inflexible education due to heavy competition for university admission. With former policy trials and various levels of failures, the current government has paid more attention to bring innovation to the public education system. The free Semester policy allows students in middle schools to break away from academic competition for one or two semesters and to receive school supports to build core competencies and explore the various field of activities. Another notable policy is called *Innovation School Program*. It aims to foster creative democratic citizens with the reformulation of school curricula and school operations based on the participation and cooperation of the educational community (S. C. Kim, 2018). It also pursues the following values: democratic operation of schools based on the sharing of a vision and accountability, the operation of a competency-based curriculum, teacher learning communities for joint curriculum research and practice, and the creation of school culture that is respectful of student autonomy (Kim et al., 2018). Various Regional Offices of Education and a few leading elected Governor officers of regional education have pushed the implementation of such model.

CONCLUSION

Accordingly, this chapter sheds light on an ongoing transformation of school education in East Asian countries. With rapid economic growth, authoritarian states, and culture of credentialism, these countries could make big progress in providing universal primary and secondary education with relatively high performance in the international competition. However, the chapter also indicates education disparities across these countries which are formulated by economic and development imbalance, social exclusion, institutional segregation, and market-driven exclusion. In the wave of global education reform movement, it is clear to see the educational reforms in these East Asian countries share similar discourses, such as "autonomy," "creativity," "critical thinking," and "competitiveness." Moreover, interestingly, in contrast to many western countries which show increasing attention to standardization and expansion of learning hours, education reforms in East Asian countries are giving more foci on holistic development of students and happiness of education.

The new reforms may enlarge the existing educational disparities between students from different socioeconomic background. Moreover, the unexpected global pandemic in 2020 caused massive school closure and educational disruption. Although East Asian countries have been actively promoting online learning and distance education since the twenty-first century or even earlier, there are increasing concerns on the digital divide which leads to educational exclusion of students who may not be able to access to internet and or be lack of knowledge and skills of using computers and Internet. This forces governments in this region to take initiatives to provide accessible, affordable, and resilient education for all.

Today, a new movement is vigorously under way all over the world to develop new modes of teaching and learning. As discussed in this chapter, it is occurring in East Asia as well, with concrete actions taken in actual classroom settings. For example, new modes of learning known as "active learning" and "collaborative learning" are practiced, based on the concept of "key competencies" or "twenty-first century skills" advocated by the OECD. Traditionally, East Asian students, despite their internationally high academic standards, have been criticized for their passive attitude to learning, a negative effect of the conventional cramming-style education centering on rote memorization that has been the dominant mode of learning in the region. However, since around the beginning of the twenty-first century, this tendency has been gradually changing or has already remarkably changed in some countries in the region. Toward a new normal in post-pandemic, besides the dominant conceptions which emphasize national development and competitiveness, it is necessary for East Asian countries to explore a more common ground for building a more collective sense and identity to share responsibility for building a resilient, inclusive, and sustainable world through global citizenship education and education for sustainable development.

NOTES

i. The most recent prior studies that we consulted with regard to the historical development of, and current challenges facing, Japan's education discussed in this chapter are Yonezawa et al. (2018) and Kitamura et al. (2019)

ii. Japan's economic bubble refers to the economic situation from the mid-1980s to the beginning of the 1990s, when assets mainly expressed in real estate and stock prices were excessively inflated as a result of speculation, irrespective of the real economy. When this period of rapid economic expansion ended, a credit crisis ensued due to the ending of speculative moves, causing stock and land prices to plummet and the economy to decline. The resultant recession continued up to the 2010s, and Japan has not yet fully recovered from the bursting of the economic bubble even today, with no noticeable signs of economic expansion or growth.

iii. The term "Newcomers" refers to immigrants to Japan who arrived in the country in and after the 1980s. They mainly include immigrants from the Korean Peninsula, those of Chinese descent, and those of Latin American nationality (descendants of Japanese immigrants to Latin America). Immigrants who arrived in Japan by the end of the first half of the twentieth century and their descendants are known as "Oldcomers."

iv. In concrete terms, about 40% of 1989 test takers obtained full or near-full marks, whereas in the 2001 test, the percentage of students achieving such results shrank to about one-third of the total.

v. Refer to Akashi (2014) for the evolution of Japan's immigration policy.

REFERENCES

Akashi, J. (2014). New aspects of Japan's immigration Policies: Is population decline opening the doors? *Contemporary Japan*, *26*(2), 175–196.

Byoun, S., Byun, K., Jon, J., & Oh, S. (2015). Institutional responses to the internationalization of higher education in South Korea: Case studies of 4 universities. *The Journal of Korean Education*, *42*(2), 55–85.

Chinese Communist Party Central Committee. (1994). Zhonggongzhongyang Guanyu Jinyibu Jiaqiang He Gaijin Xuexiao Deyu Gongzuo De Ruogan Yijian (Opinions on further strengthening and promoting moral education in schools). Retrieved from http://www.pkulaw.cn/fulltext_form. aspx/fulltext_form.aspx?Gid=c341b3533034a6dbbdfb. Accessed on September 15, 2020.

CIATE KOREA (Civil Alliance for Social Transformation through Education). (2019). Civil Society Issue Report Submitted to 2019 High-level Political Forum <Placing SDG 4.7 at the Heart for the Sustainable Development Goals. Retrieved November 1, 2020, from https://sdgforum.org/ attachment/cfile29.uf@99022B345CFE882013A1E5.pdf

Fujioka, H. (1996). "*Atarashii gakuryokukan o kangaeru: Kyoiku shinrigaku no shiten kara*" (A study of the new concept of academic achievement: From the viewpoint of educational psychology), *Shinri Kagaku* (*Journal of the Japanese Research Association of Psychological Science*), *18*(1), 15–30.

Han, J., Gao, Y., Zhang, Y., & Han, C. (2017). Urban–rural extension: Urban–rural reproduction among different groups of children. *Chinese Education & Society*, *50*(4), 315–335.

Huh, K. (2009). Understanding Korean Educational Policy. Vol. 4. Seoul: Universalization of Elementary and Middle School Education, the Korean Educational Development Institute (KEDI).

Hong, M. S. (2020). *Korean education and SDG4: Current landscapes and challenges*. Paper presented at the International Webinar Series by Tohoku University – Decade towards 2030: Experiences and Prospects of SDG4 2030, Tohoku University.

Hong, M. S., & Hwang, Y. (2020). 'Epistemological shifts in higher education post-Covid-19: South Korea's critical opportunities and challenges for renewing visions of higher education' in Reimagining the new pedagogical possibilities for universities post-Covid-19 (Peters, M. et al.). *Educational Philosophy and Theory*.

Ichikawa, S. (2002). Gakuryoku teika ronso (Controversy over the decline of academic ability) (pp. 147–169). Chikuma Shobo.

Jeon, M. J., Hong, M. S., & Hwang, Y. J. (2022). Recontextualizing internationalization of higher education in South Korea through the lens of knowledge-policy-power interface (forthcoming).

Kariya, T. (2010). From a credential society to a 'learning capital' society: A rearticulation of class formation in Japanese education and society. In H. Ishida & D. H. Slater (Eds.), *Social class in contemporary Japan: Structures, sorting and strategies*. Routledge.

Kariya, T., Shimizu, K., Shimizu, M., & Morota, Y. (2002). *Chosa hokoku: "Gakuryoku teika" no jittai* (*Survey report: The actual situation of the alleged decline of academic ability*). Iwanami Shoten.

Kitamura, Y., Toshiyuki, O., & Masaaki, K. (Eds.) (2019). *Education in Japan: A comprehensive analysis of education reforms and practices*. Springer.

Kim, S. C. (2018). Six dimensional dilemmas of innovative schools' Policy. *Journal of Education & Culture, 24*(2), 33–56.

Kim, S. E., & Lee, K. Il. (2019). Genealogy of and issues on Korean government's education policies regarding international students. *Journal of Education & Culture, 25*(5), 61–78.

Kim, Y. (2008). Understanding Korean Educational Policy, Vol. 2. Universalization of Tertiary Education, the Korean Educational Development Institute.

Ko, J. W., Wei, Y., & Moon, S. (2019a). An analysis of policies towards developing higher education hub in Korea: A case study of Incheon Global Campus. *Journal of Education & Culture, 25*(2), 415–432.

Kwak, B. S. (2008). "1945–1960 Economic Expansion and Establishment of Basic Education," Korean education: An Analysis of Expansion (2), Korean Educational Development Institute 2nd policy forum announcement, debate source.

Lee, C. J., & Kim, Y. (2016). Reflection on the education policy orientation in post-May 31 reform in Korea. *Asia Pacific Education Review, 17*(3), 413–426.

Lee, H. -Y., Choi, G.-M., Yoon, J. -H., & Kim, G. -T. (2006). 100 Years of Modern School Education in Korea: A Study (2), Korean Educational Development Institute Report, RR 98-8.

Liang, X., Kidwai, H., & Zhang, M. (2016). *How Shanghai does it: Insights and lessons from the highest-ranking education system in the world*. World Bank.

Liu, J. (2018). *Inequality in public school admission in Urban China: Discourses, practices and new solutions*. Springer.

Liu, S. (2020). *Neoliberalism, globalization, and "Elite" education in China: Becoming international*. Routledge.

Matsuoka, R. (2015). School socioeconomic compositional effect on shadow education participation: Evidence from Japan. *British Journal of Sociology of Education, 36*(2), 270–290.

Matsuoka, R. (2018). Inequality in shadow education participation in an egalitarian compulsory education system. *Comparative Education Review, 62*(4), 565–586.

Matsuoka, R. (2019). *Kyoiku kakusa: kaiso, chiiki, gakureki (Inequality in education: Social strata, communities, and educational background)*. Chikuma Shobo.

MEXT. (2001). *White paper: Japanese government policies in education, culture, sports, science and technology 2001*.

Ministry of Civil Affairs. (2018). Statistics of left-behind children in rural China 2018. Retrieved October 25, 2020, from http://www.mca.gov.cn/article/gk/tjtb/201809/20180900010882.shtml

Ministry of Education. (2018). Education in Korea, Ministry of Education, Sejong, Republic of Korea.

Ministry of Education. (2019). Education in Korea, Ministry of Education, Sejong, Republic of Korea.

Ministry of Education. (2020). Introduction of Korean Education. Retrieved November 1, 2020, from http://english.moe.go.kr/main.do?s=english

Miyajima, T. (2014). *Gaikokujin no kodomo no kyoiku: Shugaku no genjo to kyoiku o ukeru kenri (Immigrant children's education: The current situation of school enrollment and the right to receive education)*. University of Tokyo Press.

National Statistic Bureau. (2019). *China's year book 2019*. Beijing National Statistic Bureau of China.

Oh, C. (1974). *History of Korean education* (Vol. 2), Gwangmyeong Publishing.

Oh, Y. J., & Park, M. A. (2018). The role of International Education Quality Assurance System (IEQAS) and its implications. *Global Studies Education, 10*(3), 139–164.

Ren, Y. (2020). Shenhuaqiangshijucuo jifazhiduhuoli yongxinshuxiejiaoshiduiwujianshexinpianzhang (Further enhancing initiatives of teachers empowerment, stimulating the vitality of the system, and writing a new chapter in the construction of the teaching force). http://www.moe.gov.cn/fbh/live/2020/52439/sfcl/202009/t20200904_485107.html

Shimizu, K., Isa, N., Chinen, A., & Shibano, J. (2014). *Chosa hokoku: "Gakuryoku Kakusa" no jittai (Survey report: The actual situation of disparity in academic performance)*. Iwanami Shoten.

Shin, T. (2011). The administrative tasks of student exchange program for activating overseas academic exchange in Korean Universities. *Korean Journal of Comparative Education, 21*(2), 155–185.

Tan, C. (2013). *Learning from Shanghai: Lessons on achieving education success*. Springer Singapore.

UNESCO. (2019). *Global education monitoring report*. UNESCO

Van Damme, D. (2001). Quality issues in the internationalisation of higher education. *Higher Education, 41*(4), 415–441. https://doi.org/10.1023/a:1017598422297

Vickers, E., & Zeng, X. (2017). *Education and society in Post-Mao China.* Routledge.

Wang, Y., Lavonen, J., & Tirri, K. (2018). Aims for learning 21st century competencies in national primary science curricula in China and Finland. *Eurasia Journal of Mathematics, Science and Technology Education, 14*(6), 2081–2095.

Yamamoto, Y. (2014). Immigrant Children's schooling and family processes in Japan: Trends, challenges, and implications. In D. Radosveta, B. Michael, & Fons J. R. van de Vijver (Eds.), *Global perspectives on well-being in immigrant families.* Springer Social Sciences.

Yamanouchi, K. & Hara, K. (2010). *Ronshu: Nihon no gakuryoku mondai—Gakuryoku ron no hensen (Collection of theses on Japan's academic ability challenge: Evolution of views on academic ability).* Nihon Tosho Center.

Yang, L., Wang, B., Zhang, Y., Ye, Z., Wang, Y., & Li, P. (2018). Willing to pay more for high-quality schools? A hedonic pricing and propensity score matching approach. *International Review for Spatial Planning and Sustainable Development, 6*(1), 45–62.

Yang, Z., Wu, D., & Zheng, X. (2018). ICT in Education 2.0: Key historical transition of ICT in education in the new era. *Education Research (in Chinese), 459*, 16–22.

Yonezawa, A., Kitamura, Y., Yamoto, B., & Tokunaga, T. (eds.) (2018). *Japanese education in a global age: Sociological reflections and future directions.* Springer.

Yuan, Z. (2018). Exploration in reform context: Improving Gaokao system with Chinese characteristics. *Journal of East China Normal University (Education Sciences), 3*, 1–12.

Zhang, W., & Bray, M. (2017). Micro-neoliberalism in China: Public–private interactions at the confluence of mainstream and shadow education. *Journal of Education Policy, 32*(1), 63–81.

Zhao, K. (2020). Educating for wholeness, but beyond competences: Challenges to key-competences-based education in China. *ECNU Review of Education, 3*(3), 470–487.

WHEN POLICYMAKERS ARE NOT TRUE BELIEVERS: THE BOUNDED RATIONALITY OF POLICY BORROWING

Adam Nir

ABSTRACT

Based on a description of the national features of the Israeli society and educational system, this chapter will briefly describe various attempts conducted since the 1970s to decentralize the Israeli educational system and promote school autonomy. It will focus specifically, on the School-Based Management (SBM) policy, borrowed by educational policymakers and implemented in the Israeli educational system during late 1990s. The decision to borrow this policy did not follow policymakers' recognition in the limitations and shortcomings of the centralized structure of control, which characterized the educational system since Israel became an independent state in 1948. Rather, it followed pressures coming from various stakeholders who considered centralized policy plans irrelevant and not enough sensitive to the variety of local circumstances and needs (David, 1989; Hanson, 1984; Nir, 2002; Nir et al., 2016). Therefore, more than 20 years later, it appears that the implementation of SBM created limited effects in terms of teachers and school leaders' degrees of freedom and that the educational system still maintains its centralized structure and features. The main argument the present chapter will attempt to make is that borrowed policies have a limited capacity to promote significant change in the borrowing system when policymakers do not fully believe in the policy's values and ideas and are reluctant to abandon current patterns of organizational behavior. Specifically, it will describe the process that characterized the borrowing and implementation of the SBM policy in the Israeli educational system and will discuss the main

World Education Patterns in the Global North:
The Ebb of Global Forces and the Flow of Contextual Imperatives
International Perspectives on Education and Society, Volume 43A, 169–181
Copyright © 2022 by Adam Nir
Published under exclusive licence by Emerald Publishing Limited
ISSN: 1479-3679/doi:10.1108/S1479-36792022000043A011

symptoms that characterized the policy borrowing process when policymakers were not fully committed to the values and mode of operation brought by the borrowed policy.

Keywords: Education policy; Israel; bounded rationality; policy borrowing; school-based management; stakeholders; national education system; school autonomy

INTRODUCTION

If someone had doubts regarding the extent to which we live in a globalized world, the outbreak of the COVID-19 pandemic provides terrifying proof to the interconnectedness and interdependence of peoples and countries. When writing these lines, the pandemic has affected 189 countries and territories, with 1,080,840 deaths (CSSE, October 13, 2020). Although the history of humanity provides evidence regarding previous pandemics, the present one is unprecedented in its capacity to take advantage of modern globalization, allowing massive spread of the pandemic at a surprising speed.

This reality provides irrefutable evidence to the permeable borders existing among countries and to the growing interdependence of the world's economies, cultures, and populations, which inevitably increases the interactions between people living in different regions around the globe.

Since globalization has become a strong source of influence that people and countries cannot ignore, societies and states employ simultaneously two opposing reactions while attempting to cope with these global influences and pressures: on the one hand, globalization has increased countries' tendency to differentiate themselves through manifesting their national exclusivity and uniqueness. On the other hand, globalization has promoted countries' tendency to adjust their patterns of conduct in accordance with global standards and indicators and, in doing so, has enabled the conduct of international comparisons. Finding a proper balance between these two reactions is among the challenges that societies and nations are facing in our modern and global world.

While these circumstances create a challenging dilemma in all areas of public administration, they have a unique influence on policy setting and implementation in national educational systems, which are expected to establish and strengthen students' national identity and at the same time prepare them for their adulthood as citizens of the world.

One prominent influence of globalization on educational policy setting is evident in policymakers' tendency to borrow educational policies that were articulated and successfully implemented in some educational context, and implement them in their own educational context.

This chapter tells the story of a School-Based Management (SBM) policy implemented in the centralized Israeli educational system, an educational policy originated in North America and Australia. Although this story is context related, its scope is much broader. It provides a vivid example for policymakers' inclination to follow global trends that call for liberalism and pluralism through the empowerment of schools, although their willingness to abandon central patterns of control and faith in the power of a decentralized structure to promote educational effectiveness is rather limited.

CROSS NATIONAL POLICY BORROWING IN EDUCATION

The articulation of educational policies at the national level is carried out by civil servants and policymakers who operate in a political context (Nir, 2019). A political context creates a unique environment for policy planners since politicians tend to avoid risks and failures that could hamper their political careers (Haering, 2011, p. 177). This statement is supported by research findings showing that policymakers' sense of risk is a major determinant of policies (Sjöberg & Drottz-Sjöberg, 2008) and that politicians are more likely to initiate risky endeavors when they have greater confidence in their re-election (Sheffer & Loewen, 2019).

While risk and uncertainty may affect policy setting in all areas of public administration, the unique features and complexity characterizing public educational systems seem to add to the multifaceted challenge educational policymakers often face. Educational problems and objectives are ill defined, complex and wicked, and the means for their achievement are inherently unreliable and vague (Leithwood, 1994; Nir, 2000a). Ill-defined educational problems typically have multiple correct solutions, and there may be multiple methods of obtaining each (Wagner, 1994). Such qualities create an unstable foundation for policymaking (Lubienski et al., 2014) and may encourage educational policymakers to play it safe and embrace policies known for their reputation, proven accomplishments and potential to produce tangible results.

A prominent expression in both developed and developing countries to policymakers' inclination to decrease the sense of uncertainty may be evident in the widespread practice to borrow policies (Phillips & Ochs, 2003; Steiner-Khamsi, 2014). The process of policy borrowing, which appears under various terminologies (Raffe & Semple, 2011), reflects a conscious and deliberate adoption of a policy that originates in one context and is adopted by another (Phillips & Ochs, 2004). The international tendency to borrow policies seems to be a direct consequence of globalization, which fosters a unified world culture and greater interconnectedness among individuals coming from different societies. As Steiner-Khamsi notes, in the twenty-first century, globalization has become so dominant that it has reached the level of an "epidemic" (2004, p. 2). Thus, globalization semantics challenge the past conception of education as a culturally bounded system (Steiner-Khamsi, p. 5).

The literature mentions three main arguments in support of policy borrowing. Initially, borrowed policies offer solutions that worked in other educational systems and, therefore, reduce the uncertainty that typically accompanies newly created policies. Second, they save the time required for policy setting. This is an extremely significant feature of borrowed policies since public education is headed by politicians who wish to get re-elected based on their proven accomplishments. Ready-made policies, consequently, are more likely to enable meeting short-term political pressures and needs (Halpin & Troyna, 1995). Third, borrowed policies are assumed to save money, and thus are of high value to governments that constantly strive to change the cost-effectiveness ratio in public education (Steiner-Khamsi, 2014).

Nevertheless, borrowed policies are not free of limitations. A major limitation may be evident in their insensitivity to contextual features. This limitation is significant especially when the contextual differences between the lending and borrowing countries are extreme. Therefore, policymakers must take into account the cultural features from which a policy is borrowed and those in which they wish to implement it (Auld & Morris, 2014; Cheng, 1998). Large contextual discrepancies require the borrowing state to initiate fundamental changes not only to the educational system, but also in the political culture and in the perceptions, expectations, and mentality of individuals and the society as a whole. This may explain why comparative researchers warn against transplanting educational reforms that originate in one country into others (Steiner-Khamsi, 2014).

The chapter's main argument is that borrowed policies have a limited capacity to promote significant change in the borrowing educational system when policymakers do not fully believe in the policy's values and ideas and are as a result reluctant to abandon existing patterns of professional and organizational behavior. Focusing on the borrowing and implementation process of a SBM policy in the centralized Israeli educational system, the chapter discusses some of the main symptoms characterizing policymakers' lack of commitment to the values and mode of operation brought by the borrowed policy.

THE ISRAELI CONTEXT

Before I go on to describe how the SBM policy was introduced in the Israeli educational system, it seems imperative to present an overview of the Israeli national context in which the educational system operates.

Israel is a small country with an area of approximately 20,770 km² (8,019 sq mi). It is 424 km (263 mi) long from north to south, and its width from east to west is 114 km (71 mi) at its widest point. Since independence in 1948, Israel has been in almost constant conflict with its neighboring countries with periodic wars and other military activity.

The State of Israel has a population of approximately 9,136,000 inhabitants as of the end of 2019: 74.1% percent of them are Jews, 21.0% are Arab, while the remaining 4.9% are defined as "others" (including non-Arab Christians, non-Arab Muslims and residents who do not have an ethnic or religious classification) (Israel Central Bureau of Statistics, 2020a). Moreover, 10.1% of Israeli Jews define themselves as "ultra-Orthodox," 11.3% are "religious," 13% consider themselves "religious traditionalists"; 22.1% are "non-religious traditionalists," and 43.1% are "secular" (Israel Central Bureau of Statistics, 2020b).

Israeli society has evolved as a state of immigrants producing a society characterized by high fragmentation among different social groups and sectors. One primary line of fragmentation among ethnic subgroups may be found between immigrants who came from eastern and western Europe and America (Ashkenazi

Jews) and Jews who immigrated to Israel during the 1950s from Arab or Moslem countries (Sephardi Jews). A second division within the Jewish sector is along religious lines with Jews representing a range of religious outlooks from ultra-Orthodoxy to radical secularism. Another main source of fragmentation is the relationship between Jewish and non-Jewish minorities.

Before the outbreak of the COVID-19 pandemic, Israel's economy was strong with an annual growth of approximately 3% on average. However, the COVID-19 pandemic has had profound effects with significant increases of unemployment rate and public debt (OECD, 2020). The pandemic, which also increased income inequality, maintained Israel among the most unequal economies in the Western world (OECD, 2020). Although a significant portion of Israel's national budget is dedicated to security, the national investment in education has steadily increased. Nevertheless, the average public spending per student remains low compared to most other OECD countries (OECD, 2020).

The educational system has always been viewed as a primary vehicle for nation building. Ever since independence, the educational system was expected to reduce gaps and promote cohesion among the different sectors and, at the same time, to respond to the pluralistic nature of Israeli society.

To achieve these goals, a centralized structure was adopted with a system controlled by a strong central bureaucracy under the overall direction of the Minister of Education and a Director General. The Ministry of Education is legally and politically responsible for the implementation of the relevant laws and the operation of the educational system. It sets national goals, tightly controls inputs, and the allocation of budgets. The ministry monitors student achievement through national performance evaluation tests, determines the national curriculum, and is responsible for employing teachers and the construction of new schools. The educational system is divided geographically into eight districts (the Jerusalem district is divided into the region of Jerusalem and the city of Jerusalem itself), which supervise and monitor the educational processes conducted by schools to ensure the compatibility of these processes with central policies (Nir & Gillis, 2019).

The Israeli educational system is comprised of approximately 5,000 public schools with 2.4 million students and 200,000 teachers (Ministry of Education, 2018). Although great diversity exists among the different Local Education Authorities (LEAs) as a result of economic and political constraints and geographical location, uniform academic standards for high schools are employed throughout the system and controlled through national matriculation examinations conducted by the Ministry of Education. In elementary schools, in addition to school-level efforts to track student achievement, central control is obtained through national evaluation tests (Nir, 2018).

INTRODUCING SBM IN THE CENTRALIZED ISRAELI EDUCATIONAL SYSTEM

Between the 1970s and 1990s, the Ministry of Education initiated various policies that explicitly argued for the need to promote school autonomy. These initiatives followed pressures to increase schools' autonomy based on the recognition that strong centralization and curriculum uniformity may not be able to allow schools to provide adequate and relevant pedagogical solutions to the high variance of needs and expectations characterizing Israeli society. However, in practice, these initiatives have not yet made a significant change in the centralized culture and nature of the educational system (Nir, 2018).

In 1992, the Minister of Education commissioned a steering committee to explore the possibility of extending the scope of school autonomy and introducing a SBM policy in Israel. This initiative took place mainly because of pressures coming from educators, parents, community members and local authorities to increase school autonomy. These pressures and the limited ability of the Central Office to control schools (Gaziel & Romm, 1988) created a tendency to initiate SBM although central officials remained reluctant to decrease their control over the schooling system. The committee set the following guidelines for the implementation of the SBM policy in the Israeli educational system: (1) schools will develop a clear definition of focused goals; (2) schools will develop a clear work plan that corresponds with their defined goals; (3) schools will use and implement extensive monitoring and assessment methods; (4) schools will be granted full independence in using their budget; (5) schools' authority with respect to personnel matters will be broadened; (6) there will be a governing body for each school (Ministry of Education, 1993).

The implementation of the SBM policy began gradually in 1996. More than two decades later, no significant changes are evident in schools' autonomy or in the centralized structure and patterns of control characterizing the Israeli educational system (Nir, in press).

An efficient strategy allowing the evaluation of policymakers' intentions is to focus on the extent to which declarations and explicit policy messages correspond with implementation goals and procedures. The following examples will show that the introduction of the SBM policy in the Israeli educational system is characterized by significant discrepancies between policy messages and actions. As one could expect, these inconsistencies, which mostly reflect policymakers' ambivalence, led to limited changes both in the centralized hierarchical control and in schools' degrees of freedom. From a broader perspective, the analysis intends to shed light on the limited efficiency of borrowed policies when policymakers fail to fully understand the implications likely to follow the borrowing process and establish a proper balance between the values and guiding assumptions of the borrowed policy and those characterizing their own educational context.

SUPERVISION AND CONTROL

SBM is based on an assumption that schools' decision-making authority should be promoted to increase their responsiveness to local needs. Therefore, external supervision needs to be moderated and confined so as to enable schools to develop their administrative as well as pedagogical autonomy based on their local agenda. In this sense, the introduction of SBM in centralized structures suggests a significant shift in school control from external supervision dominated and administered by district superintendents to internal school-based supervision dominated by school personnel and by the inclination of school-level educators to sustain their autonomy. Traditionally, Israeli superintendents were expected to maintain centrally oriented control over schools, and to make sure that schools operate in accordance with central instructions and regulations. Although superintendents were instructed to assist schools in building their own autonomous agenda following the introduction of the SBM policy, they were still expected to fulfill their customary monitoring role, and report to the district regarding school activities and performance (Bogler, 2014). They felt obliged to maintain their control over schools mainly because the implementation of decentralization initiatives in centralized structures have always been controversial among high-ranking Israeli officials who were never eager to surrender their authority to schools and to decrease their influence over the educational system (Nir & Eyal, 2003).

In practice, however, the formal role definition of the educational superintendent was never redefined following the introduction of SBM. This may partly be explained by the superintendents' professional union's resistance to narrow superintendents' authority, and mainly because "it is believed beyond reasonable doubt that, even when increasing the independence of educational institutions, there is a need for the supervision of the superintendent" (The Avigad Report, 1984). Therefore, even when SBM was borrowed and introduced in the Israeli educational system more than a decade after this report was published, superintendents were still expected to serve as the eyes and ears of the Ministry of Education in schools. They maintained their formal role definition that included a number of central responsibilities, such as the monitoring of schools' implementation of central regulations, the evaluation of school administration and the monitoring of children's achievements, to name a few. While expected to maintain a centrally oriented control over schools, superintendents were also asked to use their professional wisdom and increase, in some mysterious way, school autonomy. These circumstances created contradictory demands, exposing them to a severe role conflict. As a result, research evidence has shown that superintendents were encouraged to adopt a coping strategy that served their professional interests rather than school autonomy. Since superintendents' formal role definition remained unchanged, their centralized socialization and inclination to prove the necessity of external supervision of schools undermined implementation of SBM and the development of the organizational autonomy of schools that traditionally operated in a centralized structure (Nir & Eyal, 2003).

THE CURRICULUM

Traditionally, the Ministry of Education determined the curriculum for all public schools comprising the national educational system. Three layers typically comprised each disciplinary curriculum: a core mandatory curriculum of basic subjects and values intending to ensure uniformity in the educational system; a selection of curriculum that consists of subjects determined by the Ministry of Education from which each individual school can choose; and, an optional curriculum that consists of subjects according to choices made by each individual school. Schools were allowed to develop their own curriculum within this category to express their individual school credos (Inbar, 1990).

One of the factors that encouraged Israeli policymakers to borrow and implement a SBM policy may be evident in the growing recognition of the negative pedagogical effect of strong centralization and curriculum uniformity (Vollansky & Bar-Elli, 1995). SBM was assumed to grant schools extended autonomy and allow them to determine their own curricular goals and processes in accordance with local circumstances and needs.

In reality, though, significant gaps are evident between the policy's manifested intentions and declarations and the implementation process. The demand stating that all schools must operate in accordance with central curricular regulations was never abolished following the introduction of the SBM policy. Decisions referring to the curriculum were still made by the Director General (Nir, 2002). Although each SBM school had to produce its annual pedagogical plan, each plan had to include a reasonable number of operational tasks, corresponding with the educational policy and national curriculum set by the Ministry of Education (Nir, 2000b). A study performed in the Bedouin sector revealed that SBM schools did not develop their own curricula because of the mandatory central curriculum set by the Ministry of Education (Mizel, 2011). Abu-Saad (2008) argued that setting an obligatory central curriculum for Bedouin schools is done on purpose, to enable the government to control schools and prevent potential conflict with the central authority. Hence, although the SBM policy was officially introduced in primary schools in 1998, the Ministry established a standardized and obligatory curriculum for primary education with uniform standards five years later (Berkovich & Bogler, 2019; Eyal & Berkovich, 2010). This inconsistency between policy declarations and practice created a paradoxical situation wherein the mandates and requirements for curriculum are still under the control of the central educational authorities, while the stated intention is to grant authority to SBM schools and allow them to develop their own school-based curriculum.

TEACHERS' EMPLOYMENT

The balance between responsibility and authority is critical for organizational leadership and a prominent expression of organizational autonomy. Therefore, broadening school leaders' authority with respect to personnel hiring and dismissal is one of the manifested features of the SBM policy. This aspect of SBM, which was part of the recommendations made by the SBM committee and later on adopted by the Ministry of Education, implies a need to significantly increase school leaders' authority regarding schoolteachers, which was extremely limited since Israel became an independent state in 1948. The Ministry of Education is traditionally the employer of all public elementary and junior high schoolteachers. Every teacher becomes automatically tenured after two years of probationary status. Once a teacher is tenured, firing is possible only in extreme cases and has to be approved by the Minister of Education or the Director General. The main reasons for dismissal are usually related to schoolteachers' behavior and are seldom related to professional performance standards. The terms and regulations of schoolteachers' employment, including salary and promotion, are specified in collective contracts and protected by work laws that guarantee job security. Teachers' employment is also secured by two powerful unions that monitor teachers' work conditions and professional rights (Rubio & Rosenblatt, 1999).

Although the articulated SBM policy suggested a significant shift in personnel control, from external supervision dominated and administered by the Ministry of Education to internal school-based supervision, in practice, central control over personnel, including hiring, dismissal and salaries, has remained centralized and the recommendation made by the SBM committee to broaden leaders' authority in this respect was never implemented. Hence, although SBM is the declared policy of the Ministry of Education for more than two decades, school leaders' control over their teachers remains extremely limited (Nir, 2002, 2006; Nir et al., 2017).

EVALUATION

SBM emphasizes school-based evaluation processes (Brown, 1990, p. 70) to allow schools greater power and legitimacy to internally monitor their activities. School-based evaluation is assumed to produce the necessary information for helping individuals, groups and the school to learn, improve and increase the matching between needs, goals, processes and outcomes. School-based evaluation allows the school staff to conduct a systematic inquiry with the intention of getting a deeper insight into the interplay among conditions, processes and outcomes as well as the possibilities for further development (Darling-Hammond, 1993).

Although school use of extensive monitoring and assessment methods is one of the key guidelines defined by Israeli policymakers for SBM implementation, it appears that policymakers have refused to abandon central evaluation and monitoring of schools. Traditionally, evaluation of school performance was under the responsibility of the Department of Evaluation and Measurement at the Ministry of Education. However, following a report submitted by the National Task Force for the Advancement of Education in Israel, which emphasized the significance of SBM and school autonomy, this ministerial department was closed and replaced in 2005 by the National Authority for Measurement and Evaluation in Education (RAMA).

According to its website, the role of RAMA is to lead the process of measurement and evaluation of the educational system through: (1) the evaluation of the educational system and the examination of standards and objectives set by the Ministry of Education; (2) the evaluation of schools according to standards outlined by the Ministry of Education; (3) the execution of GEMS tests in 5th and 7th grades, the publication of the results openly and their submission to the government and parliament; (4) the development and control of final examinations and the evaluation of the outcomes; and (5) the administration of international tests such as PISA and TIMSS. Although the reform proposed by the National Task Force was never formally implemented, the emphasis it placed on "evaluation, standards and measurement" through the creation of the RAMA is a clear confirmation of its impact and an expression of the discourse on "educational standards" constructed by the Ministry of Education (Resnik, 2011).

Hence, while the SBM policy, which emphasizes school-level evaluation, became the declared and formal policy of the Ministry of Education, the responsibility to evaluate and monitor school performance remained external and centralized. Although under SBM schools were allowed and expected to define their own goals and work plans and to self-monitor their actions and outcomes, the central emphasis placed on national and international standards and their measurement by an external agency reflects a significant discrepancy between declared intentions and practice.

THE BOUNDED RATIONALITY OF POLICY BORROWING

Policy implementation has long been recognized as key for policy impact and success. Pressman and Wildavsky (1984) were first to show that implementation dominates outcomes regardless of the quality of the policy at hand. In many cases, implementation activities fail to meet policy expectations mainly because implementation, which is an act of bargaining and transformation, is influenced by contextual factors (McLaughlin, 1987) and by the interpretation and sense making of individuals operating throughout the system (Coburn, 2004; Elmore, 1977; Spillane, 2004, p. 77). Since policy effects are indirect and mediated through interpretations and contextual features, implementation heavily depends on the unique conditions characterizing the implementing system. Therefore, the implementation of a particular policy may have different meanings and consequences in different settings (McLaughlin, 1987).

Turning to the introduction of the SBM policy in the Israeli educational system, it is evident that discrepancies are a prominent feature of the implementation process. Discrepancies are evident, in particular, when declared policy messages are compared with the actual actions taken in the process of implementation. In extreme cases, as in the case of school leaders' authority regarding teachers' employment, although this issue was included in the declared policy it was postponed even before implementation begun.

How can these discrepancies be explained? Although one could argue that they reflect improper or inefficient conduct, which may always be a point of weakness for policy implementation processes, it seems that the current case is much different.

Initially, it is important to acknowledge that the implementation of borrowed policies is always subjected to contextual influences characterizing the borrowing system. Contextual features greatly influence implementation (Murphy & Beck, 1995) since context establishes a frame of reference and a sort of membrane that absorbs changes and maintains meaning (Nir, 2009).

While the decision to borrow the SBM policy may testify to Israeli policymakers' awareness of global trends supporting school autonomy and the limitations associated with central control, it is important to acknowledge that the introduction of SBM in the Israeli schooling system requires a major change not only of the system, but also in policymakers' mindset. Such a change is essential in considering that centralization has dominated Israeli socialization processes for decades and is the main mode of operation for all governmental offices even today. In this sense, Israeli policymakers are all caught in the "centralization trap" (Nir, 2006, 2009, 2012), referring to their difficulty to reconcile between the contradictory tendencies to delegate and maintain central authority in schools at the same time. This trap is made of a wide range of contingencies intended to ensure the dominance of central control even when a policy intended to promote school autonomy is officially initiated and implemented. The power of habit and reluctance to lose control and the fear of chaos and the lack of trust in subordinates are only a few prominent examples of these contingencies.

The introduction of SBM in the centralized Israeli educational system, consequently, reflects a dialectical process in which a continuous tension exists between the different drives for educational autonomy and the highly centralized nature of the system. Paradoxically, although caught in the centralization trap and reluctant to surrender their authority, senior officials were still encouraged to follow global trends and borrow a policy plan that emphasizes the need to promote school autonomy. In an attempt to reconcile this paradox, however, Israeli policymakers seem to shape SBM and transform it from a policy plan intending to promote the authority and autonomy at the school level to a "declarative autonomy" policy (Nir et al., 2016) so that their central hegemony will persist.

It appears that the centralization trap and central socialization set rigid borderlines and narrow policymakers' perspective when considering policies such as SBM. The Israeli experience reveals that senior officials perceive and implement SBM according to a centralized logic and rationale, although this mode of operation reflects a significant deviation from the values and guiding assumptions that a SBM policy intends to establish. It is therefore hardly surprising that almost 20 years after the initial implementation of SBM in the Israeli educational system was set in motion, the system still maintains its centralized patterns of control and confines the degrees of freedom granted to schools (Nir et al., 2017).

Although policy borrowing has become nowadays a widespread practice in education both in developed and developing countries (Ball, 1998; Phillips & Ochs, 2003; Steiner-Khamsi, 2014), it is suggested that policymakers use caution before a final decision is made. Specifically, the values and guiding assumptions of the policy they intend to borrow must be confronted with those characterizing their own context to allow a rational evaluation of anticipated consequences which are likely to follow implementation. Reliance on professionals who are external to the educational hierarchy may be useful in this respect and may allow policymakers to consider the consequences of a proposed policy for their own context from different angles that are beyond their personal views and professional perspectives.

REFERENCES

Abu-Saad, I. (2008). Present absentees: The Arab school curriculum in Israel as a tool for deeducating indigenous Palestinians. *Holy Land Studies: A Multidisciplinary Journal, 7*(1), 17–43.
Auld, E., & Morris, P. (2014). Comparative education, the 'new paradigm' and policy borrowing: Constructing knowledge for educational reform. *Comparative Education, 50*(2), 129–155. https://doi.org/10.1080/03050068.2013.826497

Ball, S. J. (1998). Big policies/small world: An introduction to international perspectives in education policy. *Comparative Education, 34*(2), 119–130.

Berkovich, I., & Bogler, R. (2019). DESCP factors: The "invisible" impediments to reforms in education. *Journal of Educational Administration and History, 51*(3), 239–255.

Bogler, R. (2014). The elusive character of the school superintendent role: The Israeli case. In A. E. Nir (Ed.), *The educational superintendent: Between trust and regulation: An international perspective* (pp. 75–90). Nova Science Publishers.

Brown, D. J. (1990). *Decentralization and school-based management*. The Falmer Press.

Cheng, K. M. (1998). Can education values be borrowed? Looking into cultural differences. *Peabody Journal of Education, 73*(2), 11–30.

Coburn, C. E. (2004). Beyond decoupling: Rethinking the relationship between the institutional environment and the classroom. *Sociology of Education, 77*(3), 211–244.

CSSE. (2020). Coronavirus COVID-19 Global Cases by the Center for Systems Science and Engineering (CSSE) at Johns Hopkins University (JHU). Retrieved October 13, 2020, from https://gisanddata.maps.arcgis.com/apps/opsdashboard/index.html#/bda7594740fd40299423467b48e9ecf6

Darling-Hammond, L. (1993). Reframing the school agenda. *Phi Delta Kappan, 74*(10), 752–761.

David, J. L. (1989). Synthesis of research on school-based management, *Educational Leadership, 46*(8), 45–53.

Elmore, R. (1977). Lessons from follow through. *Policy Analysis, 1*(3), 459–484.

Eyal, O., & Berkovich, I. (2010). National challenges, educational reforms, and their influence on school management: The Israeli case. *Educational Planning, 19*(3), 44–63.

Gaziel, H. H., & T. Romm. (1988). From centralization to decentralization: The case of Israel as a unique pattern of control in education. *European Journal of Education, 23*(4), 345–352.

Haering, B. (2011). From research to practice: How can science contribute to politics. In L. Goetschel (Ed.), *The politics of peace: From ideology to pragmatism* (pp. 175–182). Lit Verlag.

Halpin, D., & Troyna, B. (1995). The politics of educational policy borrowing. *Comparative Education, 31*(3), 303–310.

Inbar, D. (1990). Is autonomy possible in a centralized system? In I. Friedman (Ed.), *Autonomy in education: A conceptual framework and process implementation* (pp. 53–71). Henrietta Szold Institute (Hebrew).

Israel Central Bureau of Statistics. (2020a). *Population in Israel at the beginning of 2020*. National Bureau of Statistics, December 31st, 2020, publication no. 413/2019. Retrieved October 31, 2020, from https://www.cbs.gov.il/he/mediarelease/pages/2019

Israel Central Bureau of Statistics. (2020b). Israel in number at the evening of the New Year. Jerusalem, September 16th, 2020, publication no. 296/2020. Retrieved October 23, 2020, from https://old.cbs.gov.il/reader/newhodaot/hodaa_template.html?hodaa=202011296

Leithwood, K. (1994). Leadership for school restructuring. *Educational Administration Quarterly, 30*(4), 498–518.

Lubienski, C., Scott, J., & DeBray, E. (2014). The politics of research production, promotion, and utilization in educational policy. *Educational Policy, 28*(2), 131–144.

McLaughlin, M. W. (1987). Learning from experience: Lessons from policy implementation. *Educational Evaluation and Policy Analysis, 9*(2), 171–178.

Ministry of Education. (1993). *School-based in-service training*. Director General's Special Memorandum. Ministry of Education (Hebrew).

Ministry of Education. (2018). *Transparency in education*. Administration of Economics and Budgeting and Administration of Teleprocessing and Information. Jerusalem (Hebrew).

Mizel, O. (2011). Curriculum development in self-governed Israeli Arab-Bedouin elementary schools. *Language, Culture and Curriculum, 24*(2), 105–123.

Murphy, J., & Beck, L. G. (1995). *School-based management as school reform*. Corwin Press.

Nir, A. E. (2000a). The simplification trap in educational planning. *Planning and Changing, 31*(1 & 2), 70–83.

Nir, A. E. (2000b). The annual plans of school-based management schools operating in a centralized educational system: Planning for ambiguity. *Educational Planning, 12*(4), 19–38.

Nir, A. E. (2002). The impact of school-based management on school health. *Journal of School Leadership, 12*(4), 368–396.

Nir, A. E. (2006). Maintaining or delegating authority? Contradictory policy messages and the prospects of school-based management to promote school autonomy. *Educational Planning, 15*(1), 27–38.

Nir, A. E. (Ed.). (2009). *Centralization and school empowerment: From rhetoric to practice.* Nova Science Publishers.

Nir, A. E. (2012). School-based management and the centralization trap: An evidence-based perspective. *Curriculum and Teaching, 27*(2), 29–45.

Nir, A. E. (2018). Using the system thinking approach in educational policy setting: A choice among compromises. In H. Shaked, C. Schechter & A. Daly (Eds.), *Leading holistically: How schools, districts, and states improve systemically* (pp. 178–195). Routledge.

Nir, A. E. (2019). Professional political and contextual considerations of policy borrowing. In Rosemary Papa (Ed.), *Oxford research encyclopedia of education.* Oxford University Press.

Nir, A. E. (2020). Educational centralization as a catalyst for coordination: Myth or practice? *Journal of Educational Administration, 59*(1), 116–131.

Nir, A. E., Ben-David, A., Bogler, R., Inbar, D., & Zohar, A. (2016). School autonomy and 21st century skills in the Israeli educational system: Discrepancies between the declarative and operational levels. *International Journal of Educational Management, 30*(7), 1231–1246.

Nir, A. E., & Eyal, O. (2003). School-based management and the role conflict of the school superintendent. *Journal of Educational Administration, 41*(5), 547–564.

Nir, A. E., & Gillis, M. (2019). From idealism to pragmatism: Transitions in Israeli public education. In K. G. Karras & C. C. Wolhuter (Eds.), *International handbook of teacher education worldwide* (2nd ed., Vol. 2, pp. 109–124). H&M Publishers.

Nir, A. E., Kondakci, Y., & Emil, S. (2017). Travelling policies and contextual considerations: On threshold criteria. *Compare: A Journal of Comparative and International Education, 48*(1), 21–38.

OECD. (2020). *OECD economic surveys: Israel 2020.* OECD Economic Outlook: Statistics and Projections Database, September 2020. Retrieved October 25, 2020, from file:///D:/Google%20Drive/Desktoph/Israel-2020-OECD-economic-survey-overview.pdf

Phillips, D., & Ochs, K. (2003). Processes of policy borrowing in education: Some explanatory and analytical devises. *Comparative Education, 39*(4), 451–461.

Phillips, D., & Ochs, K. (2004). Researching policy borrowing: Some methodological challenges in comparative education. *British Educational Research Journal, 30*(6), 773–784.

Pressman, J. L., & Wildavsky, A. (1984). *Implementation* (3rd ed.). University of California Press.

Raffe, D., & Semple, S. (2011). *Policy borrowing or policy learning? How (not) to improve education systems.* Publication 57. Centre for Educational Sociology.

Resnik, J. (2011). The construction of a managerial education discourse and the involvement of philanthropic entrepreneurs: The case of Israel. *Critical Studies in Education, 52*(3), 251–266.

Rubio, A., & Rosenblatt, Z. (1999). Job insecurity of Israeli secondary-school teachers: Sectoral effects. *Journal of Educational Administration, 37*(2), 139–158.

Sheffer, L., & Loewen, P. (2019). Electoral confidence, overconfidence, and risky behavior: Evidence from a study with elected politicians. *Political Behavior, 41*(1), 31–51.

Sjöberg, L., & Drottz-Sjöberg, B. M. (2008). Risk perception by politicians and the public. *Energy & Environment, 19*(3–4), 455–483.

Spillane, J. P. (2004). *Standards deviation: How schools misunderstand education policy.* Harvard University Press.

Steiner-Khamsi, G. (2004). Globalization in education: Real or imagined? In G. Steiner-Khamsi (Ed.), *The global politics of educational borrowing and lending* (pp. 1–6). Teachers College Press.

Steiner-Khamsi, G. (2014). Cross-national policy borrowing: Understanding reception and translation. *Asia Pacific Journal of Education, 34*(2), 153–167. https://doi.org/10.1080/02188791.201 3.875649

The Avigad Report. (1984). *The supervision in the educational system.* The Ministry of Education Culture and Sports, Jerusalem (in Hebrew).

Vollansky, A., & Bar-Elli, D. (1995). Moving toward equitable school-based management. *Educational Leadership, 53*(4), 60–62.

Wagner, R. K. (1994). Practical problem-solving. In P. Hallinger, K. Leithwood & J. Murphy (Eds.), *Cognitive perspectives on educational leadership* (pp. 88–102). Teachers College Press.

INDEX